Resisting explanations of Japanese "self" through Western assumptions, the contributors to this volume use on-the-ground experiences with Japanese people to trace the parameters of selves in their own social contexts. The authors find these selves to be multiple and changing, inextricable from the kaleidoscope of everyday life. They reinterpret what Westerners have viewed as oppositions in Japanese life – the contrast between public and private life, ritual and informality, group consensus and personal strength – and demonstrate that the Japanese nurture multiple sides of themselves to reconcile these alternatives. The Japanese people emerge from this book as a complex, multifaceted people, vulnerable to the influences that surround them, yet shaping selves creatively around a broad spectrum of people and situations.

Japanese sense of self

Publications of the Society for Psychological Anthropology

Editors
Robert A. Paul, Graduate Institute of the Liberal Arts, Emory University, Atlanta

Richard A. Shweder, Committee on Human Development, The University of Chicago

Publications of the Society for Psychological Anthropology is a joint initiative of Cambridge University Press and the Society for Psychological Anthropology, a unit of the American Anthropological Association. The series has been established to publish books in psychological anthropology and related fields of cognitive anthropology, ethnopsychology, and cultural psychology. It will include works of original theory, empirical research, and edited collections that address current issues. The creation of this series reflects a renewed interest among culture theorists in ideas about the self, mind–body interaction, social cognition, mental models, processes of cultural acquisition, motivation and agency, gender, and emotion. The books will appeal to an international readership of scholars, students, and professionals in the social sciences.

Japanese sense of self

Edited by

Nancy R. Rosenberger

Oregon State University

CAMBRIDGE
UNIVERSITY PRESS

Published by the Press Syndicate of the University of Cambridge
The Pitt Building, Trumpington Street, Cambridge CB2 1RP
40 West 20th Street, New York, NY 10011–4211, USA
10 Stamford Road, Oakleigh, Melbourne 3166, Australia

First published 1992
First paperback edition 1994

Printed in Great Britain at the University Press, Cambridge

A catalogue record for this book is available from the British Library

Library of Congress cataloguing in publication data

Japanese sense of self / edited by Nancy R. Rosenberger.
    p.   cm. – (Publications for the Society for Psychological Anthropology)
Includes index.
ISBN 0 521 41520 9 (hardcover)
1. Self-perception – Japan. 2. Social perception.
I. Rosenberger, Nancy Ross. II. Series.
BF697.5.S43J36   1992
155.8'952 – dc20   91–26271 CIP

ISBN 0 521 41520 9 hardback
ISBN 0 521 46637 7 paperback

UP

Contents

Figures

Contributors

NANCY R. ROSENBERGER
Oregon State University

JOSEPH TOBIN
University of Hawaii, Honolulu

DORINNE KONDO
Pomona College, Claremont, California

AUGUSTIN BERQUE
Ecole des Hautes Etudes en Sciences Sociales, Paris

TAKIE SUGIYAMA LEBRA
University of Hawaii, Honolulu

TAKAMI KUWAYAMA
Virginia Commonwealth University, Richmond

JANE BACHNIK
University of North Carolina, Chapel Hill

Preface

The idea for this volume grew out of a panel at the American Anthropological Association in 1987 entitled "Japanese Selves: Creating and Receiving Culture." Previous studies had restricted the idea of self in Japan to the Western, oppositional, and implicitly essentialist categories of "individual" and "society." Although this opposition continues to haunt us – and, given the rhetorical necessities, is almost impossible to escape – our purpose was to ask new questions about the constitution of self in Japan, drawing upon our own experience and observations.

Originally, Takie Lebra was the discussant for papers given by Dorinne Kondo, Takami Kuwayama, Nancy R. Rosenberger, and Joseph Tobin. Later, Dr Lebra generously donated a paper that had been part of another panel because it spoke directly to the issues we were addressing. Jane Bachnik, who had been unable to participate in the panel, composed her paper in relation to others in the volume. At her suggestion, we invited the French scholar Augustin Berque to contribute to the volume in order to broaden our American perspective and to add the aspect of environment to our understanding of how selves are constituted along with other domains in Japanese life.

I would like to thank Dr. Robert Paul for his constant support for this project. I am grateful to Jane Bachnik, Takie Lebra, Joseph Tobin, and Clint Morrison for their help at various stages. Claire Younger gave support to the entire volume through her clerical skills. I also appreciate the help of Jessica Kuper of Cambridge University Press in bringing this work to fruition.

1 Introduction

Nancy R. Rosenberger

In this volume, self and the social are studied as interactive rather than opposing processes. We ask: How do the self and the social constitute one another? What does the self look like if we locate it not in a domain separate from society but at the very nexus of shifting relationships, changing economies, and mobile views of nature? Pictured in this way, what meanings do selves have and where is their power? By analyzing specific instances in Japan, we show what a study of Japanese lives can offer to the anthropological efforts to understand the issue of self outside of Western assumptions, while suggesting to students of Japanese society the parameters to consider in understanding the various constructions of self in Japan.

In the postwar period, Western-trained anthropologists have struggled to reconcile what they observe and experience in Japan with assumptions of the opposition between individual and society that underlie both our theories and our common sense views of the world. In terms of this opposition, Japanese people appear contradictory in the negative sense. Ruth Benedict outlined the problem in the opening pages of *The Chrysanthemum and the Sword*:

All these contradictions ... are true ... The Japanese are, to the highest degree, both aggressive and unaggressive, both militaristic and aesthetic, both insolent and polite, rigid and adaptable, submissive and resentful of being pushed around, loyal and treacherous, brave and timid, conservative and hospitable to new ways. They are terribly concerned about what other people will think of their behavior, and they are also overcome by guilt when other people know nothing of their misstep. Their soldiers are disciplined to the hilt but are also insubordinate. (1946: 2)

That Americans would perceive the Japanese in terms of individual will versus societal norms is not surprising: these are categories through which we organize knowledge, and they have informed not only the construction of these "contradictions" by Western scholars but also their attempts to bridge them. The authors in this volume break with these categories, emphasizing themes of multiplicity and movement in their attempts to construct alternative views of Japanese selves from their experiences and observations.

Western dualities

The dichotomy between individual and society emerged from Galileo's and Copernicus's refiguring of the world on a mathematical and mechanical basis. Cause-and-effect logic replaced metaphorical correspondence as the explanation for the social and natural world. As the divine was eliminated from matter, the rational individual displaced God at the heart of this world, becoming the origin of true knowledge by virtue of transcendent reason (Venn 1984: 133–6; see also essays in Carrithers et al. 1985, Dumont 1986, Lutz 1988, Tambiah 1984).

To attain scientific objectivity, this individual had to set aside parts of the immediate world that would disturb the rational intellect: body, emotion, fantasy, nature, everyday context, and social relationship. Thus, the ideal individual was conceptualized as acting according to abstract principles, eschewing decisions made by emotion, intuition, or social influence.

A dichotomy of Western ("us") versus non-Western ("them") became embedded in the dichotomy of individual versus society, with the first term superior in each case. Westerners living in industrial, economically "modern" societies idealize themselves as individuals, in control of emotions and social relations, able to think abstractly by cause-and-effect logic. Westerners often affirm this ideal by viewing non-Westerners as swayed by emotion, relation, and context – only able to think in the specific case and then only by metaphor. It follows that Western societies can take the "higher" form of democracy because decision making can be entrusted to the hands of rational individuals, whereas non-Western societies require a strong collectivity for cohesion and control of people enmeshed in the immediacy of relationship and superstition.

This point of view remains with anthropologists, even those studying complex, industrialized non-Western societies. Whether anthropologists characterize Japanese as disciplined and submissive (overcontrolled from without) or as resentful and insubordinate (undercontrolled from within), we still tend to locate them on the negative side of the individual/society dichotomy. We often portray Japanese as the opposite of our ideal selves: as concrete thinkers, particularistic moralists, situational conformists, unintegrated selves; as intuitive rather than rational, animistic (undivided from their environment), and unable to separate body and mind. The temptation of such general conclusions continually bedevils Western-trained scholars of Japan.

At the other extreme, scholars sometimes try to save Japanese people from other-ness by showing them as completely like us: individuals who feel the repression of society, who think reasonably, who make moral judgments based on abstract principles, and who indeed have integrated selves.

In this volume, we attempt to render these dichotomies unnecessary by conveying the complex processes involved in the relationships between selves and the social in Japan.

Politically, our attempt to escape these false dichotomies is helped by a milieu that is increasingly open to viewing Japanese people as equally human because of their corporations' phenomenal economic growth. Through the media, Americans are beginning to share an urge to delve into the behind-the-scenes, inner life of Japanese people, if only to figure out the secret behind their threatened economic superiority. However, such information is often used to debunk Japanese ways as something Americans would never stand for or, on the opposite side, it is used to translate their ways into our ways so Americans can keep up with Japanese. Again, false dichotomies easily re-emerge.

Conceptually, the present authors are aided in this attempt to overcome individual/society and Western/non-Western dichotomies by trends in Western thought from phenomenology to poststructuralism that attempt in various ways to displace the Western subject from its privileged position of reason and essentiality. Objectivity itself is challenged as not being transcendent but rooted in the male, Western perspective of a historic world-view (MacKinnon 1982). The subject as an essential center of principles seems to make little sense when we understand selves and principles as heterogeneous, making sense only in relation to other socially constructed meanings (Derrida 1989 [1966]). We are finding that the "Western individual" is a concept squarely rooted in culturally con-structed and historically changing perceptions, social relations, and ideologies (Weedon 1987).

Rather than a naturally unfolding destiny that must fulfill its own isolated essence, in this view self attains meaning in embodied relations to other people, things, and ideas (Rosaldo 1984; see also Geertz 1973, Shore 1982, Keeler 1987, White and Kirkpatrick 1985, Heelas and Lock 1981, DeVos 1985, Shweder and Levine 1984). People are subjects, creations of a particular social, political, and economic world at a certain time (Althusser 1971). Yet they are creative, as they produce as well as reproduce culture, albeit within social and historical parameters (Giddens 1979). Self is emotionally invested in the cultural world, learning to use it creatively through language and actions in relational contexts (Urwin 1984). In such a conception of self, integration gives way to multiple dimensions and identities. In short, people take up multiple positions in social, political, and economic worlds that are highly differentiated and constantly changing (P. Smith 1988, Kristeva 1982).

The study of Japanese concepts of self helps us as Western-trained scholars to understand the self as firmly embedded in the culturally constructed world. The very word for self in Japanese, *jibun*, implies that self is not an essentiality apart from the social realm. *Jibun* literally means "self part" – a part of a larger whole that consists of groups and relationships. *Jibun* is always valued in relation to that larger whole (cf. Dumont 1970). We are forced to understand that self attains form through relating to others, but, as we shall see, by relating in a variety of ways. It is in this multiplicity of relationships that meaning and power emerge.

Since World War II, Western-trained anthropologists, grappling with self as part of a social whole in Japan, have overcome only gradually and with difficulty the ideology of the individual which is embedded in their theories and common sense views.[1]

Re-viewing inherited approaches: Benedict, DeVos, and Caudill

The earliest studies of self in Japan were done in the forties by scholars working with the theories of the culture and personality school. Accepting the division of individual and society, they linked these through personality – its formation in early childhood and its subsequent projections and anxieties in societal institutions. Indeed in this model, culture is inferred from a sample of persistent individual behavioral traits and is integrated like a personality (Bock 1980: 42–4). The more Freudian scholars center their approach around individual drives of sex and aggression that are socialized early on and either defended against or expressed in adult social institutions. If these drives are successfully channeled, the adult can develop a rational intellect and independent relationships.

Such theories were not innocent of the political ideologies of World War II. Geoffrey Gorer (1943) claimed that harsh toilet training and weaning inflicted early repression and guilt on Japanese people. As a result, the Japanese were alternately disciplined and wild. Near the end of the war, the government called on Ruth Benedict to explain Japanese war actions and advise on the future Occupation. As we will see, her conclusions also reproduced a sense of overly harsh controls (though not in early childhood) contrasted with enjoyment of emotion and activities associated with sex and drink. Such analyses gave ample rationale for American war efforts and later economic and political domination over Japanese as the inferior, foreign "other."

Benedict's *The Chrysanthemum and the Sword* (1946) has remained influential in Japanese studies to this day. Benedict had developed an approach in which she generalized personality patterns to characterize cultures as integrated systems – some as excessive Dionysians, others as rational Apollonians (1934). The Japanese, who showed both extremes, challenged her rather reductive theory.

To her credit, she allowed the conundrum of the "contradictions" she perceived in Japan to push her toward a solution that went beyond culture as a collection of personality traits: a meta-framework of hierarchical organization. For example, in politics, citizens must obey unquestioningly at the state level, but they participate in a kind of democratic "community responsibility" at the local levels – a proper place for the will of the people (1946: 83).

Benedict posits that Japanese distinguish and prioritize their actions through multiple "circles" – an idea that anthropologists still build on today (see Lebra, this volume). "Circles of obligation" represent duties to various people and groups from emperor to parents. A "circle of human feeling" consists of emotional and physical pleasures, subordinate to circles of obligation.

Hierarchical relations among circles help to explain how contradictions can coexist but they remain the negative contradictions of the irrational individual versus the controlling society. Benedict identifies the circles of obligation with societal norms typical of "other" societies – orderly but repressive. She characterizes the circle of human feelings as "impulse gratification," expressions of "natural" drives. Although she recognizes the great pleasure Japanese derive from bodily experiences such as bathing, drinking, and sex, she suggests Japanese have "dangerous selves" (p. 290) in need of restraint, perhaps because of their supposed lack of guilt (cf. Lebra 1983).

Benedict employs personality formation to make sense of the seeming paradox between institutionalized enjoyment and conformity to obligations through personality formation. She finds a "deeply implanted dualism" in upbringing: the spontaneity and acceptance of childhood as against the "great threats of ostracism and detraction" from parents and peers as one gets older (p. 293). Thus, repression is not internalized, but rooted in "shame" stimulated by external sanctions. This accounts for acceptance of obligation in public but unbridled enjoyment in private.

In short, for Benedict hierarchy remained a static structure imposed on frustrated individuals, rather than a creative field for the expression of meaningful values. In terms of the issue of control – so vital to understanding identity in the US – Benedict maintained the Japanese as the "other," lacking control from within, yet, still human, suffering under control from above.

Benedict's characterization of Japan as a shame culture spurred other scholars to save Japanese from being seen as primitive people without internalized guilt.[2] Ironically, the stimulus to make Japanese seem more Western came from the effort to explain why Japanese were by then competing successfully with white middle-class people in the heartland of America (Caudill and DeVos 1956). DeVos, a psychologist and anthropologist, has explored the question of achievement throughout his career (1986 [1960], 1985, DeVos and Wagatsuma 1959). DeVos argues that Japanese do indeed have a sense of guilt, but that it is induced by the extreme intimacy between mother and child rather than by a superego with integrated principles. The mother's devotion frees the child (usually male) for the present, but indebts him in the long run. In adult life he must return the debt by achieving through company and marriage, but always in predictable ways that do not threaten the relationship with the mother (1986 [1960]).

The result is an image of contradiction that appears to Westerners as negative and self-defeating: Japanese seem to be rational, controlled individuals able to achieve, but underneath they are frustrated and suppressed. On the surface, they are like us, but ultimately they are thwarted. Concentrating on the gap between the individual psyche and societal actions, DeVos's work loses sight of the positive value that Japanese give to relationships of both spontaneity and obligation in adult life. He recognizes the importance of interpersonal relationships, but reduces them to fit into a Western theory.[3]

In the fifties and sixties, William Caudill, a psychoanalyst and anthropologist, edged away from seeing Japanese in terms of social discipline and tightly controlled individual expression. Although in an early study of mental hospital caretakers and patients he explained Japanese as denying pleasure and emotion (1962: 116) with few channels for impulse gratification, he also conveyed that for some Japanese libidinal pleasure may not mean genital sex, but bathing, eating, and sleeping together.[4]

Deeply influenced by Doi in later articles (see below), Caudill pushes beyond his theory's biologically driven individual to explore satisfaction derived from mutual dependency in intimate relationships. Caudill finds a warm nexus of relationship in the everyday life of families. In a study of co-sleeping arrangements (Caudill and Plath 1986 [1966]) and in a study of Japanese and American infant–child relationships (Caudill and Weinstein 1986 [1969]), he acknowledges the very early importance of non-sexual intimate relationship and its continued dynamism in family life. Caudill pushes back the time line for the development of a cultural self to three months, making way for Doi to push it back to birth. Caudill's conclusions remain true, however, to oppositions pointed out above that identify differences between Westerners and non-Westerners. Japanese babies are trained to be other-oriented and interdependent, stressing emotion and intuition in decision making, whereas American babies are trained to be individual-oriented and independent, emphasizing the rational in decision making (1986 [1969]: 204).

Group cohesion united with desire: Nakane and Doi

Although not explicitly about self, Nakane's *Japanese Society* has been central to an interpretation of self as rooted in the group. A Japanese anthropologist trained in British structural functionalism who has done fieldwork in India, Nakane is concerned with finding the structural principle underlying cohesion or group consciousness. Although in India common group attributes of caste or occupation allow individuals free expression outside of certain rules, Nakane concludes that in Japan individual autonomy is inimical to group cohesion. The group's cohesion depends on people's daily integration within the frame (*ba*) of one group or locality – not only through work but through emotional participation that "disregards objective intellectual observation and analysis of individual qualities" (p. 123). Built on personal relationships between superiors and inferiors, the group consciousness provides emotional security, but the group "alters people's ideas and ways of thinking" (p. 10).

Nakane's analysis constitutes the Japanese as the epitome of the West's "other": lacking autonomy, immersed in emotional relationship within a group. She has been roundly criticized for her elite male group model of verticality that has ideologically served both Americans and Japanese in rationalizing Japanese economic superiority (cf. Mouer and Sugimoto 1986). Yet by discrediting individual autonomy in Japanese society, she has opened a space for questions about the processes of interaction between selves and groups. Unfortunately, her critique does not reconstruct an alternative idea of self (nor does it suggest that the Western self may not be entirely autonomous either). However, as other scholars attempt to reconstruct an alternative idea of self, Nakane's concept of frame or locality helps in the understanding of the Japanese self in terms of multiple relationships, groups, and contexts (cf. Bachnik, this volume).

If Nakane legitimized a Japanese form of group cohesion through vertical relationships, Doi Takeo, a Japanese psychoanalyst, invested those relationships with individual desire – the desire to be passively cared for by another (*amae*). Based on his experience with Japanese mental patients seeking such indulgence and with US mental patients threatened by their unknowing need for such indulgence, Doi (1977) proposed a desire that he thought was more basic than either sex or aggression – the desire to be loved and indulged. All people have this desire but Japanese are conscious of it, verbalize it, and have ways to achieve it partially through their hierarchical relationships.

Doi relieves the individual of the necessity to find meaning as an isolated entity by locating the development of psychological desire and its (partial) satisfaction in relationships. Desire for indulgence or passive love (*amae*) is born in the prelinguistic union with the primary "object-choice," the mother, who indulges the infant completely (1977: 20). After initial unconscious acceptance of indulgence, the child becomes aware of its lack, and demands it. Conscious of separation, the child becomes aware of self (*jibun*: the "self" part of the whole). The child is not doomed to separation, however. Doi posits that Japanese can actualize their desire to receive passive love at a prelinguistic level through the non-verbal relations of intimacy they construct in private groups (*uchi*). In more formal relationships outside the intimate group, the child must learn restraint, although limited indulgence might occur. Even Japanese never fully overcome separation, but relationship with nature offers yet another possibility for union.

For Doi, then, no dichotomy exists between relationship and the "individual." In fact freedom for the individual is found in relationship – a freedom found by presuming on the good will of the other (1986: 19). Duality exists, but the difference is between ways of relating: between outer contexts where one relates with restraint and deference (*soto*) and inner contexts where one unharnesses spontaneous expression (*uchi*) – always framed within the limits of another person's indulgence. Doi (1986) claims that consciousness itself is split similarly between "front" and "back" (*omote/ura*) type of relationships, according to restraint versus expression of *amae* or dependence (cf. Tobin, this volume). He thus maintains a mutually constitutive dualism in the Japanese world. Benedict's circles of obligation (*giri*) become for Doi vessels of form which are filled to varying extents with the content of the circle of human feelings – the desire to be indulged. *Amae* humanizes the world of obligation, while the world of obligation and restraint offers protection to the intimate side of mind and relationship.

Doi challenges central assumptions of Western theory in stating that the self develops and satisfies desire in relationship. Yet he still hints at essentiality in that he focuses on individual desire, attempting to explain everything in terms of psychic needs. At the same time, he can be accused of legitimizing Japanese claims to cultural uniqueness by giving the close, non-verbal relationship in Japan a mystical and ubiquitous power.

Doi shows Westerners in their own terms why Japanese invest themselves in hierarchical relationships. Significantly, he fails to focus on the person giving the indulgence (Kumagai 1981), thus masking dynamics of dominance in the relationship – both the immediate dominance by the person who is indulged and the future dominance by the person who gives indulgence, who will be paid back in some way. This imbalance may result from his focus on the masculine side of relationships.

The significance of Doi's work for anthropology lies in his method of following linguistic associations to trace the significant connections among ideas and practices in a culture. His work, as well as those reviewed in the next section, shows the importance of using Japanese words and concepts to avoid the assumptions inherent in Western theories which focus on definitions of hierarchy, power, collectivity, individuality, and morality.

Getting around Western theory: Lebra and Befu

Takie Lebra is a Japanese-born, Western-trained anthropologist who has largely focused on indigenous terms and actions to avoid the pitfalls of locating Japanese on the negative side of dichotomies drawn from Western theories. In her introduction to *Japanese Patterns of Behavior* (1976), Lebra politely agrees with Parsons that at the "cultural" level, obligation and desire are "logically contradictory," but goes on to argue that they are "functionally complementary" at the "behavioral" level – the level of her analysis. Although the cultural/behavioral split may seem a false dichotomy, Lebra uses it as a rationale to present Japanese society as she understands it from a native point of view – without ever challenging Western theory.

Lebra posits that contradictions such as those mentioned by Benedict are foreclosed by social situationalism – shifts in action in accord with important differences in relationship, group, and context. Accommodating themselves to ritual, intimate, and anomic contexts, Japanese people take on the guise of discriminating social actors.

Despite this insight, Lebra still differentiates "self" in isolated introspection "at the opposite pole from social involvement" (p. 158). She seems to be searching for an essential core of individuality that fits with Western theory. In her chapter below, however, Lebra clarifies the interaction between self and the social as she shows Japanese selves working in multiple aspects within and apart from relationships.

Harumi Befu, another Japanese-born, Western-trained anthropologist, also tries to convey the interaction between selves and the social in Japan by using indigenous terms, but without fully escaping Western assumptions. He uses *seishin*, spiritual strength developed through self-discipline, to link what Western theory differentiates: conformity to group consensus and personal strength. He argues that *seishin* is not only the backbone of loyalty in relationship, but also a source of strength for a Japanese in personal networks of power, "strategically allocating his resources ... to bring him bountiful returns" (1980: 180). Befu shows us that the Japanese self is not only involved in intimate relations of warmth, but intimate relations of competition and manipulation as well. In using social exchange theory, however, he risks making the self seem too rooted in isolated self-interest, an individual agent separable from social norms which exist only at a separate level of ideology (cf. Kondo, this volume).

Both Lebra and Befu illustrate the problems that can result in trying to remain loyal both to the theories of the Western academy and at the same time to indigenous observation and experience.

Mead's theories of relational self: Smith and Plath

A number of anthropologists studying Japan, including Robert Smith (1983) and Plath (1980) as well as Lebra (above), have used George Herbert Mead's ideas of self to blend Western theory with cultural ideas and actions. Mead (1934) is appealing because he theorizes relationality as basic to self, an idea which fits much of what anthropologists perceive in Japanese life. Anthropologists using his ideas have deepened our under-standing of Japanese self. Mead posits the self in two parts: "me," the internalized reflexive view of self as seen by others (the generalized other), and "I," the non-reflexive reaction in the midst of that interaction from which innovation arises (Cronk 1987). Other people are not simply external; they are part of one's own selfhood (Taylor 1989: 509).

Following Mead, anthropologist Robert Smith (1983) describes Japa-nese as having self as recreated in relationship. He claims that "there is no fixed center from which ... the individual asserts a noncontingent existence" (p. 81). Oriented toward cooperative aspects of relationship, Japanese gain a strong sense of self by approximating ideal role types, joining groups, and situating themselves in relation to others (cf. Kuwayama, this volume). However, Smith does not escape hints of the Western essential self with individualistic drives. He agrees with Reischauer (1977, quoted in Smith 1983) that the "cooperative, relativistic Japanese is a product of firm inner self control – a master of anti-social instincts" (pp. 56–7); and thus, that "Japanese pay a price for their cooperative society in an underlying psychological malaise from uniform-ity" (p. 103).

Also influenced by Mead, Plath uses oral history to portray the depth and vitality of relationship in Japanese life. Building on Benedict's work, he adds the grace of human feeling to her circles of obligation, claiming that Japanese are not sociocentric (tied to roles), but people-centered: "the lifelong struggle is to carry out one's responsibilities to others without diminishing one's playful responsiveness toward them" (1980: 217).

Plath's relational self remains to some extent essentialist, separated from a judging society and finding unity in itself. As in Mead's work, although relationships are important and vital to development, it is not clear for Plath how relationships *constitute* the self. Others are "a jury who evaluate and confirm the course of your becoming and being" (p. 10) – representatives of society's changing norms.

For Plath, society and self are different in nature: society is fragmented through multiple points of view and violent historical changes while the individual rises above this fragmentation as the agent of unity in a fragmented world (p. 181). Augmenting Mead's rather unclear idea of agency, Plath uses Erikson's concept of identity as developed through adulthood and across changes in history. Thus, for Plath the Japanese people may not stress individuality to begin with, but in bringing together a fragmented history, they attain a unified identity. He presents the Japanese self as a product of relationships, but remains within Western theory of the individual by emphasizing consistency.

The threat of individualism

Scholars such as those discussed above have made convincing cases for the importance of relationality in Japanese self. New questions are emerging about individualism, however, as Western goods and lifestyles seem, at least to the foreign eye, to be pervading Japanese life. Although the Japanese have mastered the world economically in terms of Western-style goods and technology, there may be an ironic reverse as Western styles begin to master Japanese conceptions of self and relationship (Rosenberger 1992). Scholars begin to ask: are the Japanese proceeding toward an ideology of self as separate and essentialist? Are alienation and anomie overwhelming conceptions of self based on relationship?

There is no doubt that Japanese have imported certain ideas about individualism in a historical process that has been going on since the Meiji restoration of 1868, but with renewed vigor since the end of World War II. Ohnuki-Tierney (1987) argues that Japanese self and society have always brought in outside influences, because they define themselves reflexively, that is, in relation to the outside or the other. Ohnuki-Tierney describes the Japanese conception of the universe as divided into two parts – the inside of Japanese society and the outside peopled with gods, foreigners, and so on. The boundary between the dualities is permeable; what is outside should be able to pass through to purify and become purified in the inner realms of Japanese society, often through the mediation of marginal beings. The relation of self with outside others is based on opposition with the outside world, but synthesis within the Japanese world. Thus, Japanese have taken on the accoutrements and concepts of the Western world such as Western clothes and individualism, only to tame or purify them by bringing them into the reciprocity and unity with others internal to Japanese society.

Now that Japan is gaining economic mastery in Western terms, however, there are hints that Japanese people may be losing the ability to tame outside influences and make them part of their inner reciprocity. Ohnuki-Tierney proposes that the popular film "Tampopo" symbolically acts out the danger of Japanese losing the collective self built on the give and take of personal relationship to the sterile silence of individuality (1990: 208). Likewise, in a study of Japanese railway advertisements, Marilyn Ivy (1988) suggests that the Japanese are losing their culture, but, defining it as merely style, are not admitting it. Rather than seeking self in relationship, they search for identity through being what is different than themselves – the "other," the exotic – whether that be foreign or a reinterpreted version of their own "tradition." The result is a marginalization of "traditional" Japanese interaction. Even studies of preschools indicate that children are found lacking in discrimination of shifts between contexts of formality and informality – a skill that formerly they would have learned at home (Tobin et al. 1989).

Indeed, various scholars point to behaviors that show increasingly alienated people searching for meaning as relationships and institutions that undergird relational selves are threatened. We can see evidence of this to varying degrees in school phobias (M. Lock 1986) and high school failures (Rohlen 1983), in the alienation of the factory worker (Clark 1979) and the part-time worker and artisan (Kondo 1990), in the search for meaning among salarymen (E. Vogel 1971) and housewives (S. Vogel 1978, Imamura 1987, Rosenberger 1987), in the threat of anomie in city living (Bestor 1989), and in the loneliness of the elderly (Bethel 1992).

Many Japanese-trained scholars reject such alienation, emphasizing Japan's concept of the collective self, embedded in social context and the Japanese natural world. In Berque's essay in this volume, he mentions Watsuji's "interpersonal relationship" (*aidagara*) (1935), Hamaguchi's "contextual man" (*kanjin*) (1977), Makino's "extended ego" (*kakudai ego*) (1978), and Doi's "indulgence" (*amae*) (1971).

Western-trained scholars sometimes criticize these authors' over-emphasis on the concept of collective or interpersonal self when Japanese use it to build a myth of the uniqueness of Japanese culture. Yet even those Western-trained writers who perceive alienation agree that the Japanese conceptions of self are still embedded in interpersonal relationship in comparison with the American conceptions of self. Moeran (1986 [1984]) argues that individualism is practiced in name in Japan, but remains a part of a reciprocal Japanese self. Individualism links with spontaneous feelings of the heart that have always been an alternative to the devoted loyalty that demands giving up one's heart. Now individuality is expressed as sincere feelings of the heart – still well within the traditional Japanese way of purity. Rohlen (1976) also suggests that Japanese find their "individuality" in activities relating to the building of spirit or *seishin*. Thus, growth toward individuality consists of aesthetic polishing that builds toward the final unity of non-self rather than individualism in a sense of essentialism and consistent identity.

Studies of early childhood also indicate the crafting of selves embedded in reciprocal relationship. Although the increasing number of genteel families in league with institutions aimed at high scores on entrance examinations may not teach group-oriented cooperation, preschools and elementary schools seem to create atmospheres that constitute the self in terms of cooperation with peers and superiors (Lewis 1984, Tobin et al. 1989, Le Vine and White 1986). Even when it comes to marriage, though far from the unseen arranged marriages of their grandparents, young people's unions are based on the idea of the incompleteness of self (Edwards 1989). Despite their questioning and complaining, part-time workers (Kondo 1990), heirs of agricultural households (Bachnik 1992) and middle-aged housewives (Rosenberger, in press) also find meaning in being part of a defined set of obligatory and reciprocal social relationships.

In this volume the authors present examples of Japanese people who are not essentialized individuals despite economic and social changes. In a variety of ways, they portray Japanese people as shifting among modes of experience – sometimes spontaneously expressing inner opinions and unique characteristics in intimate relations, and sometimes disciplining themselves to enliven more formal, hierarchical group life. Japanese self emerges as neither entirely collective nor completely individualistic. In fact, these essays imply that whether or not Japanese are becoming individualistic in an American sense is the wrong question, one itself rooted in Western dichotomies. The more appropriate question is, what shifts occur as Japanese people make Western lifestyles and concepts of individuality part of their own processes of self and social relationship.

Themes

Throughout the volume, each author presents self as multiple, moving, and changing. They show people grounded in meanings beyond themselves, meanings that shift in relation to other people, close and far, to nature, wild and tamed, and to the political economy, past and future. People continually create themselves and are created in terms of the multiple pictures that people weave with others and their environment as they move through life.

These shifting interactions of self and the social have parameters defined by a range of cultural values. This range defines movement much like the universal movement proposed by Andrew Lock (1982): between inner and outer and between lack of control and control. In Japanese terms, this range of values measures movement and multiplicity according to degrees of distance or closeness, difference or fusion. Most of the present authors convey this range through indigenous terms such as *soto/ uchi* (outer/inner), *omote/ura* (front/back), or *tatemae/honne* (on-stage/ back-stage), the first term implying contexts and relationships that are more distant with differences emphasized, and the second term implying those that are closer with fusion stressed (Doi 1977, Lebra 1976, Bachnik 1992, Rosenberger 1989). Inner and outer are not understood only in terms of self versus group, but also in terms of groups that one belongs to with varying degrees of intimacy (Wetzel 1984). According to this distance, control – or restraint, in Japanese terms – increases and decreases. Some authors, such as Lebra, present a continuum of dualities, while others, such as Bachnik, suggest a continuum between polar extremes of distance and intimacy. Kuwayama proposes a continuum ranging from *jibun* (self) through increasingly distant others to *seken* (public opinion). Although emphases and meanings change over time, the general parameters of this range of values appear to extend over a long period of history.

The authors are concerned with the multiplicity of self, or the multiple and changing positions that constitute self. Multiplicity of self can be perceived in various dimensions – in relation to other individuals, other groups, objects, aspects of nature, and historical ideologies. Almost all writers discuss examples of Japanese people defining and redefining themselves in relation to the distance or difference from other people or other groups. For example, Tobin develops this multiplicity in the shifts between contexts of work and play within the preschool environment; Bachnik in movements between the nuclear family group and the family with outside guests; Rosenberger in shifts among a middle-aged woman's friends, students, nuclear family, and in-laws; Kondo in movements of an artisan among relations with boss, other artisans, and part-time workers; Kuwayama in shifts between one's own and others' agricultural households; and Lebra in movements between relations of "face" and relations of "belly." In all of these, the shifting of relative differences between people in terms of gender, age, and status are important indicators of what position will be taken for the moment.

In addition to this shifting relational self, Lebra emphasizes that the multiple self, as conceived by the Japanese, also includes an "inner self." The inner self is "more immune from social relativity" and "a focus for self-identity and subjectivity." Kuwayama also hints at this in the *jibun* or self in his model. In both, this inner-oriented realm of self exists in relation to the interactional self, but is juxtaposed to it. Both authors emphasize the feelings of vulnerability (Lebra) and shame (Kuwayama) experienced in the outer dimensions of self and the need to escape these in inner dimensions. Lebra proposes a hierarchy linking shame and guilt to these outer and inner dimensions, thus resolving Benedict's dilemma concerning shame and guilt as an apparent dichotomy.

Although other contributors do not deny the existence of an inner realm of self, they emphasize its cultural constitution and social embeddedness. Tobin, for example, agrees with Doi that the inner realm of consciousness itself is divided in ways that are similar to the outer realm of social interaction. Kondo proposes that self is not autonomous apart from the historical ideologies that constitute it. In short, debate continues as to the constitution and autonomy of inner aspects of self.

Multiplicity of self also emerges in relations with material objects. Objects are invested with cultural meanings and therefore their use helps construct various aspects of selves and social relations. In both Kondo and Kuwayama, for example, the use of machines leads to the construction of certain images by which people relate with others. In Tobin's chapter, chopsticks and uniforms constitute the context for one aspect of self while mud and empty pop cans construct the context for another. Different teapots signal shifts in self-relationship in Bachnik's chapter and the tightness of one's kimono measures another such difference in Rosenberger's analysis. Berque's chapter extends this idea into different arrangements of nature – cherry blossoms around a temple or urban greenery – that also constitute various interactions of self and society.

Some chapters demonstrate the multiplicity of self in relation to the changing political economy. Kondo shows a male artisan creating and being created in identities of both artist and organizational man as factory life changes. Rosenberger presents a female teacher and housewife establishing identities in relation to both long-accepted ideologies of women's familial roles and postwar ideologies of women working independently.

Both analyses reveal that each gender has heterogeneous positions and that these positions may well be conflictual.

The chapters give several ideas as to the significance of this view of self as multiple. First, it suggests that thinking will emphasize indexing rather than referencing. Bachnik and Tobin contend that indexing multiple places along a range of meanings is more important to Japanese than defining oneself consistently according to fixed meanings. Second, a multiple concept of self implies the idea that power is inherent in the creation of selfhood. If self is not essential, but depends for meaning on differences and likenesses with other selves, then, as Kondo and Kuwayama show, power in interrelations is inevitable.

Third, these multiple identities concern not only power but meaning as well. Rosenberger argues that as people relate in multiple ways to people of different ages, genders, and social statuses, to various arrangements of nature, and to changing demands of the political economy, they create larger patterns that carry cultural meanings important to their ongoing understandings of society and the universe. Last, a conception of self as multiple aims toward purity as a goal to be reached through dissolving dualities. Both Lebra and Berque discuss the ultimate ideal of multiplicity: entry into a space beyond difference, at the level of the cosmos rather than self or the social.

In conclusion, the essays in this volume present a view of Japanese self as multiple and moving which urges a reconsideration of concepts of self in other societies as well. As Shweder and Bourne (1984) have pointed out, the definition of self in terms of contextuality and relationship or again in terms of generality and essentiality is a difference in emphasis, not a difference in kind. Like Yin and Yang, elements of each exist in the other. It is hoped that these studies of Japanese self will expand Western-trained scholars' conceptions of self to include multiplicity, change, and interaction with others, not only in non-Western societies such as Japan, but in Western cultures as well. If, as scholars, we never examine the common sense presuppositions that guide our theories and interpretations, we will continue to ask either–or questions of individualism versus collectivity, placing "them," the non-Western others, on the negative side of apparent dichotomies – or else making them like us.

NOTES

1 I have chosen to use the term self in this essay, focusing on "the human being as a locus of experience" (Harris 1989: 601). Such a focus privileges ways in which people interpret and construct themselves in relation to others. Harris has suggested that the term individual suggests a member of humankind and

the term person, an agent-in-society. I do not mean to de-emphasize the social as a result of this focus on self, for self is constituted by the social and has agency only through the social. Unlike Harris, I use the term individual to imply the Western concept of essential, consistent identity.

2 As Doi (1986) has pointed out, the guilt/shame dichotomy is related to Western dichotomies of individual/social discussed above. Feeling guilt is objectified in abstract principles and is thus superior to feeling shame which is subjectified in concrete personal relationship. The sanction of external shame seemed to place Japanese on the far side from reason in a situational morality that denied the transcendent individual.

3 In his 1985 article in a book about the interactional self, DeVos still emphasizes "actualization of social self among the Japanese" through its "role dimension"; the circle of human feelings is a "secret self . . . of unshared secrets or personal fantasies" (1985: 181). The individual/society dichotomy remains as the Japanese either conform to normative roles or retreat to the unconscious.

4 Through specially constructed TAT tests given to employees and patients in a mental hospital, Caudill finds that Japanese emphasize non-sexual satisfaction and deny pleasure and emotion. Bias toward a Westernized male point of view seems evident. Only three male doctors differentiate and enjoy both sexual and non-sexual encounters; the rest – many of them women – deny pleasure and sexual feeling because they are forced to restrain their sexual impulses in physical yet non-sexual situations such as the bath.

REFERENCES

Althusser, Louis. 1971. Ideology and Ideological State Apparatuses (Notes towards an Investigation). *Lenin and Philosophy*. New York: Monthly Review Press.
Bachnik, Jane. 1992. *Family, Self and Society in Modern Japan*. Stanford, Calif.: Stanford University Press.
Befu, Harumi. 1980. The Group Model of Japanese Society and an Alternative. *Rice University Studies* 66. Houston, Tex.
Benedict, Ruth. 1934. *Patterns of Culture*. Boston, Mass.: Houghton Mifflin.
    1946. *The Chrysanthemum and the Sword: Patterns of Japanese Culture*. Boston, Mass.: Houghton Mifflin.
Bestor, Theodore. 1989. *Neighborhood Tokyo*. Stanford, Calif.: Stanford University Press.
Bethel, Diana. 1992. Alienation and Reconnection in a Home for the Elderly. *Remade in Japan*. (J. Tobin, ed.), New Haven, Conn.: Yale University Press.
Bock, Philip. 1980. *Rethinking Psychological Anthropology*. New York: W. H. Freeman.
Carrithers, Michael, Collins, S., and Lukes, S. 1985. *The Category of the Person*. Cambridge: Cambridge University Press.
Caudill, William. 1962. Patterns of Emotion in Modern Japan. *Japanese Culture* (R. Beardsley and R. Smith, eds.), Chicago: Aldine.

Caudill, William and DeVos, George. 1956. Achievement, Culture and Personality: The Case of the Japanese Americans. *American Anthropologist* 58: 1102–26.

Caudill, William and Plath, David. 1986 (1966). Who Sleeps by Whom: Parent–Child Involvement in Urban Japanese Families. *Japanese Culture and Behavior* (T. S. Lebra and W. P. Lebra, eds.), Honolulu: University of Hawaii Press.

Caudill, William and Weinstein, Helen. 1986 (1969). Maternal Care and Infant Behavior in Japan and America. *Japanese Culture and Behavior* (T. S. Lebra and W. P. Lebra, eds.), Honolulu: University of Hawaii Press.

Clark, Rodney. 1979. *The Japanese Company*. New Haven, Conn.: Yale University Press.

Cronk, George. 1987. *The Philosophical Anthropology of George Herbert Mead*. New York: Peter Lang.

Derrida, Jacques. 1989 (1966). Structure, Sign and Play in the Discourse of the Human Sciences. *Modern Literary Theory: A Reader* (P. Rice and P. Waugh, eds.), London: Edward Arnold.

DeVos, George. 1985. Dimensions of Self in Japanese Culture. *Culture and Self: Asian and Western Perspectives* (A. Marsella, G. DeVos, and F. Hsu, eds.), New York: Tavistock.

    1986 (1960). The Relation of Guilt towards Parents to Achievement and Arranged Marriage among the Japanese. *Japanese Culture and Behavior* (T. S. Lebra and W. P. Lebra, eds.), Honolulu: University of Hawaii Press.

DeVos, George and Wagatsuma, A. 1959. Psychocultural Significance of Concern over Death and Illness among Rural Japanese. *International Journal of Social Psychiatry* 5: 6–19.

Doi, Takeo. 1977. *The Anatomy of Dependence*. Tokyo: Kodansha.

    1986. *The Anatomy of Self*. Tokyo: Kodansha.

Dumont, Louis. 1970. *Homo Hierarchicus*. Chicago: University of Chicago Press.

    1986. *Essays on Individualism: Modern Ideology in Anthropological Perspective*. Chicago: University of Chicago Press.

Edwards, Walter. 1989. *Modern Japan Through Its Weddings*. Stanford, Calif.: Stanford University Press.

Geertz, Clifford. 1973. *Interpretations of Culture*. New York: Basic Books.

Giddens, Anthony. 1979. *Central Problems in Social Theory*. London: Macmillan.

Gorer, Geoffrey. 1943. *Themes in Japanese Culture*. Transactions of the New York Academy of Science, Series F, pp. 106–24.

Harris, Grace Gredys. 1989. Concepts of Individual, Self and Person in Description and Analysis. *American Anthropologist* 91: 599–612.

Heelas, Paul and Lock, Andrew. 1981. *Indigenous Psychologies*. London: Academic Press.

Imamura, Anne. 1987. *Urban Japanese Housewives*. Honolulu: University of Hawaii Press.

Ivy, Marilyn. 1988. Tradition and Difference in the Japanese Mass Media. *Public Culture Bulletin* 1: 21–9.

Keeler, Ward. 1987. *Javanese Shadow Plays, Javanese Selves*. Princeton, N.J.: Princeton University Press.

Kondo, Dorinne. 1990. *Crafting Selves: Power, Gender, and Discourses of Identity in a Japanese Workplace*. Chicago: University of Chicago Press.

Kristeva, Julia. 1982. Women's Time. *Feminist Theory: A Critique of Ideology* (N. Keohane, M. Rosaldo, and B. Gelpi, eds.), Chicago: University of Chicago Press.

Kumagai, Hisa. 1981. A Dissection of Intimacy: A Study of "Bipolar" Positions in Japanese Social Interaction, Amaeru and Amayakasu, Indulgence and Deference. *Culture, Medicine and Psychiatry* 5: 249–72.

Lebra, Takie Sugiyama. 1976. *Japanese Patterns of Behavior*. Honolulu: University of Hawaii Press.

   1983. Shame and Guilt: A Psychocultural View of the Japanese Self. *Ethos* 11: 192–209.

LeVine, Robert and White, Merry. 1986. *Human Conditions: The Cultural Basis of Educational Development*. New York: Routledge & Kegan Paul.

Lewis, Catherine. 1984. Cooperation and Control in Japanese Nursery Schools. *Comparative Education Review* 28: 69–84.

Lock, Andrew. 1982. Universals in Human Conception. *Indigenous Psychologies: The Anthropology of the Self* (A. Lock and P. Heelas, eds.), London: Academic Press.

Lock, Margaret. 1986. Plea for Acceptance: School Refusal Syndrome in Japan. *Social Science and Medicine* 23: 99–112.

Lutz, Catherine. 1988. *Unnatural Emotions*. Chicago: University of Chicago Press.

MacKinnon, Catherine. 1982. Feminism, Marxism, Method and the State: An Agenda for Theory. *Feminist Theory: A Critique of Ideology* (N. Keohane, M. Rosaldo, and B. Gelpi, eds.), Chicago: University of Chicago Press.

Mead, George Herbert. 1934. *Mind, Self, and Society*. Chicago: University of Chicago Press.

Moeran, Brian. 1986 (1984). Individual, Group and Seishin: Japan's Internal Cultural Debate. *Japanese Culture and Behavior* (T. S. Lebra and W. P. Lebra, eds.), Honolulu: University of Hawaii Press.

Mouer, Ross and Sugimoto, Yoshio. 1986. *Images of Japanese Society*. London: Routledge & Kegan Paul.

Nakane, Chie. 1970. *Japanese Society*. Berkeley: University of California Press.

Ohnuki-Tierney, Emiko. 1987. *The Monkey as Mirror: Symbolic Transformations in Japanese History and Ritual*. Princeton, N.J.: Princeton University Press.

   1990. The Ambivalent Self of the Contemporary Japanese. *Cultural Anthropology* 5: 197–216.

Plath, David. 1980. *Long Engagements: Maturity in Modern Japan*. Stanford, Calif.: Stanford University Press.

Rohlen, Thomas. 1976. Promises of Adulthood in Japanese Spiritualism. *Daedalus* 105: 125–43.

   1983. *Japan's High Schools*. Berkeley: University of California Press.

Rosaldo, Michelle. 1984. Toward an Anthropology of Self and Feeling. *Culture Theory: Essays on Mind, Self and Emotion* (R. Shweder and R. Levine, eds.), Cambridge: Cambridge University Press.

Rosenberger, Nancy R. 1987. Productivity, Sexuality and Ideologies of Menopausal Problems in Japan. *Health, Illness and Medical Care in Japan* (E. Norbeck and M. Lock, eds.), Honolulu: University of Hawaii Press.

1989. Dialectic Balance in the Polar Model of Self: The Japan Case. *Ethos* 17: 88–113.

1992. Messages of Western Style in Home Magazines. *Remade in Japan* (J. Tobin, ed.), New Haven, Conn.: Yale University Press.

In press. Reversals in Japanese Gender Relations: Indexing Contexts and Universal Powers. *Inside and Outside: Defining a Situated Social Order in Japan.* (J. Bachnik and C. J. Quinn, eds.), Princeton, N.J.: Princeton University Press.

Shore, Bradd. 1982. *Sala'Ilua: A Samoan Mystery.* New York: Columbia University Press.

Shweder, Richard and Bourne, Edmund. 1984. Does the Concept of the Person Vary Cross-culturally? *Culture Theory: Essays on Mind, Self and Emotion* (R. Shweder and R. Levine, eds.), Cambridge: Cambridge University Press.

Shweder, Richard and LeVine, Robert (eds.). 1984. *Culture Theory: Essays on Mind, Self and Emotion.* Cambridge: Cambridge University Press.

Smith, Paul. 1988. *Discerning the Subject.* Minneapolis: University of Minnesota Press.

Smith, Robert. 1983. *Japanese Society: Tradition, Self and the Social Order.* Cambridge: Cambridge University Press.

Tambiah, Stanley. 1984. *The Buddhist Saints of the Forest and the Cult of Amulets.* Cambridge: Cambridge University Press.

Taylor, Charles. 1989. *Sources of the Self.* Cambridge, Mass.: Harvard University Press.

Tobin, Joseph, Wu, David, and Davidson, Dana. 1989. *Preschool in Three Cultures: Japan, China, and the United States.* New Haven, Conn.: Yale University Press.

Urwin, Cathy. 1984. Power Relations and the Emergence of Language. *Changing the Subject* (J. Henriques, W. Hollway, C. Urwin, C. Venn, and V. Walkerdine, eds.), New York: Methuen.

Vogel, Ezra. 1971. *Japan's Middle Class.* Berkeley: University of California Press.

Vogel, Suzanne. 1978. Professional Housewife: The Career of Urban Middle Class Japanese Women. *The Japan Interpreter* 12: 16–43.

Venn, Couze. 1984. The Subject of Psychology. *Changing the Subject* (J. Henriques, W. Hollway, C. Urwin, C. Venn, and V. Walkerdine, eds.), New York: Methuen.

Weedon, Chris. 1987. *Feminist Practice and Poststructuralist Theory.* Oxford: Basil Blackwell.

Wetzel, Patricia. 1984. Uti and Soto (In-Group and Out-Group): Social Deixis in Japanese. Ph.D. dissertation, Cornell University.

White, Geoffrey and Kirkpatrick, John (eds.). 1985. *Person, Self, and Experience: Exploring Pacific Ethnographies.* Berkeley: University of California Press.

2 Japanese preschools and the pedagogy of selfhood

Joseph Tobin

Preface: a myth of Japanese childhood

To many Westerners, childhood in Japan is a tragic tale, part *Paradise Lost*, part *1984*, part *Civilization and Its Discontents*. The way the story goes, Japanese infants leave the peace and security of the womb to find an even more obliging world awaiting them, a world of unbounded maternal indulgence. Japanese infants and toddlers have their every wish to be cared for granted, their every dependency appeal answered. Jumping ahead to the end of the story (since we seem to know little about the middle), these overindulged and undercontrolled infants and toddlers somehow are transformed by age seven or eight into spiritless, unimaginative schoolchildren capable of little other than memorizing facts for exams.

The current Western wisdom has it that it is the Japanese school system which is the key agent of this transformation. The Japanese school system is viewed by most Westerners (and not a few Japanese) as a Godzilla-like monster with Mombusho (the Ministry of Education) for a brain and preschools for a mouth, each spring swallowing alive whole cohorts of happy, spoiled kids, chewing them up, and then spitting out armies of robot-like businessmen, bureaucrats, office ladies, and housewives.

Western scholars end up echoing these tropes of tragedy and horror when they begin their research into Japanese early childhood with the question "How do Japanese preschools transform spoiled toddlers into overly-restrained elementary school students?" Several assumptions that inform this question are ethnocentric and just plain misinformed.

Are Japanese toddlers spoiled and overindulged? Based on reading Benedict (1946), misreading Doi (1977), over-reading Caudill and Weinstein (1969), and overgeneralizing from personal experiences in Japan, many Western scholars as well as laymen are convinced that Japanese young children are spoiled. But to label Japanese mothering as spoiling

21

is to ignore the substantial variation to be found in Japanese child rearing. The image of the Japanese mother as unstintingly indulgent and at all times available to her toddler is in part a by-product of an over-reliance by Western researchers on urban, upwardly mobile, white-collar informants. Clearly, young urban middle-class housewives have more time and energy to lavish on their infants than do their working-class, professional, and rural peers. And even the ideal-typical Japanese urban middle-class *sarariman* (businessman's) wife may be less sweet with her young child behind closed doors than she shows to others.

There is also ethnocentrism in the implicit suggestion that there is something strange, something amiss, something in need of explanation, about the attention Japanese mothers give their children and in the use of the pejorative terms "spoiling," "dependence," and "indulgence" to describe this parenting style. Are Japanese children unusually, strangely, or dangerously indulged, or just more indulged, or indulged in a different way, than Western children (who may after all be the strange ones)? Indulgence and spoiling are poorly defined concepts, hard to identify and measure even within a culture.

Like the notion that Japanese babies and toddlers are spoiled and undercontrolled, the notion that Japanese older children are dull, over-controlled, and lacking in individuality is an ethnocentric stereotype that tells us more about Western values and concerns than about Japanese character. The Western assumption that Japanese children by age five, six, or seven are better behaved than their American peers is unsupported by comparative study and instead based largely on over-generalizing from seeing Japanese children in contexts that call for good behavior.

My research in Japanese *yōchien* (nursery schools) and *hoikuen* (daycare centers) suggests that Japanese children are neither as spoiled and indulged going into preschool nor as subdued and controlled coming out as our stereotypes suggest. After several years of studying Japanese preschools I have come to view them less as Marine-style boot-camps dedicated to breaking headstrong, spoiled recruits' spirits to the yoke of group domination than as outward-bound programs intended to provide sheltered, home-bound children with a chance to learn to function as members of a group. Japanese preschools do not seek a renunciation of individuality or selfhood so much as they offer children the chance to develop dimensions of self difficult to cultivate at home. The question we should ask is not "How do Japanese preschools transform spoiled toddlers into overcontrolled elementary school students?" but rather "How do Japanese preschools help today's home-reared toddlers develop a culturally appropriate sense of self?"

Omote and ura as dimensions of self

In *The Anatomy of Dependence* (1977) Doi Takeo suggests that in infancy Japanese develop a dyadic, interdependent dimension of self which Doi discusses in terms of the Japanese concept of *amae* (dependence). This first level of self, learned largely through repeated dyadic interactions between mother and child, includes the sense of being lovable and the sense of being a person able both to give and receive pleasure in intimate, interpersonal relationships.

In *The Anatomy of Self* (1986), Doi explains that the paired terms *omote* and *ura*, which mean, literally, front and rear, are used in common phrases to distinguish that which is presented to the outside world from that which is hidden from public view. (For example, *omote-ji* is the outer fabric, *ura-ji* the lining of a kimono.) Following a line of thought he introduced in a 1973 paper on ". . . the Japanese 2-fold Structure of Consciousness," Doi suggests that the Japanese self is two-tiered, with *omote* and *ura* dimensions. *Omote* is the front-side of the self, the side of the self one shows in public; *ura* is the private side of the self, the side one shows only to family and friends.

Putting Doi's theories into a developmental context would suggest that the Japanese child's first two years of life are focused on learning *amae* while the years from three to six are focused on learning *kejime* – the ability to make distinctions (Hendry 1986), distinctions between *omote* and *ura* (front and rear), *tatemae* and *honne* (appearance and real feelings), and *uchi* and *soto* (home and outside) (Lebra 1976). Japanese children begin to learn these distinctions at home as infants, begin under their parents' and siblings' tutelage to learn to bow, to use polite language, and to be polite with, but a little leery of, outsiders. But to develop the second dimension of self more fully children need to move outside the boundaries of mother and home and become members of more complex social groups.

During the second stage of the development of the self Japanese children are asked not to reject their desire to *amaeru* as infantile, but instead to learn to seek satisfaction of their dependency drives in relationships beyond the boundaries of the family and to cultivate a sense of self not only as a son or daughter in a family but also as a person in society. During this second stage of development Japanese children, already competent in the informal, spontaneous give and take of family life, develop a more outward-facing sense of self that will allow them to interact comfortably with non-kin and strangers. The ability to shift levels of intimacy and restraint learned in the inner circle of family relations as a toddler is expanded during the preschool years to the larger circles of peers, teachers, and neighbors.

Is any of this uniquely Japanese? Westerners, like Japanese, also ideally have multifaceted selves, selves able to adjust to different people and different situations. Western children also learn the difference between indoor and outdoor voices, learn the need to be circumspect and polite in formal contexts, learn to control the display of their emotions and to channel the gratification of their impulses.

The difference may be less one of psychology than of ethnopsychology, less a difference between Japanese and Western psyches than in the way the dimensions of the self are portrayed and evaluated in Japan and the West. In Japan, unlike in America, circumspection, circumlocution, formality, ceremony, ritual, and manners are viewed as vehicles for expressing as well as masking pleasure and for realizing rather than for binding the self. Less likely than Americans to view social conformity as a sign of weakness of character, joining the group as a betrayal of individuality, or ritualized public discourse as hypocrisy, Japanese value the *omote*, formal dimension of the self, as well as the *ura*, more spontaneous dimension.

On the road to adulthood Japanese children must learn lessons more complex than simply distinguishing inside from outside, front from back, public from private, and family from strangers. To have a proper, two-tiered Japanese sense of self one must learn to make much more fluid and subtle distinctions, learn to step back and forth across the gap dividing *omote* from *ura* in the course of a single conversation, or indeed, even in the midst of a single phrase, as a slight wink of an eye or a change in the level of politeness of a verb ending suddenly signals a slight but crucial warming up or cooling down of relations. As Doi suggests, *omote* and *ura* are complementary rather than opposing. There is *omote*, inevitably, in *ura* and *ura* in *omote*. In even the most formal, public interactions (*tatemae*) there is the potential for experiencing real human feeling (*honne*). In even the closest of relationships there is always a hint of *omote*, an unspoken awareness of the chasm that separates all human beings and that makes a degree of restraint necessary even among family members. As the Japanese saying puts it, "Strangers begin with siblings."

Thus the most crucial lesson to be learned in the Japanese preschool is not *omote*, not the ability to behave properly in formal situations, but instead *kejime* – the knowledge needed to shift fluidly back and forth between *omote* and *ura*. "To be Japanese," Doi writes in *The Anatomy of Self*, "is to be aware that things have an omote and an ura, and a person is not considered an adult until he or she has grasped this distinction" (1986: 33).

I suggest that the Japanese preschool helps children develop and integrate this twofold selfhood not by offering a world completely unlike the world of mother and home, but instead by offering a world that is simultaneously home (*uchi*) and not-home (*soto*), front (*omote*) and rear (*ura*), a world of both spontaneous human feeling (*honne*) and prescribed, formal pretense (*tatemae*). If preschools were purely a world of *omote* and home purely a world of *ura*, Japanese children might never learn to integrate the two sides of the self. Without an opportunity to integrate the *omote* and *ura* dimensions of the self, Japanese children might grow up to be the caricatured human being of this paper's preface, spoiled and impulsive at heart, externally overcontrolled.

An approach to studying preschools and the self

As part of a larger study of preschools in Japan, China, and the United States (Tobin et al. 1989), my colleagues and I videotaped in a classroom in a Kyoto daycare center and then took an edited version of the tape back to the school for the teachers and administrators to discuss and explicate. In this paper I will describe some of what we saw and taped during our visits to Komatsudani Hoikuen and present Principal Yoshizawa's, Assistant Principal Higashino's, and classroom teacher Fukui's explanations of these scenes to show how Japanese preschools, or at least one Japanese preschool, attempt to help children develop a traditionally Japanese sense of self in a world most Japanese perceive to be rapidly changing. Using Komatsudani's staff's explanations, I will suggest that structural features of the Japanese preschool including teacher/student ratios, disciplinary practices, and the ordering of space, time, and words function to help contemporary Japanese children cultivate what Doi calls a "twofold consciousness," a self combining *omote* and *ura*, front and rear dimensions.

The shrinking world of the Japanese child

In today's Japan preschools are being asked to provide a socializing function provided by other institutions in earlier eras. Preschool in Japan is a relatively recent phenomenon: the first *hoikuen* (daycare centers) and *yōchien* (nursery schools) were opened less than a hundred years ago (Shoji 1983) and it was not until the last twenty years that a majority of Japanese children began to attend preschool. Currently 95 percent of

Japanese children attend at least one year of *hoikuen* or *yōchien* before entering primary school.

Traditionally the process of growing up and becoming a person was thought to take place metaphorically if not literally on the road. (The Japanese word *dō*, like the English words "way" and "path," has the meaning not only of road, but also of praxis or regimen, as in *bushidō* – the way of the samurai.) To learn to be a man, a boy would have to venture outward, to embark on a journey where he would be forced to encounter and deal with strangers. Japanese proverbs such as "If you love your child, send him to the wide world," "Travel teaches friendship, life teaches compassion," and "It's good to be made to endure hardship" suggest that there are dimensions of the Japanese self that cannot be developed at home in the bosom of the family and that cannot be taught by parents. These lessons can only be learned on the road where one can experience the life of the outsider.

"To become a (mature) person one must eat a stranger's rice" means that to achieve personhood a child must learn to fuse the (*ura*) intimacy of receiving food with the (*omote*) formality of being a guest and bearing a debt. In Doi's terms, eating a stranger's (as opposed to mother's) rice means learning to function outside the world of *amae*, outside the world governed by *ura* relations, in the world of *omote*, the world not of family love but of social exchange, a world mediated not by uninhibited expressions of human feeling (*honne*) but rather by restrained, conventional rules of discourse (*tatemae*). Until a child has been outside the home, interacting with strangers, he not only cannot understand *omote*, he cannot appreciate *ura* either. There can be no true expression of spontaneity without the prior experience of restraint, no understanding of informality without an experience of formality, no appreciation of the significance of selfless motherly love without first-hand knowledge of debt, obligation, and exchange. Having learned on the road to behave properly in the outside world, the Japanese child proceeds to the higher developmental stage of finding human feeling (*honne*) behind the facade of manners (*tatemae*), and family-like pleasures in interactions with non-kin. Finally, returning to the bosom of the family, the developing Japanese child comes to accept the inevitability of there being a degree of formality in family interactions, and to appreciate the added depth this hint of restraint adds to heartfelt relationships.

In earlier eras Japanese children were not literally sent out on the road, literally to dine with strangers. But in earlier eras Japanese children had more opportunities than they do today to spend time outside their homes, apart from their mothers, in play away from the eyes of parents, in interactions with children and adults in their community who, though not literally strangers, were also not immediate family.

In the last twenty-five years or so the world of the Japanese family has shrunk: nuclear families have become more common, as young people have moved to cities, leaving parents and grandparents behind. In this modern "my home" era, extended family households have been replaced by urban condominiums ("mansions") and apartment complexes (*danchi*) and by suburban "bed towns" composed of single family homes. The birth rate has dropped from four children per family a few generations ago to fewer than two children per family today (Iritani 1979). Some scholars argue that the pervasiveness of this urbanization, family nuclearization, and gentrification of Japan has been exaggerated. For example, Keith Brown (1987) suggests that the nuclear family is far more representative of urban than of rural Japan and that the trend toward nuclearization may have peaked in the 1960s. But this does not significantly alter the argument I am making about the link between preschools and family change. As a force affecting the Japanese preschool, more important than the actual shrinking and nuclearization of the Japanese family is the Japanese perception of the world of the family as shrinking. Whether or not the lives of contemporary Japanese children have become objectively narrower, Japanese widely believe this to be the case and act accordingly.

Principal Yoshizawa of Komatsudani Hoikuen, like many other Japanese preschool administrators, teachers, and parents we spoke with, told us that with the shrinking of the world of the Japanese family since the war and especially in the last twenty years, the world of the Japanese child has become too sheltered: "Children's lives have become so narrow. Most of our children live in apartments, with just their parents, and their parents tend to spoil them and make things easy for them." In interviews, many Japanese parents we spoke with told us that they fear that their children are missing out specifically on the kind of spontaneous, unsupervised interactions with other children that they recall experiencing as children growing up in families of four and five children surrounded by a friendly sea of cousins, family friends, and neighbors. For example, a preschool parent in a suburb of Tokyo told us:

When I was a little girl I was outside all day. As soon as I would wake up, I would be outside, playing with my friends until dark. But it is not like that these days. At least not here, in Chiba. I don't know my neighbors that well. People move in and out so much and we live so high up, we only really meet people who share this stair-well.

In earlier eras, in eras when Japanese children grew up in extended families, with lots of siblings, in neighborhoods where the feeling of community was strong, children did not need to be sent to preschool to learn to interact with peers and adults other than their parents. But in today's Japan most parents believe that their child's best chance to experience *omote* and *ura* outside the limited context of the home lies in the preschool. To an American observer Japanese preschools are strikingly obliging and hospitable, and yet they are structured to represent to Japanese children the challenges of the outer world, the complexity of the road, the richness of life in a rural *buraku* (hamlet) or urban *chō* (neighborhood) in the idealized past.

A muddy field at the end of the road

Preschools like Komatsudani self-consciously attempt to compensate for the shrinking of the child's world at home by expanding the child's world at school. This strategy was apparent on a morning I observed group exercise being held away from the school.

On this day when I arrived at Komatsudani at 9 a.m. with several visiting American educators, Principal Yoshizawa told me that "Instead of having *taisō* (exercise) on the playground, as we usually do, today the older children will take a walk and have *taisō* at a different place." "A park?" I asked him. "No, not a park, exactly," Yoshizawa responded. I assured the American educators that Yoshizawa must be planning to take the children and us to an especially beautiful setting this morning for us to watch and film morning exercise. Perhaps we were heading for nearby Kiyomizu Temple or Okazaki Shrine.

At 10 a.m. the 60 four- and five-year-old children, their two teachers, and my delegation of American educators left the grounds of Komatsudani in a long line behind Principal Yoshizawa. We walked for nearly twenty minutes through the city streets, past the turn-off for Okazaki, past the road to Kiyomizu, and finally past the grounds of Kyoto Women's College where I momentarily thought (hoped) the exercises might be held. We doubled back two or three times across our path before finally arriving at an unpaved lot, about 60 meters square. The lot, marked for future construction, was covered with debris from houses that had previously stood on the site. Rain from the night before had settled into depressions across the gouged and pitted lot, leaving several mud puddles and ditches of standing water.

Under their teachers' direction the children formed a large circle, taking care to avoid the mud, the pools of standing water, and the piles of litter and construction debris. Without the benefit of the recorded music they usually have to guide them through the morning song and exercises the children and teachers seemed awkward and a bit at a loss, but they persevered through ten minutes of song and calisthenics. *Taisō* completed, the children, teachers, and their confused and disappointed American observers (this was not what we had anticipated videotaping) stood around apprehensively, looking to Yoshizawa to see what would happen next. Finally, a five-year-old boy said to Yoshizawa, "Well, what do we do now?" "Play," answered Yoshizawa.

The children gradually began to break ranks. Some started games of *junken* (paper, rock, scissors). Several boys discovered empty soda cans and began to fill them with muddy water. Other children threw rocks and sticks at cans. Children trying to broad-jump small puddles often missed, muddying themselves and others. Some children continued to stand around, confused, while others grew more bold and excited, making mud pies, purposely splashing each other, and collecting interesting litter and debris. Several children, muddied by others, ran to their teachers who gave them a quick wipe-off, a pat on the back, and encouragement to enter the fray, "to play." After twenty minutes of play on the muddy, littered lot, the teachers got the children lined up and we returned, by a more direct route this time, to the school.

Back at Komatsudani, over tea, Yoshizawa explained the morning's activity:

TOBIN: Why did you take the children to that place for *taisō*?
YOSHIZAWA: These days children only know how to play if they are given special toys and playground equipment. We took them to that field so they could learn how to play without special equipment. The idea was for them to discover that they can have fun even on an empty lot.
TOBIN: Did you know it would be so muddy?
YOSHIZAWA: It's because I knew it was muddy that I chose to take them there today. I went by there this morning and saw the mud and decided to bring the older children. You noticed that most of them were afraid of getting dirty? These days many children don't know how to be children. Especially for *hoikuen* children like ours who are in school all day, everyday, they grow up not having the opportunity to play in the mud if we don't arrange for them to get it here with us.

All of Komatsudani's excursions are not to muddy fields. Every month the children walk to a nearby temple, where they participate in a formal Buddhist ceremony (Komatsudani is a Buddhist preschool and Yoshizawa a Buddhist priest). Higashino, the assistant principal, explained: "The idea for all our excursions is to give the children experiences they don't get at home and don't get on the usual days in school. We go out on excursions to widen the children's world." Widening a preschool child's world involves giving him a chance to experience both the *ura* of mud-play and the *omote* of a temple service. Yoshizawa took only the older children in the school to the muddy field on the day we videotaped because the lesson for the day was the advanced course in *omote* and *ura*: having learned during their first and second years at Komatsudani to think of morning exercise as a formal, *omote* activity and excursions to public places as *omote* contexts, Yoshizawa purposely complicated the distinction between *omote* and *ura* for the older children by challenging them to discover that even outside, in public, with teachers, administrators, and foreign visitors looking on, there is the potential to enjoy spontaneous, silly, uninhibited play. Similarly, monthly excursions to the temple adjoining the school are used at Komatsudani to teach children that even where no strangers are present and one is among friends and under the supervision of a priest as easy-going as Principal Yoshizawa, it is appropriate to practice a degree of self-restraint and observe a certain level of formality.

Behaving and misbehaving

At Komatsudani a child who frequently misbehaves and who does not know how to behave in contexts (such as visits to a temple) that require order and restraint is viewed as inadequately socialized. But the staff of Komatsudani are less concerned about these children who do not know how to behave than they are about children who do not know how to misbehave (Lewis 1984). Principal Yoshizawa views misbehaving as a lost art for today's sheltered, nuclear-family raised children, as we can see in his discussion of the behavior of Hiroki, a wild and unruly four-year-old boy we videotaped:

I worry more about some of the other children who never misbehave, than I worry about Hiroki. He'll be okay. It's easier to teach a mischievous child to behave than to teach a too good child to dare to be naughty. In the old days children had more chance to play freely, without adults always peering over their shoulders. These days, children don't know how to really play, to play like children, which includes being mischievous, right?

Yoshizawa responded similarly to our questions about the way the staff of Komatsudani responded (or rather, seemed not to respond) in our videotape to children's fighting:

TOBIN: Isn't fighting a problem?
YOSHIZAWA: No, fighting's not a problem. Fighting at this age is natural. If there were no fights, that would be a problem. Children need to learn how to fight when they're young so they won't have to fight when they get into junior high school and could really hurt someone.

To put Yoshizawa's philosophy in terms of Doi's Japanese self-psychology, children who behave too well, like children who behave too badly, are one-dimensional, lacking a sense of *ura* in one case, a sense of *omote* in the other. The role of a preschool like Komatsudani is not to make bad children good or good children bad but instead to provide an environment structured so as to facilitate the development in children of a two-dimensional sense of self, a self able to integrate playing wildly in the mud in the morning with sitting quietly in a temple in the afternoon. A child who develops such a two-tiered sense of self in preschool will do well in other contexts in Japanese society, including, for example, in the life of the Japanese company man. The Japanese company man, like the Japanese preschooler, is a member of an institution that is both home (*uchi*) and not-home (*soto*), an institution that requires fluid shifts between *omote* and *ura*, between the formality of a management meeting and the spontaneous good fellowship of a section drinking party (Rohlen 1974).

Student/teacher ratios and group life

Komatsudani, like most other Japanese daycare centers and nursery schools, has ratios of thirty students to one teacher in the three-, four-, five-year-old classes. (In the United States ratios of sixteen children to one teacher are considered too high.) Our interviews with Japanese preschool staff suggest that student/teacher ratios are kept high in part to provide children with a large, complex peer group with whom to interact (Tobin et al. 1987). A *yōchien* teacher in Kyoto told us: "It seems to me that children need to have the experience of being in a large group in order to learn to relate to lots of kinds of children in lots of kinds of situations." Another young teacher explained:

I envy the way the American teachers, with such small classes, have time to play so affectionately with each child. That's how I like to play with my nieces and nephews. That's a good way for aunts and uncles and parents to play with their children. But I don't think that's necessarily the best way for a teacher to relate to children. Teaching is different from being a parent or aunt or friend to a child. Sometimes I feel like playing very warmly in a down-on-the-floor, barefoot sort of way with my students ... I'm a human being, as well as a teacher, and I'm not suggesting that teachers should be cold or formal. What I'm trying to say is that I believe a teacher should emphasize relating to the class as a whole, rather than to each student, even if this is a little sad for the teacher sometimes.

Large class sizes and high student/teacher ratios generally are disliked by Americans because they make intense dyadic relationships between teachers and students more difficult. But in Japanese preschools this loss of dyadic intensity, rather than being an undesirable by-product of large ratios, is an intended effect. If the ratio were to fall below twenty students or so per teacher, the teacher would become increasingly accessible and her attention increasingly attainable by individual students. This not only would threaten the group ethos that Japanese expect preschools to provide and interfere with children's play with peers, it also would make the teacher more mother-like and thereby encourage children to behave more like dependent sons and daughters, thus blurring the critical distinction between school and home, teacher and mother.

Most of today's home-reared, indulged Japanese children come to preschool having already developed the dyadic, *amae* dimension of self. At preschool children are helped to develop the group dimension of selfhood. The Japanese preschool's large student/teacher ratios and the emphasis on encouraging the development in children of group-living skills (*shūdan seikatsu*) are intended to foster in each child an identity as a member of a group.

To function in a Japanese group requires both *omote* and *ura*. Groups in Japanese preschools as in Japanese companies call on the *ura* as well as the *omote* dimensions of the self. Children doing morning exercise are a group, but so are children playing wildly in the courtyard after lunch. Quality control circles in a factory are groups but so are five or six workers in a section going out to a bar to get drunk after work. The Japanese preschool prepares children for the group life they will encounter in elementary school, junior high, and beyond by giving children many opportunities to participate in both formal, ceremonial, highly structured (*omote*) group activities led by teachers and in informal, unstructured, spontaneous (*ura*) group activities.

Space

The use of interior and exterior space in the Japanese preschool contributes to the children's developing an intuitive understanding of inside–outside and front–back. In Japanese architecture much emphasis is placed on the creation and definition of transitional areas and spaces (Itoh 1973). The *genkan* (entrance-way) of Komatsudani is a good example.

As children arrive at school each morning with their mothers, fathers, or grandparents, they rise together up two concrete steps to Komatsudani's front patio. This partially covered yet still outside area leads through large fully opened double temple doors into the *genkan* proper, the inner hallway. Teachers and sometimes the principal or assistant principal take turns standing just inside, outside, or astride the doorway, greeting parents and children as they arrive and helping children make a smooth transition each day from outside to inside, from family to school. In this critical moment of each child's day, custom and architecture combine to facilitate separation, as the child slips out of his street shoes and steps across the threshold to the inside in one motion, leaving his mother or father, still shod, standing in the doorway. It is much more cumbersome for a mother or father to get to the inside for to do so would require the parent to find a place to put her shoes and then to locate the slippers that guests wear inside. Children in Japanese preschools either go about as they do at home in their bare feet, or change into special indoor shoes some schools provide. In either case, a cubbyhole with the child's name awaits just inside the entrance-way, giving the entering child a place to put away his shoes. This symbolically gives the child the status of insider rather than (like his parents) guest and declares that for the child the school is a kind of *uchi*, a second home.

Here Japanese preschools differ from preschools we visited in China and the United States in the greater formality and definition of the transition process from home to school that is both provided and required by Japanese architecture and footwear customs. In American preschools parents usually walk all the way into the classroom with their children, help their children put away their things, and often stay for two or three or sometimes even for ten or fifteen minutes before finally saying a last goodbye. In Japan, in contrast, these separations are generally more formally and more precisely orchestrated and defined, each a little ceremony of entrance and exit occurring in spaces that symbolically express transition and the distinction between in and out. The architecture of the school mirrors the architecture of the self, suggesting not a clear delineation between inside and out, but instead, a significant overlap, as there are areas that are outside but have a feeling of being in and areas that are inside but have a feeling of being out. Standing just outside the school doorway with his mother, the Japanese child is in the world of *soto*. But stepping across the threshold and crossing the transitional space of the *genkan*, the child is once again home, putting away his shoes in their familiar spot.

Time

The distinctions between family and school and between *omote* and *ura* are reflected in the temporal as well as the spatial structures of the Japanese preschool. The school year begins in April with a formal event, the *nyūenshiki* (entrance ceremony), in which parents (usually mothers), dressed in kimono or their finest Western-style clothes, turn their children over to the care of the teachers and administrators. In a scene reminiscent of Rohlen's description of a Japanese company entrance ceremony (1974: 35–40) speeches are made by representatives of each of the parties involved: a PTA mother asks the teachers to please take care of the children and she pledges, on behalf of all of the parents, to support the school in every way possible. A teacher goes next, stating that the preschool staff members are honored by the trust and responsibility the parents are giving them to care for and educate their children and she pledges, on behalf of all of the teachers, to work hard and energetically. A child from the oldest class thanks the parents, teachers, and administrators for all they have already done and promises, on behalf of all of the children, to play and work hard throughout the year.

The principal, the day's final speaker, thanks the parents for all they have done for the children and for having confidence in his preschool, and thanks the teachers, in advance, for doing all of the real hard work in the coming year. He then says to the children: "This is a special day, isn't it? It's only once in your life you will enter preschool. You will be doing many things this year, making lots of friends, playing lots of games, singing lots of songs, even climbing some mountains. Really! So please do your best. Welcome to our school." The principal bows, and by this time many of the mothers are crying, their babies having formally left the nest. The end of the year graduation ceremony is very similar, but this time the focus is on the oldest children who are about to begin primary school. And this time all of the mothers and most of the teachers cry unabashedly. The Japanese school year is punctuated by many other smaller rites of passage: holidays such as Girls' Day, Boys' Day, and 7-5-3 Day are each celebrated with special foods and rituals. Parents also come to school for sports day (*undōkai*) in the fall, for the school play in the spring, and for a pre-New Year's vacation party in December. At each of these occasions Japanese preschool children are given opportunities to learn about *omote* and *tatemae* as they participate in shared, public, ceremonial expressions of feeling and emotion.

Time itself is given a formal, *omote* meaning as children learn to punctuate their lives and record their development less according to their birthdays, as children do in the United States, than according to their year in school. For example, if you ask a Komatsudani child his age he is likely to respond not "six-years-old" but instead, "ōkii-gumi" (oldest class). In Japanese preschools, as in Japanese society in general, decisions about whether to wear summer or winter school uniforms (*aifuku*) or whether to drink warm or cold tea with lunch most often are based not on individual preference or even on the day's weather, but rather on the calendar, the most public, formal definer of time. Holidays and seasons are stressed and formally and ceremonially enjoyed, thus introducing preschool children to the nationally shared rhythms by which Japanese of all ages move through their lives.

The relativity of *uchi* and *soto* (inside and outside), *tatemae* and *honne* (formal appearance and spontaneous feeling), and *omote* and *ura* (front and rear) are reinforced by the daily schedule of a preschool like Komatsudani that divides the day into school-wide, class-wide, and undefined periods of activity. Children play freely from when they arrive until 9.30 each morning when the clean-up song is played and children assemble for *taisō* (morning exercise). *Taisō* in preschools, as in large companies, functions to create a sense of shared identity and of common purpose. As the children run and jump and bend more or less in unison with all the other children and teachers in their school, they participate in a ritualized yet no less heartfelt expression of being one, of being members of the same organization, the same *uchi*.

As *taisō* ends, the children and teachers disassemble, reassembling moments later in their classrooms where they again go through a round each day of ritualized greetings, greetings which this time stress their common identity not as members of the same school, but as members of the same class. As the children at Komatsudani each morning shout out together, "Sensei, ohayō, minna-san, ohayō" ("Teacher, good-morning, everyone, good-morning"), the word "everyone" suddenly shifts meaning from "everyone in our school" to "everyone in our class." Thus the Japanese preschool child, guided by a daily routine featuring the same songs and choral recitations at the same time every day, and by formal rites of transition that lead him from activity to activity, moves each day through a world composed of both adjoining and concentric circles of group identity, a constantly changing and yet predictable world of family and school, large group and small group, inside and outside.

In addition to the calendar and the clock, another sort of time, tempo, is used by Japanese preschools to reinforce the meaning of *omote* and *ura*, of front-door (polite, formal) ways of behaving versus back-door (relaxed, spontaneous) modes of feeling and interacting.

Americans viewing the Japanese preschool find themselves faced with a conundrum: the Japanese preschool strikes us as an institution at the same time both too chaotic and too structured for American tastes. This is no accident. Like a conductor leading his musicians through a symphony by Stravinsky, the Japanese preschool leads children through wildly changing yet carefully composed, orchestrated, and directed changes in tempo and mood. When Japanese preschools are structured, they are highly structured (though not somber, rigid, or joyless). And when Japanese preschools are chaotic they are wildly chaotic (Lewis 1984) (though even this chaos is anticipated and planned). These swings back and forth throughout the day from highly structured, teacher-directed, class-wide group activities such as work-book sessions and origami projects to the anarchy of the post-lunch period when nobody seems to be in charge and children are allowed to run about, to scream, and even to fight, suggests not that the Japanese and their preschools are in any way inconsistent or inscrutable but rather that they place a great emphasis on the cultivation of a sense of self capable of integrating *omote* and *ura*, *tatemae* and *honne*, *soto* and *uchi*.

Structured activities such as *taisō*, work-books, and *happyōkai* (the end of the year celebration) are times for *omote*, for public behavior, times in the Japanese preschool for cultivating the public dimension of the self. The word *omote* does not carry with it nearly as much of the negative connotations as does the English word "formal" of being constrained or pleasureless. Rather *omote* and *ura* refer to different kinds of pleasures and satisfactions and to different aspects of the self. To become a person in Japan is to learn to be comfortable in each of these worlds, to be able both to receive and to give satisfaction in each of these kinds of relationships.

Unstructured activities such as early morning and late afternoon playground play and free time after lunch provide children with the chance to explore the limits of their uninhibited pleasures and moods. During these periods of chaos, children gradually learn to limit and modulate their expressions of *ura*. *Ura*, like *omote*, requires learning and adaptation to others and to reality. *Ura* is not the id, not unrestrained impulse and emotion. Rather, *ura* refers to the dimension of the self that can comfortably be shared and indulged with one's friends and family. In four-year-olds *ura* naturally at times finds expression in fighting but it has many other expressions as well.

Japanese preschool administrators like Higashino and Yoshizawa and teachers like Fukui believe that in an increasingly impersonal and pressured Japan it is especially important for preschools to help children cultivate not just their *omote*, their ability to function in formal settings, but their *ura* as well, their ability to make friends, to relax, to find pleasure outside as well as inside the world of school and work. Japanese preschools strive to give children the chance to cultivate *omote* and *ura*, and the ability to move comfortably back and forth between the two.

Words

The distinctions between *omote* and *ura*, *uchi* and *soto*, and *tatemae* and *honne* also are reinforced daily in the way language is used in Japanese preschools. Formal language and the style of honorific speech, posture, and comportment that Japanese adults are expected to use in their interactions with social superiors and in *omote* encounters in general are introduced in the preschool not by demanding, encouraging, or expecting children to speak formally to their teachers, but rather by the teachers joining the students several times throughout each day and on special occasions throughout the year in stylized group recitation using formal speech. For example, each day before lunch at Komatsudani the children and teachers recite aloud and in unison, "Otōsama, Okāsama, arigatō gozaimashita" ("Honorable Father, Honorable Mother, we humbly thank you"). Japanese children never directly address their parents nearly so honorifically. In fact, to do so would ring ludicrously false. Many Japanese believe that even expressions such as "I love you," "thank you," and "I'm sorry" (Doi 1977, 1986) sound strange when used within the family, as they suggest a distance between family members, a denial of the taken-for-grantedness and mutual interdependency that is highly valued in family life and close friendships. Thus when the children in Komatsudani use honorific language each day at school to refer to their parents, the point of the ritual is not so much to honor their parents as to learn to participate in a shared, public, ceremonial world, the world of *omote* and *tatemae*. It is the social order, not their parents, that is being honored by this use of formal language. The most important distinction being taught and learned is not, as it might appear to be, the Confucian one between high-status parents and low-status children, but rather the distinction that exists between the side of the self that finds expression in one's private, *ura* relationship to one's family at home and the side of the self that finds expression in the public, *omote* relationship to one's family that is shown to the outside world, through stylized, formal words and gestures.

Japanese children speak two distinct languages at school: the language of *ura* with friends and with teachers during the informal segments that make up the great majority of the school day and the language of *omote* during the formal ceremonial moments that punctuate the day and the year. In American preschools teachers work hard to model, correct, and elicit from children words as self-expression ("Sally, don't hit. Use words. *Tell* Molly how you feel"). In contrast, Japanese teachers put a great deal of effort into correcting, modeling, and eliciting the language of *omote*. Formal greetings, honorific terms of address, and ceremonial phrases are drilled, practiced, and endlessly repeated, especially during the first few weeks of the school year (Peak 1986). Because Japanese preschool teachers, unlike American preschool teachers, do not explicitly teach self-expression, because they do not often encourage children to handle interpersonal problems with words, and because they rarely enter into or attempt to arbitrate children's disputes (Lewis 1984), Japanese children's "free" speech is very free. Uncorrected and unconstrained by adult interference, Japanese children's *ura*-talk is almost always loud, often naughty and rude, and strikingly unlike formal (*omote*) Japanese speech.

Conclusion

A dominant American image of Japan is that Japanese young children go into preschool overindulged and undercontrolled and come out overcontrolled, unimaginative, and spiritless. Our research in Japanese *yōchien* (daycare centers) and *hoikuen* (nursery schools) suggests in contrast that the primary function of the Japanese preschool is not to break children's spirit or will but instead to help children add to the dyadic, interdependent sense of self learned at home in the first three years of life a more group-oriented, outward-facing sense of self. This second level of self, which Doi calls the *omote* (front) dimension, complements rather than displaces the *ura* (rear) dimension of self that developmentally precedes it.

The ideal Japanese child, like the ideal Japanese adult, is not always or even usually under tight self-control. Japanese preschools function to give children a chance to cultivate the *ura* as well as the *omote* dimensions of the self. A well-balanced Japanese child should be able to move easily back and forth between control and emotionality. In contemporary Japan it is in preschools where Japanese children have their best chance of developing and integrating a twofold sense of self, a sense of self capable of fusing *omote* and *ura*. The large class size, the hands-off approach to dealing with children's misbehavior, the fluctuations between structure and chaos during the school day, the use of language and even the ordering of space and time, each of these features of the Japanese preschool contributes to the creation of an environment structured to help children learn to feel themselves, to be themselves, in front-door, formal contexts as well as in interactions which are back-door, informal, and spontaneous.

REFERENCES

Benedict, Ruth. 1946. *The Chrysanthemum and the Sword: Patterns of Japanese Culture*. Boston, Mass.: Houghton Mifflin.

Brown, Keith. 1987. Farm Life in a Japanese Village. *Japan Society Newsletter* 34 (5): 2–5.

Caudill, William and Weinstein, Helen. 1969. Maternal Care and Infant Behavior in Japan and America. *Psychiatry* 32: 12–43.

Doi, Takeo. 1973. *Omote* and *Ura*: Concepts Derived from the Japanese 2-fold Structure of Consciousness. *Journal of Nervous and Mental Disease* 157: 258–61.

   1977. *The Anatomy of Dependence*. Tokyo: Kodansha.

   1986. *The Anatomy of Self*. Tokyo: Kodansha.

Hendry, Joy. 1986. *Becoming Japanese*. Honolulu: University of Hawaii Press.

Iritani, Toshio. 1979. *The Value of Children: A Cross-national Study*, Vol. VI. Honolulu: East–West Center Press.

Itoh, Teiji. 1973. Tradition in Formative Culture. *Listening to Japan* (J. Bailey, ed.), New York: Praeger.

Lebra, Takie Sugiyama. 1976. *Japanese Patterns of Behavior.* Honolulu: University of Hawaii Press.

Lewis, Catherine. 1984. Cooperation and Control in Japanese Nursery Schools. *Comparative Education Review* 28: 69–84.

Peak, Lois. 1986. Training Learning Skills and Attitudes in Japanese Early Educational Settings. *Early Experience and the Development of Competence* (W. Fowler, ed.), San Francisco: Jossey-Bass.

Rohlen, Thomas. 1974. *For Harmony and Strength.* Berkeley and Los Angeles: University of California Press.

Shoji, Masako. 1983. Early Childhood Education in Japan. *Comparative Early Childhood Education* (G. Lall and B. Lall, eds.), Chicago: Charles C. Thomas Co.

Tobin, Joseph, Wu, David, and Davidson, Dana. 1987. Class Size and Student/ Teacher Ratios in the Japanese Preschool. *Comparative Education Review* 31: 533–49.

1989. *Preschool in Three Cultures: Japan, China, and the United States.* New Haven, Conn.: Yale University Press.

3   Multiple selves: the aesthetics and politics of artisanal identities

Dorinne Kondo

It was, of all places, on the annual company trip to an *onsen*, or hot springs resort, when I began to realize how significant work could be in the lives of my informants. I was a *pāto taimā* (part-timer) at a small confectionery factory in Tokyo, a family-owned concern that made "traditional" Japanese sweets and Western pâtisserie, and we had gone en masse to a mountain inn for our revels. It was much like other company trips: the sumptuous banquet, where men drank impressive quantities of beer and sake, where people were enjoined to "Sing!" to entertain the others, where we stayed up late for yet another game of *mah-jongg* or yet another dip in the sulfurous baths. At breakfast time, I stumbled downstairs to the communal tables in the dining room, and found myself face to face with Ohara-san, the head of the *wagashi*, or Japanese sweets, division of the company. At that point, I had been working in *wagashi* for only a week or so, and Ohara-san was, quite frankly, a daunting presence. He embodied a stereotype my informants often invoked: the stern, silent, severe artisan. In the factory, he would work for hours without a word, occasionally stalking about to glower at his subordinates as he inspected their creations. Above all, he appeared unapproachable, and seven in the morning seemed no time to make my first try. But, summoning my courage, I asked him about our one shared experience: work. I was astonished, in the course of our conversation, to see how animated he could be. The gaunt, stiff countenance now assumed a variety of expressions: frowns as he described the hardships of his childhood and his apprenticeship; an air of pride and confidence as he spoke of his craft, a softness, even, as he poetically described the delicate, aesthetic emotions he expressed in his art. In fact, he was so loquacious (and, no doubt, so happy to have such a captive audience) that we were the last ones left at the breakfast table, and I had to scramble to prepare myself for the day's outing. Long afterwards, my head still spinning, I began to recall, in bits and pieces, conversations and interviews with other artisans, who often spoke in tones of affection and respect for their craft, even the tools and

40

the materials they used. Ohara-san and his breakfast monologue directed me toward an investigation of the ways selves are constructed at the workplace, and, in particular, toward a specifically artisanal idiom of work.

Self, work, and meaning

Anthropological studies

To understand Ohara-san's narrative of work and life requires rendering intelligible the hardships and the aesthetics of work he so vividly described. At the same time, these meanings must be placed within a particular, changing political/economic context. Too often, our folk ideologies encourage a separation of studies which aims to "convey other cultural experience" on the one hand, and studies of world historical political economy on the other (cf. Marcus and Fischer 1986). Most research on "the concept of self ...," beginning with Mauss's original formulations of *la notion de personne* (1986) to the spate of work in the last fifteen years on selfhood in other cultures, is no exception. These analyses tend to emphasize static, essentialized, global traits disconnected from power relations in the society.[1] Though they provide important guides to certain inescapable refrains in any culture, a more critical approach might ask to what extent general "essences" of selfhood can be distilled out from the particular contexts in which they took place, and whether ambiguity, multiple interpretations, and contradictions might complicate – or even shatter – the impressions of a smooth totality. And surely, investigations of selves in the domain of work cannot ignore struggles over the meanings of power, hierarchy, and discipline (cf. Kondo 1987).

Another approach would aim to challenge the distinction between the personal and the political by moving from the level of "a concept of self" in a global sense to more finely grained, contextual studies of selfhood in specific, historically located situations. When one studies people in family enterprises in Japan, a single, monolithic idiom fails to capture the complexity of my informants' lives. One must continue a quest to further decenter the self, seeing not simply a "concept of self" related to other abstracted domains of social life, but how selves are constructed variously in specific situations, how these constructions can be fragmented by multiplicity, contradiction, and ambiguity, and how these constructions shape, and are shaped by, relations of power. Yet in so doing, we must not lose sight of the importance of meanings and meaningful action in social life.

Workers' identities

A number of such attempts emerge in sociology and in European social history from the literature on skilled artisanal work. Much of this literature, primarily focused on eighteenth- and nineteenth-century Britain and France, examines the collective identities of skilled male artisans (Sewell 1980, Scott 1974, Thompson 1964, Prothero 1979, to name only a few). Revising theories which linked membership in the proletariat with class consciousness and revolutionary potential, this new literature tied skill – and membership in artisanal "corporations" and guilds – to workers' solidarity and to participation in political protest.[2] Skill is linked in a romantic way with community, political consciousness, and a collective worker identity.

If much of the European literature on artisans and politics celebrates the communities of artisans in the eighteenth and nineteenth centuries, another discourse relates workers' identities to changes in the political economy through an examination of the fate of skilled work in industrial, capitalist societies. How does skill become redefined under regimes of industrial capitalism and mass production, and how do these redefinitions shape one's personal identification – one's investment in work? Labor process theorists such as Harry Braverman (1974) see the growth of capitalism linked with the introduction of scientific management, mass production technology, and the development of professional classes of "mental" workers – engineers, designers, and the like. These changes rob craftsmen (and I use the gendered term intentionally) of their skill, relegating them to ever more monotonous, meaningless, atomized tasks. Others, such as Piore and Sabel (1984), accord less omnipotence to capital, and point to the success of alternative models of production, particularly a craft "paradigm" of work organization they call "flexible specialization." Flexible specialization, they say, is to be preferred to mass production, because "flexible specialization is predicated on collaboration. And the frequent changes in the production process put a premium on craft skills. Thus the production worker's intellectual participation in the work process is enhanced – and his or her role revitalized. Moreover, craft production depends on solidarity and communitarianism . . ." (Piore and Sabel 1984: 278).

Among these investigations of worker identity, several common themes emerge. Mass production technologies are associated with worker alienation. Worker solidarity, community, and skilled work, however, foster positive worker identities. Sociologists and historians alike share a romantic view of work. They see solitary artisanal communities realized in a Golden Age of the past or in a utopian future. Artisans' lives are depicted as undifferentiated and uncomplicated, another unproblematic totality.

My analysis confirms aspects of such explanations and questions others. Braverman soft-pedals the ways workers often impose meaning on the world and derive satisfaction in industrial settings. Piore and Sabel are right in pointing to the existence of craft traditions in industrial work. On the other hand, they, along with Braverman, tend to over-romanticize the craft model of the work process and neglect its "cultural force":[3] its distribution in society, and who participates in these cultural meanings. As a growing revisionist literature, much of it written by feminists, has pointed out, solitary craft communities have another, less romantic side. To create solidarity means to exclude the "unskilled" (cf. Stark 1982), and unskilled, all too often, means women (cf. Gray 1987, Berg 1987, Rule 1987). Celebrations of artisanal community beg the question of how jobs are labeled "skilled" or "unskilled" in the first place, and how becoming a full-fledged artisan means becoming a man, involving a specifically masculine pathway to maturity and a masculine work identity. Indeed, Phillips and Taylor (1980), in an important programmatic essay, argue that labels of skill have little or nothing to do with the actual complexity of the work involved. Instead, work is labeled skilled or unskilled, depending on the sex of the workers, not on its intrinsic degree of difficulty. Yet, because these scholars are sketching out a position rather than offering a case study, they leave in abeyance questions about how these labels get put into place, how work classifications are reproduced or challenged in everyday life, how these attributions of skill might shape, and are shaped by, the construction of self in work.

So Ohara-san's paean to his artisanal aesthetic must be taken seriously, as deeply meaningful and suggestive of nuanced, deeply felt emotion. But it must also be set more precisely in the context of our interaction and, especially, within the context of the workplace. As Jacques Rancière has argued, "Whenever workers speak in the name of work, affirm its rights or glorify its greatness, we run the risk of inferring a false picture of the collectivity they represent or of the realities that underlie their speech, unless we determine very precisely who is speaking, who is being addressed, and what the stakes are" (1986: 327).

Let us begin, then, with Ohara-san and his story, keeping a critical eye on its ambiguities and ironies, as well as its positive construction of a life at work.

Ohara-san and artisanal idioms of work

My breakfast conversation with Ohara-san was relatively brief, but during its course he revealed these outlines of a tale.

Ohara-san was born in the thirties in the cold, poor northeast of Japan. Shortly after he graduated from middle school, both of his parents died tragically in an accident, forcing Ohara-san to quit school and find a job. He knew it would be as an artisan, because from childhood, he loved making things. In fact, his favorite childhood hobby was building ships in glass bottles, the more complicated the better. An uncle, a confectioner in a neighboring town, took pity on the orphaned Ohara-san and took him on as an apprentice. A few years at his uncle's workshop taught him the basics of the trade, and Ohara-san decided to move on. All of life, he said enthusiastically, is a form of learning (*benkyō*), and each shop had its own *yarikata*, its own way of doing things. Learning these different *yarikata* kept him moving, first within the same province, and then, in his late teens, all the way to Tokyo to try his fortunes. There too he moved regularly from establishment to establishment, about once a year during his early years of apprenticeship. After his skills were honed, however, he sometimes quit sooner; once, because the level of expertise was so low (*teido ga hikui*) he walked out after a single day. The quest to pursue his craft took Ohara-san to ten or twelve different workshops, from the posh suburbs of neighboring Shizuoka Prefecture to the livelier areas in Shitamachi, the old downtown. But when he got married and, especially, when his children were born, Ohara-san began to think better of his itinerant ways, and decided to settle down (*ochitsuku*) in one spot. That was twelve years ago, and he has been with the Sato establishment ever since.

Ohara-san spoke in nostalgic tones about his early period of apprenticeship, though it sounded grueling, hardly the material for nostalgic reminiscence. Because the master was showing his benevolence and largesse in teaching tyros the trade, a salary of any substance would have been unthinkable. Free room and board and a pittance of a wage sufficed. The work was demanding, beginning at dawn and lasting until late at night. Yet, according to Ohara-san, these years of perseverance were a necessary part of his training. Those who stuck it out were the truly dedicated. What enabled them to endure was a dream of becoming master craftsmen themselves, and one day opening their own shops. "You have to have a goal," he stated emphatically. (*Mokuhyō o motte yaranai to, dame mitai.*)

For Ohara-san, work was the reason for living, his *ikigai*. In art (*geijutsu*), his expertise and artistic sensibility found expression. The proper practice of his craft requires skill and a delicate sensitivity to the changes in the seasons, for *okashi* (Japanese sweets) change according to seasonal rhythms. This feeling for the seasons (*kisetsukan*) he extolled as wonderful, one of the greatest pleasures of his work. The more mundane tasks, making *okashi* for everyday consumption, can be done equally well by the younger men, who possess the necessary strength and stamina. The attitude of most young people today, he assured me, is very different from his own. "They're in it for the money. A craftsman's attitude today is rare."

Ohara-san, many people thought, was an embodiment of a "traditional" artisan. People in the factory admired his skill, but often kept their distance. Those outside the trade, such as my landlady and her family, nodded when I provided descriptions of Ohara-san and the atmosphere in the *wagashi*, or Japanese sweets, division. "Traditional" (*dentōteki*), they pronounced. A "traditional" artisan who made "traditional" Japanese confections. But what makes him a "traditional artisan"? And what is the meaning of his tale within a factory setting?

Ohara-san's story refracts motifs from a larger, composite story of artisanal work. Exploring general themes of work, skill, and workers' identities draws our attention to: first, a discourse on creative self-realization through work, through the polishing of the self through hardship; second, an artisanal aesthetic which connects selves to material objects and to the natural world. Later, we must more clearly situate these discourses within the particular situation of the Sato factory. For Ohara-san's tale of aesthetic self-realization in work also begins to tell us how some people come to be defined, in certain contexts, as less fully human than others.

Artisanal idioms of work: a collective story[4]

Work as maturity and self-realization

One important way my informants talked about the process of maturation is through the notion of *ichininmae*, literally one complete portion for one person. It can refer, among other things, to becoming a mature human being (*ichininmae no ningen*), a mature gendered being (*ichininmae no onna*), or in the factory setting, a mature practitioner of the trade (*ichininmae no shokunin*). This process is an arduous one. It means having to undergo hardship (*kurō*) for only in this way will the inner self be tempered; only in this way will the hard edges of immaturity be planed into the roundness of adulthood. *Kurō* can be found in carrying out the requirements of a social role, whether it be the role of bride, mother, or worker. The hardship of a young person in "training" for the university entrance exams can be a form of *kurō*. So can economic hardship. So can the tribulations of a young bride who leaves her natal family to become a member of a new household.

In a work setting like the Sato factory, however, *ichininmae* and *kurō* are implicated in a particular artisanal system of apprenticeship. In the Tokugawa period, and according to informants, through the prewar period, the apprenticeship system for artisans (*totei seido*), as well as apprenticeship service in merchant households (*detchi bōkō*), followed general patterns, informed by more general notions of *shugyō*, perfecting a trade, paying one's dues in order to become a skilled worker and a mature person.

The most exemplary form of *kurō* takes place outside the natal home, for separation from one's circle of attachment and belonging is itself a form of suffering. The theory is that outside the home, people must monitor their behaviors more carefully, polishing their skills as social beings. Typically, young apprentices lived with their masters and took their meals together. Living conditions were often demanding and difficult, intensifying the degree of hardship. As in Ohara-san's story, work is described as demanding, occupying nearly all one's waking hours. Mythic tales of masters' cruelty abound. The master and his family, went one oft-repeated story, took lavish meals, complete with fish, vegetables, and steaming bowls of soft, white rice, while the apprentices made do with bowls of cold leftovers, or even worse, rice mixed with barley.[5]

The pedagogies of the workplace were another kind of *kurō*. Like other forms of pedagogy linked to processes of self-realization, artisans sometimes began their training with cleaning, sweeping, cooking, and other tasks with no apparent relation to their chosen trade. Even when they began to take more active part in learning appropriate artisanal techniques, there might be little explicit verbal instruction from the master.[6] Learning through observation (*minarai*, literally "seeing and learning") was and often still is the primary mode of instruction. This serious task of learning the trade required full energy, and holidays were infrequent: the first and the fifteenth of the month, according to the older men. "They were like slaves" (*Dorei mitai na mon datta n desu yo*), averred Tanoue-san, a man in his sixties and a third-generation woodworker. Other artisans told tales of their humiliations on the job. One man, a maker of umbrella handles, described with thinly veiled distaste a master who constantly berated him with the epithet stupid (*don*). On the surface, such stories decry the apprenticeship system, as exploitative. But the condemnation is ambiguous. For an artisan's claim to special powers of endurance and fortitude – and, therefore, a special claim to maturity and toughness – is also heightened in the telling of these tales.

Formally, the apprentices' progress in honing their skills and, presumably, furthering their maturity as human beings could be calibrated through a system of hierarchical ranks. During the Tokugawa period, Japanese artisanal careers followed the apprentice–journeyman–master progression familiar to us from the European system. A similar trajectory existed among merchant households, where young boys entered as *detchi* (apprentice), rose to the status of *hanninmae* – half a portion for one person, half a person – before the young man could become a full-fledged clerk (*bantō*), often around the age of thirty.

Prevailing notions of skill among artisans – in the present day as in earlier times – stress physical idioms of technical capability. The aim is to go beyond a purely cognitive level of learning, and to learn with the body (*karada de oboeru*). A multiplicity of idioms indicate that this is a kind of physical knowledge. An artisan's skill and technique is known as his *ude*, his arm, and to hone a skill is to polish one's "arm" (*ude o migaku*). Both the male artisans in the confectionery factory and the female hairdressers at the salon where I worked for a few months spoke of, literally, "attaching the technique to the body" (*gijutsu o mi ni tsukeru*). For the women, their specialized knowledge and practical abilities were part of their dowry (*yomeiri dōgu*); if they had to work to support the family or supplement the family income they would be able to do so. The assumption is that the technique becomes one with the person, and that once learned, this physical knowledge can never be effaced. It becomes one's property, if you will, a palpable part of the self. Those who have put in their years of training, those who have seasoned and tempered their skills to the point where skill is "attached to the body," have also become more mature persons in the process.

The portability of skill dovetailed with common ideals of traveling from workshop to workshop to learn new techniques, thus highlighting mobility as an integral part of artisans' self-definitions. Clearly this presents a career trajectory quite different from that of today's Organization Man or even from the merchant households, where in order to rise in the hierarchy apprentices had to come in at a young age and remain with the same firm. Gordon (1985) describes the difficulties of early factory owners in the Meiji period, who constantly complained of problems of labor discipline. The independent artisans hired to work in the factories were unaccustomed, and often hostile, to this more regimented work setting.

The pattern of moving from workshop to workshop died hard – and in some cases, never died at all. Many of the older artisans in the factory had long histories of job mobility. Matsumoto-san, the chief of the baking division, had been to at least ten different places to learn, all of them in the Shitamachi section of Tokyo. He quit his various jobs for a variety of reasons: disputes over job responsibilities (too much delivery, not enough time to actually make confections) and personality conflicts with the master (he and the *dannasan* just didn't get along) seemed the most frequently cited reasons. To find new jobs, Matsumoto-san did not have to rely on personal connections. Five years ago he simply got out of the subway, saw a sparkling, well-appointed sweet shop, thought "Isn't this a pretty shop across from the station?" (*Eki mae ni kirei na mise ga aru zya nai?*), and went in to talk with the head of the factory. He has been with the Satos ever since. His skill in the midst of a shortage of skilled artisans meant that Matsumoto-san could always find another job, and not surprisingly, he radiated confidence.

Having polished the heart and the "arm" through hardship, having learned new techniques at a variety of establishments, having acquired in the process a certain confidence and a pride in his work, an artisan could be described as possessing the artisanal spirit (*shokunin katagi*). Such artisans are, according to prevailing images, totally identified with their work. They are said to feel their *ikigai* (raison d'être) in the pleasure of creation. If I mentioned this quality to artisans I knew, the remark inevitably produced similar results: a modest denial, followed by a smile – which I usually read as an expression of scarcely concealed pleasure. The complete involvement in creation should far outweigh the importance of monetary gain; indeed, I found the phrase *shokunin katagi* (artisanal spirit) most often invoked to describe older artisans who made objects for which there was a declining market. Far from letting this situation discourage them, they continued to produce finely crafted works. Accordingly, a true artisan possessed of artisanal spirit should practice his craft even if the financial reward were small. This dedication to creation above all else clearly entails a lack of worldliness, and indeed, this is another commonly invoked cultural image of the artisan, as naive and pure (*tanjun*), unschooled in the ways of the world.

When I discussed artisanal work with artisans and people outside the trades, more often than not they would make some reference to a quintessential *shokunin* (artisan) personality, a logical corollary of this artisanal dedication to creation. Conventional wisdom depicts artisans as taciturn, a bit rough in their manner, not quite skilled at the niceties of social interaction. Again and again, my interviews with artisans turned up the recurrent theme of their ineptitude at business dealings, prey to the easy conviviality and flowery phrases of wily merchants or the machinations of cruel masters. A common ruse (common, at least, in "traditional" times – which for my informants tended to mean the early years of the Meiji Restoration) was for a master to say he would give his apprentices the capital to start up their own shops, in the "ideal" pattern. "But if the master had ten or twelve apprentices, he wasn't about to shell out money for all of them. So after ten years or so he'd say, 'I was going to set you up in business, but you did this and this and this wrong. So forget it,'" said Tanoue-san, a woodworker who lived in my neighborhood. And in the face of such deceptive (*inchiki*) masters, artisans often described themselves as, literally, having a heavy mouth, lacking skill at conversation (*kuchi ga omoi*), or not saying much (*kuchikazu ga sukunai*). Though this verbal "ineptitude" was talked about in some ways as a failing, in another it embodies the culturally valued traits of actions and no words (*fugen jikkō*). This remains a defining feature of masculinity and a highly respected trait in any person; nothing is less respected than "big talk and no action," and many have written on the high value placed on silence and verbal repose in other domains of Japanese culture. Whether or not these stereotyped images are "true" in some empirical sense (on the basis of life histories and observations, there seems to be enough truth to sustain the stereotype), they possess a mythic reality, and these images certainly form part of the self-images of at least the older artisans I interviewed.

People in the ward of Tokyo where I lived and worked still clearly believed in the salutary benefits of *kurō* through an apprenticeship-based system of pedagogy. Typically, successors to merchant households, for instance, were sent away, perhaps to a larger company in a related trade, in order to learn the business. For the local sake shop owner's son, for instance, it meant working for years in the Kikkoman soy sauce company[7] before he came back to take over the family business. The owner of the beauty salon where I also worked for a couple of months planned to send her son to a cosmetics firm to work for a few years before calling him back. In the Sato company, *kurō* was also invoked as a positive good, leading people to maturity. It was most often used by the older women when discussing the foibles of the younger artisans. Once, for example, the owner (*shachō*) caught Suzuki-san, one of the younger artisans, smoking in the factory – a capital offense in a factory where rules of hygiene were critically important. "What will the customers think if they find cigarette ashes in the cake!" yelled the owner. Suzuki-san hung his head and listened meekly, but as soon as the owner stepped outside, the young artisan exploded, "I'll quit on that bastard!" The division chief then approached, and in tones of world-weary resignation, reprimanded him with "You're the one at fault." (*Omae ga warukatta n da yo.*) The part-timers murmured their approval in the background. To them, Suzuki-san was still *namaiki* (fresh, cocky); he hadn't suffered enough yet (*kurō ga tarinai*) for his own personal growth, he should be made to suffer (*kurō o saseta hō ga ii*). In fact, Suzuki-san was already taking the first step, by apprenticing himself to a firm far away from the north country village where he was born, so that he could learn to be a more mature human being in the process of becoming a skilled artisan.

To become a mature practitioner of the trade (*ichininmae no shokunin*), then, involves a particular kind of hardship and training through an apprenticeship system. To older artisans, in particular, the system may have had its exploitative side, but surviving its rigors attested to their reserves of endurance and perseverance. Selfishness is tempered through the hardships of going outside one's natal home, trying to learn until the knowledge becomes one with the body, yet continually striving to find better ways to make beautiful objects. A full-fledged artisan is also a full-fledged man: able to make a living by his "arm" or technique, tough and able to withstand long hours and deprivation; in stereotype and sometimes in actuality, a strong, silent type, the embodiment of one sort of masculinity. He is no longer the soft, selfish being he might have been had he avoided the hardships of the trade. A mature artisan is a man who, in crafting fine objects, crafts a finer self.

Work and the material world

In Ohara-san's narrative of work and life, the ultimate satisfaction was to be found in experiencing work as *ikigai*, a reason for living. This artisanal ideal, based on certain forms of learning and on a notion of maturity forged through the hardships of apprenticeship, involves another level of meaning. Self-realization through one's art arises from certain kinds of relationships between people, their tools, the material world, and nature. Ohara-san, in particular, insisted upon the links to the seasons as one of the most wonderful (*subarashī*) aspects of his work. In so doing he articulated a compelling, personally meaningful aesthetic of work. For artisans like Ohara-san, a work aesthetic, resting upon a creative construction of a self engaging with tools, machines, and nature, is centrally implicated in the definition of a mature artisan at the workplace.

Seasonality and the factory

The passing of the four seasons (*shiki*), like the term "island country" (*shimaguni*), almost inevitably enters the conversation when Japanese people talk about Japan's uniqueness. Certainly, even if one were oblivious to changes in climate, it would be difficult to miss the humanly fashioned seasonal markers. Like the general emphasis on aesthetics in certain arenas of everyday life, attentiveness to the passing seasons is an integral part of everyday existence and cuts across class and regional boundaries (Lebra 1976: 21).

Along the busy commercial street where shoppers passed the shiny glass and metal doors of the Sato confectionery, the seasons unmistakably announced their presence. Luridly colored plastic floral decorations dangled from every lamppost of the arcade: pine and plum blossoms in the winter, shimmering with tinsel; shocking pink cherry blossoms in spring; gracefully curving willows in the summer; the primary reds and yellows of autumn's maple leaves. But we could measure the passage of the season equally well inside the factory for the confectionery business is connected closely to the seasons via the cycle of yearly rituals and holidays, many of which are associated with a particular kind of sweet.

The Japanese sweets (*wagashi*), in particular, express an appreciation for nature and for the changing seasons. Toroya, one of the most famous manufacturers of *wagashi* and suppliers to the imperial household, describes the relationship of the confections to the passing of the seasons. "The Japanese people have always highly valued the emotions evoked by the different seasons of the year. The traditional *'wagashi'* themselves express this delicate awareness of the four seasons. One of the main characteristics of these cakes is that they each possess their own descriptive and evocative names."

The Sato confectionery, like Toroya, made seasonally appropriate cakes with evocative names. "Iwashimizu," a spring issuing from the rocks, was a summer cake decorated to represent a mountain stream, the clear, pure water revealing a few scattered pebbles underneath. The harvest moon, a round, golden chestnut barely visible through its dark casing of bean jelly, was called "Moonlight" (*Gekkō*). Full-bodied confections of winter might resemble "Snowflake": a round, white mound of steamed dough, a snowflake pattern burned into the top. Sweets that mimicked seasonal flowers were always sure seasonal markers, and spring could bring out a narcissus or a plum blossom or, in March, sweets tinted pink and wrapped in a leaf from a cherry tree. Fall could take the form of a gold-colored gingko leaf tinged with red, or a lavishly petaled chrysanthemum, the flower associated with the month of October. Western confections, too, sometimes marked out the passing of seasons: for example, lighter fare like coffee-flavored gelatin (*kōhī zeri*) or a white cake with orange-flavored frosting, called "L.A.," Los Angeles, presumably for the Sunkist oranges it used, were summer desserts; in the winter these were abandoned for heavier, creamier pastries and cakes – éclairs, "decoration cakes" of all sorts, and marzipan-based confections.

Seasonal rituals are often associated with a particular kind of confection, creating enormous variations in seasonal demand. Christmas and New Year, the vernal and autumnal equinoxes, the midsummer Festival of the Dead, and the festivals of Girls' Day and Boys' Day, are occasions when people buy special sweets. The rice cakes and auspicious symbols of the New Year sweets change to the cherry blossom sweets of Girls' Day, the rice cakes wrapped in oak leaves (*kashiwa mochi*) of Boys' Day, to the heavy rice cakes (*ohagi*) for the equinoxes, on to the decorated Christmas cakes (which, Japanese are convinced, are an American tradition) topped with plastic houses, candy canes, and Santa Claus. These products are physical reminders of the passage of the seasons, Ohara-san explained to me over breakfast. The greatest plus in his work, he assured me, was the way it fostered a wonderful feeling for the season (*kisetsukan*).

Ohara-san claimed a connection to the natural world and to the passage of the four seasons as an integral element in a work identity. For now, let us take him at his word. Certainly, the importance of a sensitivity to the seasons is critical in the confectionery business and finds expression in many ways in Japanese society. A delicate aesthetic sensibility does not surprise in this milieu. Yet an artisanal aesthetic of work is not limited to the passing seasons, but extends to the assumptions some artisans hold about their relationships to tools, machines, and the material world.

Work: artisans and machines

This idiom of work depends on the interconnectedness of persons and the material world.[8] Artisans gracefully transform nature, and there can be a relationship of respect, a kind of cooperation, between human beings and their tools. For example, Tanoue-san, the woodworker, used to talk of the "personality" of each piece of wood. Perhaps this close interrelationship was most evident in the factory on ritual occasions. During the New Year, offerings are made to the tools. At the confectionery, the center of the factory was the boiler (*kama*). Here one could find the New Year's display of rice cakes (*omochi*) topped by a mandarin orange (*mikan*). Artisans like Tanoue-san also make a New Year's display in their workrooms, to indicate their gratitude to their tools. They give thanks to the machines for aid in the previous year, and make requests for the same benevolence in the coming year. Another example occurred during the dedication of the new Sato factory, when the equipment was moved from the old site to the new. A ritual of purification made the boiler (*kama*) ready for its new home. Tools and machines can, then, participate in the human domain.

This mutual affinity between human being and machine can be seen even in seemingly atomized, industrial contexts. Lest readers think this is a function only of size, I quote extensively from the field notes of Matthews

Hamabata, who, in his research on large family enterprises (*dōzoku gaisha*), visited a brewery that manufactured a well-known variety of Japanese liquor. This particular factory was viewed as a model for all other breweries owned by the company; from conception and design to management techniques, it was the most efficient and productive in the chain. Even here, or perhaps especially here, there is a close relationship between men – the gendered term is used intentionally – and their machines, for the machines are considered extensions of human beings.

The odd thing is: all three managers felt that there was a special spiritual presence in all of their machines; and they stressed over and over again that their major concern was the maintenance of their machines ... But it wasn't a love of machinery as machinery, but of machinery as some kind of spiritual extension of themselves: *kikai o migakeba, kokoro mo migakimasu* (if you polish the machines, you're also polishing your heart) ... for them, machines were extensions of themselves as spiritual beings, as creators of things, things of high quality. Quality was their main goal ... quality over speed and productivity. At any rate, there is a connectedness between men and machines, not only between men and men; there is a constant transcending of the self to create a beautiful product, a community product. (Hamabata 1981)

The penchant for humanizing the machine implies that human beings and machines partake of the same world, and that people are very intimately identified with the process of production, for the very machines they use in creating their products – even if the product is made on an assembly line – can be thought of as parts of, or representatives of, themselves. The quality of the product reflects on its maker. The worker has many avenues, then, for identifying with the product: through his or her own skills, through the machine that helped produce it, and as a creation of both a particular individual and a larger company community. Thus machines both partake of the human world and, through their use in the work process, are part of the ways human beings reaffirm their connectedness to one another. By cooperating in the creation of a product, these artisans can reaffirm their social identities. Far from contributing to alienation, artisans like these at the brewery and Ohara-san in the confectionery factory can find satisfaction in their connectedness to nature, tools, and machines.

Becoming a full-fledged artisan and a full-fledged human being at the workplace means engaging with the world in a particular way, cultivating a close relationship between men – again, I use the term intentionally – and the material and natural worlds. Solidarity is created between men and the world, and between men and men: those who share this engagement with tools, materials, and the seasons.

But locating these romantic tales in the contexts of their telling arouses our suspicions. Ohara-san was talking to a foreign researcher and trying to persuade me of the value of his work. The brewery "managers" were in a similar position as representatives of an exemplary factory. Surely under these circumstances they, too, would accentuate their romantic connections to work. On the other hand, one cannot dismiss their evident enthusiasm as mere sham, conscious exploitation, or false consciousness. Though we (specialists in "mental" work, accustomed to thinking of machines as instruments of drudgery and alienation) may find a combination of aesthetics, spirituality, and industrial work odd, it may not be so in every culture. Machines and tools are not necessarily harbingers of alienation, but instruments of artistic creation. The enthusiasm and poetry animating these tales demand to be taken seriously. They clearly form part of a mature artisanal identity.

Yet such stories also lead us to another series of questions: How are idioms of romantic connectedness and participation implicated in relations of power in particular situations? Do all workers share this same vision of work? And what of the potential ambiguities in even a single tale? Does even Ohara-san feel connected and fulfilled in his work all of the time? In order to address such doubts, we must return to the Sato factory.

Hierarchy exclusion and an idiom under siege

Skill and hierarchy

The Sato company, where Ohara-san and I were both employed, seemed, from a Western point of view, an interesting place to investigate such matters. Family-owned for three generations (really four, if you count the number of successions), its sparkling, well-appointed shop near the subway station and the dazzling white, three-story factory/residence across the alley at the back, were a testament to the firm's hard-won prosperity. The Satos employed thirty full-time workers, including several young men on contract to learn the trade before they went home to take over their own family confectioneries, and seven to eight part-timers, with one exception married women with school-age or grown children.[9] In this milieu of family business, there were pronounced structural and gender hierarchies in the assignment of work.

At this point, one must begin to ask how a "center" and, therefore, the "margins" come to be in the Sato company. Skilled artisans form the "core," or – to use a vertical metaphor – occupy "the top" of the hierarchy. Their greater claim on artisanal maturity through apprenticeship and an aesthetic engagement with the natural and material worlds legitimate the hierarchy. At the apex were the chiefs of the Japanese and

Western sweets divisions. They were the only ones who "knew" the ins and outs of the work processes of their divisions as a whole. They were marked by their abilities to do all required jobs, from folding boxes, if need be, to crafting the most exquisite and unusual confections. For the Western sweets, this consisted of French-style pâtisserie, as well as decorating cakes in imaginative ways. And when the *wagashi* division received an order for tea ceremony sweets, for example, only the chief could create them – even if such an order came in once a week at most. Skill meant that hierarchy was based on these artisans' greater experience and greater knowledge.

Perhaps the supreme expression of the chief artisans' superiority lay in their abilities to creatively adapt their skills in order to develop new varieties of confection. Changing consumer tastes made this constant innovation imperative: "if you don't go along with the times ..." (*jidai ni notte ikanai to*), said Ohara-san, shaking his head, "you just won't be able to make it." This factory seemed particularly innovative in that regard. Many new cakes and pastries had been developed, often a mixture of the Japanese types, based on sweet beans and rice, and Western pâtisserie. For example, a chestnut could be surrounded with sweet bean paste and a flaky pastry shell; or a sweetened pancake, ordinarily filled with bean paste, was slathered with sweet butter instead. These were creations of the Western division chief and the Japanese division chief, respectively. The owner sometimes came up with ideas, but lacking the necessary know-how, he could only suggest, not execute. A small, round banana cake, named "plumeria" after the flowers the owner saw in Hawaii, was one such suggestion come to life. The creative component of work gave the division chiefs an opportunity to use their expertise to devise new products, and they spoke with satisfaction of seeing the new project through, from conception to execution to commercial success.

The presumably skill-based hierarchy was pervasive at the factory, the symbolic chain of command apparent at a glance. The "chief" stayed mostly in his own completely enclosed small work space, accessible through a glass sliding door. Everyone addressed him in relatively polite language (*desu/masu* forms). It was easy, too, to discern the relative seniority and rank of the younger artisans. Only one other person besides the chief was allowed to answer the phone. This was Yamada-san, who worked at his own table, positioned in such a way that he could see the entire Western sweets (*yōgashi*) section. Two other artisans, each in his own particular work station, stood at adjacent tables placed at a right angle to the "subchief," Yamada. Eventually Yamada-san left our division in order to learn Japanese sweets (*wagashi*) and, predict-ably, the young man next in line assumed Yamada-san's former position at the "head" table. In the *wagashi* division the chief and his assistant staked out a table at one end of the finishing/packaging room (*shiage*), facing the baking rooms and the room where sweet bean paste (*anko*) was made. Given Ohara-san's stern exterior, the use of more formal, hence deferential, language levels was even more apparent. In both Western and Japanese divisions, the women "part-timers" were all together at a single table, or occasionally, depending on the work we were assigned, spread out over two tables. This circumscribed our use of space – though it also provided an excellent opportunity to talk and socialize, particularly valuable for the anthropologist. Still, our greater spatial constraints symbolized our lesser status.

In the factory, hierarchy was a familiar fact of life. But was hierarchy always based on skill alone?

Divisions of labor?

In fact, daily work rhythms could be quite fluid, and consequently, the divisions of labor were not always clear. Depending on the day's orders, the artisans might spend much of their time working alongside the part-timers. A variety of tasks were performed by both; for instance, a part-timer and a young artisan worked together making *yakigashi*, the kind of sweets baked on a large griddle. One part-timer actually did some of the same decorating jobs carried out by younger artisans: making designs on petits fours, for instance. In *wagashi* in particular, many of the everyday sweets were not elaborately decorated, so artisans could in fact spend much of their day doing work that, as the part-timers explained to me, "anyone can do" (*dare de mo dekiru*).

Consequently, the romantic artisanal aesthetic is vibrant with meaning for only a few artisans for work they do for a relatively short period of time. Older, more experienced artisans often perform tasks which do not make use of their artisanal skills, rather spending a considerable amount of time performing tasks more "properly" suited to younger artisans or to the women part-timers. Within this setting, legitimating the hierarchy of work through skill is for Ohara-san an ambiguous enterprise. On the one hand, his "superiority" can be clearly demonstrated when certain kinds of tasks are required. But on the other, he must daily engage in numerous less "artistic" activities which do not make use of his superior skills. Indeed, a good deal of work is something "anyone can do." Under these circumstances, one way to ensure the perpetuation of hierarchy is to elaborate and celebrate the aesthetic dimension of work, thereby pointing out the lack of this delicate sensibility on the part of others.

I realized in retrospect that I was an active agent in reinforcing his hierarchy of skill. Here was a foreign student/researcher, from a prestigious university, no less, wide-eyed and impressed with what she saw. Ohara-san made full use of my presence. During my stint as a *pāto* (part-timer) the *wagashi* chief would periodically bellow out, "Kondo-san!" and I would drop what I was doing to scurry over to look at his newest creation. In the summer, for instance, I remember clearly the tiny blue cubes of gelatin mimicked the petals of *ajisai*, or hydrangea. One sweet depicted a *tsukubai*, or water basin that is part of the tea ceremony garden – complete with a curving green vine and a single, small ivy leaf, again made of tinted gelatin. Ohara-san's deftness never ceased to amaze me. A few hand movements, the strategic placement of the stick, the impress of a thumb, and the shapeless dough was suddenly transformed into a work of art. Sometimes, he would ask, "Do you know what this is?" and when I guessed right, he would say, "*Sō sō*" with a pronounced air of satisfaction. On another occasion, soon after I began working in the *wagashi* division, Ohara-san removed from one of the top shelves a very real-looking artificial peony. Then he got out what must be the tiniest of torches and began bending a leaf here, adjusting a petal there. It was a flower made principally of sugar, a flower the owners would often take to the shop to display in a special glass case. "This was done by 'uchi no shokunin'" (our company's artisan), Mrs. Sato would say proudly, on more than one occasion when I stopped off to buy some sweets on my 10 percent employee discount. These beautifully crafted objects were Ohara-san's hobby and a profound source of pride. It is also apparent to me, after the fact, that Ohara-san did use my presence as a way of "showing off" his skills to me and to the others in the factory. Eliciting my exclamations was a sure way of "making his stock go up."

Artisanal celebrations of apprenticeship and an artisanal aesthetic thus reinforce the notion of a hierarchy based on superior skills. Yet in a milieu where those skills may find infrequent expression, artisans may try to protect their surprisingly fragile worker identities through a series of exclusionary practices. Ohara-san's demonstrations of artisanal prowess were just one example. The most striking strategies distinguish the male artisans as a group from the female part-time workers.

Exclusionary practices

From the outset, artisans were set off from part-timers through their training. Younger male artisans immediately embarked on a workplace trajectory based on the actual making of the confections, not merely wrapping them. On numerous vivid occasions the younger artisans received explicit instruction. On one memorable day Yamada-san, the subchief of Western sweets, tried to show Kitano-san, his immediate subordinate, how to make a rose from buttercream frosting. Yamada demonstrated, Kitano tried his hand. The central, infolding petals of the rose began to take shape. Then it collapsed. Again Kitano tried, and this time it was worse – the central core was lopsided. Again the rose collapsed. Three, four, even five times – and finally, a barely recognizable rose took form. "Aa, it's not good" (*Aa, dame da na*), said Kitano; "I just can't do this," as he stared rather ruefully at the tiny lump of frosting. Yet with time and practice, he eventually acquired speed and expertise, to the point where a few deft movements gave life to a perfectly shaped flower.

Similarly, in *wagashi*, I was witness to a session where young artisans tried their hands at a sweet decorated with a tiny narcissus, a symbol of the New Year. The stem was made of thin strips of tinted green gelatin, the center of the narcissus from the tiniest smidgen of dough in which the pointed end of a stick, about the size of a pencil point, was inserted to make a miniscule hole. Instructed by Ohara-san's example, several young artisans stood intently, bent over the metal work tables, first rolling tiny balls of dough and then pricking them with the tiny point of the stick. Suddenly one of them, a lively young man named Hiratsuka, stood up, threw up his hands, and shouted at the ceiling, "*Ore, konna komakai shigoto ga dame na n da yo*" (I [the informal or vulgar, masculine term for "I"] just can't do this detailed work!). He stomped up and down the workroom, "letting off steam," as we all chuckled at his antics, and finally returned to his work station. The interesting thing to note here is that both situations were limited to male artisans alone. No attempt was made to include the women, and the women themselves made no attempt to join in – too many trays of sweets were stacked before us, and our duty, in those circumstances, was to perform these less "skilled" tasks. Developing an aesthetic approach to craft work and the teaching of skill to the *male* workers guarded the boundaries of this select group.

Exclusionary practices could assume a verbal form. Who was an artisan, who wasn't, what could be expected of these different categories of people could be rendered starkly apparent. One day, during a lull in his work, Ohara-san came over to help me package the *monaka*. His fingers moved at least twice as fast as mine, and observing this, I blurted out, "My hands are a little slow." "Oh that's all right," he said with a startled look. "Because you're not an artisan" (*Ii n da yo, betsu ni . . . shokuninsan zya nai kara*). The remark, in some ways, was kind and tolerant but had a patronizing air, for my impaired competence could be excused because we occupied separate categories.

One incident revealed to the part-timers the disturbingly low esteem in which we were held. I was standing at the work table with one of the older

women. Nomura-san, a woman in her fifties, had just come in a little after
9.30. She began to describe her exhaustion, the reason for her later than
usual arrival. "About this time of the week I always get tired," she said.
"Housewives really get exhausted, because we have to do all the work at
home before we come to work – then stand on concrete floors all day, then
go back and do more work at home. If only we had two days of vacation,"
she said. "In only one, you just can't recover." (*Ichinichi zya, tsukare ga
torenai*.) Iwata-san chimed in, "All of us have errands (*yō*), and you can't
exactly sit in the house on your day off. You have to get your errands done
on a day when you're still tired."

Later, after we had dispersed to do separate tasks and then came back
to a central work table, Iwata-san was fuming. Apparently one of the
young artisans had overheard our conversation about our exhaustion and
made a scornful remark, "But you don't even work eight hours" (*Hachi
jikan hataraitē nē zya nē ka yo*). Iwata-san was clearly infuriated by this
remark. First of all, they didn't actually "work" eight hours, because they
didn't get paid for their lunch hour, but they did come to work around 9
and left around 5. And besides, she said, "That's what being a *pāto* means!
We are paid cheap wages, we don't get the same bonuses and rest breaks
that regular workers do, but our time is our own (*jikan ga jiyū*) ... It's
BECAUSE we can't really work eight hours a day that we're *pāto*!" By this
time, another woman, Teramura-san, had come to our table, and she
nodded emphatically. At that point, the conversation took an interesting
turn. Yamada-san was a young man almost thirty years their junior, and
no doubt his scornful remark was even more insulting given his youth.
They began to impugn Yamada-san's maturity – he was selfish (*waga-
mama*), and he expected the *pāto* to do everything for him, an especially
damning accusation in light of his denigration of their work. To quote
from my field notes:

Iwata-san was obviously disappointed and angry that "otoko no hito" (the men,
and she used this more general term, not confining herself to Yamada-san alone)
were thinking about them. That they had so little understanding. Lots of repetition
of "sore wa pāto da" (that's what a part-timer is), someone who can't work the full
eight hours ... They said that if they worked until 6, they got too tired, not while
they are there, but when they went home. If the company needed people to stay
longer, they should hire another *pāto* instead.

According to the young man's logic, the so-called less demeaning,
repetitive work should tire us less. It was as though he gave no recognition
at all to the classic double burden the part-timers had to shoulder. At the
very least, Yamada-san clearly accorded little importance to the part-
timers' work at the factory and their work in the home.

The artisans, then, excluded women by identifying themselves as a collectivity of full-time, skilled workers. As a collectivity, they could protect their terrain by downplaying the many contributions of the women to the work process and to "human relations" at work. The artisanal notion of maturity through apprenticeship, and a work aesthetic emphasizing engagement with tools, machines, and nature, create a center based on a full-fledged, male artisan connected to and fulfilled in his work. Ohara-san embodies this central figure in the workplace. Yet his existence simultaneously creates shifting peripheries in the organization, occupied by those who by definition are not quite fully human. The margins are occupied by women, who are tied to the home and are structurally temporary members of the organization. Yet these women are also necessary members of the company, who in some ways constitute a threat to artisanal articulations of a skill-based hierarchy. In incidents of conflict, such as I have described, women questioned the legitimacy of this hierarchy, recognizing the valuable contributions they made to the firm and the fact that they sometimes knew more than the artisans did. Moreover, women part-timers did not fully accept the proposition that artisanal "superiority" was based on maturity, for some of the artisans were in fact young and, from the women's point of view, terribly immature. Perhaps it is precisely *because* of these slippages that artisans so strongly reasserted their distinctiveness.

Definitions of center and periphery are not under siege from the women alone. Larger changes in work organization, practices of worker apprenticeship, and the older generation's evaluation of younger artisans also create shifting definitions of center and periphery, highlighting the subtexts for Ohara-san's narrative of self-construction in artisanal work.

Embattled idioms, historical change, and the construction of identities

In one of the more poignant moments of Ohara-san's breakfast narrative, he expatiated on the "artistic" (*geijutsuteki*) aspects of his work. The peony made of sugar, he said, was something artistic, something he could use his expertise in making. But as far as regular sweets were concerned, the young people would one day overtake him. Some of it just takes strength, he said. Only the art (*geijutsu*) separated him from the younger, more resilient men. His fear of aging and his fear of waning strength were also evident in a remark he later made: "When my body gives out, they may tell me, 'we don't need you any more.' " (*Karada ga motanaku naru to, omē ga mo iranē kara to iwareru ka mo shirenē.*) Capitalizing on his aesthetic connection to the craft helped Ohara-san to protect his place in the company hierarchy, to reassert his in fact quite fragile work identity, and to fend off vaguely envisioned future threats from younger workers.

Ohara-san's artisanal aesthetic was becoming an embattled idiom – not just in the face of young workers or a work process that made little use of his skill, but by the organizational structure of the company itself. Ohara-san the artisan found himself placed within an increasingly management-oriented, bureaucratic company. The owner was not a master artisan working alongside apprentices and journeymen; he was the "president" of the enterprise (*sachō*), a prosperous businessman. Ohara-san was an employee with an official title in an official company hierarchy. He was "head of the factory" (*kōjōchō*) and also division head (*buchō*) of *wagashi*. In short he was a "company officer." Like their counterparts in a government bureaucracy, "company officers" in the Sato factory could put their titles on their name cards and, also like company officers in any corporation, they received a flat salary, with no extra compensation for overtime. Ohara-san and his immediate subordinates spent more time in formal learning about management than in studying new developments in making confections. Once a month, the owner compelled his "chiefs" to attend a seminar led by a management consultant. None of the officers evinced any enthusiasm for this duty. Yet even formal learning about their craft was mediated through the company. Once a year, the *okashi* industry held a trade show, displaying the wares of various confectioners through-out the country, and the Sato artisans attended the show as a group, "on company orders."

Moreover, few companies offered the "rigorous apprenticeships" of old. No longer were young artisans in the position of supplicant learners. All received a salary – about $500 a month (10 *man*), plus room and board. Whereas in the past artisans and masters would take their meals together, perhaps even live in the same building, now the workers had their own company dormitory. Ohara-san viewed these developments with some regret, explaining that young men tended to identify more as *shain*, company employees, than *shokunin*, artisans. Admittedly, some younger artisans possessed clearly pragmatic attitudes toward work. Ito-san, a young artisan from the north country, heard Ohara-san's remarks, and emphatically concurred with Ohara-san's assessment of the younger generation. Ito-san pointed to himself as a good example. He wasn't in it because he liked it, he assured me. He was working just to work, as an interim pastime, before he could realize his dream of sailing around the world with his wealthy relatives.[10] Certainly Ito-san failed to embrace a vision of work as tempering the self through hardship and engaging in aesthetic relations with the material world.[11]

Indeed, this was one of the great ironies of the situation. Ohara-san in one sense represented an artisanal ideal. Yet it may be an ideal on the way to becoming a mild anachronism, as definitions of self as "company employee," the desire for "clean work," and an avoidance of *wagashi* as "too traditional" seem increasingly prevalent, especially in Tokyo. Most of the recruits who were learning *wagashi* were successors to their own families' enterprises, and would leave the company after five or six years. Of the employees not attached to a family firm, most of them were in Western pâtisserie, a division with a reputation in this company as more "akarui" (cheerful) – partially because of the personalities of the two chiefs, but partially because of cultural images that created a self-fulfilling prophecy. Western sweets, like some stereotyped images of the West in Japan, were considered more "with it," more "kakkō ī," unlikely to require the painful apprenticeships of Ohara-san's cohort. Some younger men may view Ohara-san's love of his craft as "tradition-al," even admirable, but few are likely to view it as a model for their own lives.

Discussion

Ohara-san's story provides a way for us to explore, finally, the complexi-ties, ambiguities, and subtexts in any narrative of self-construction, indeed in any "concept of self." Taken seriously, his romantic tale of hardship through maturity and aesthetic engagement with the world is a testament to the meaningful aspects of his work. Clearly, work mobilizes emotion and draws upon aesthetic sensibilities, even a certain spirituality, in ways that controvert our expectations about "mere craft" or industrial work. Ohara-san's narrative undercuts teleologies of inevitable, overwhelming worker alienation in industrial settings. His work is a source of identity and pride, both in and of itself, and in the value it has for the company. An economic situation of labor shortage heightens this value. Unless Japanese tastes undergo a drastic change, the Satos will continue to be able to make their special sweets, tailoring new products to consumer demand as well as attempting to "educate" consumers to develop new tastes. Indeed, since my stint in the factory, the Satos have only increased their prosperity. Two new branches of their shop have opened in a neighboring prefecture just outside the Tokyo city limits. Consequently, we can expect the demand for skilled workers like Ohara-san will only increase, augmenting his sense of centrality to the organization.

Yet one must also attempt to give a sense of the complexities of meaning contained in a construction of self in work. Ohara-san's story was also an active attempt to reassert his identity as a skilled artisan and buttress his claims to legitimacy as head of the factory. It is a way of creating a center for the organization, by providing one definition of who is most fully human in the workplace. Thus, artisanal celebrations of work identity are persuasive attempts to aggrandize status and legitimize practices excluding other kinds of workers, especially the so-called "unskilled," from admission to the community of mature, full-fledged male artisans. Solidary worker communities, or satisfying worker identities, though compelling for certain people in certain contexts, have their less romantic sides. The aesthetics of work cannot be separated from its politics.

Paradoxically, definitions of artisanal work are under siege, precisely from the quarters of the excluded. For example, women part-timers sometimes accept certain aspects of artisanal claims on maturity, but they do not accept an absolute hierarchy based on the superiority of all artisans. For the younger men are precisely that: younger, less mature. In the women's hands, the *artisanal* idioms of maturity through hardship and aesthetic skills and knowledge, provide the tools with which part-timers can criticize the artisans for failing to live up to this ideal.

Historical and economic changes also assail the univocity of Ohara-san's narrative. Artisanal maturity through apprenticeship and aesthetic sensibility is an embattled idiom within this larger setting of threatened obsolescence, increasing emphasis on hierarchical company-based forms of organization, and a division of labor in which similar tasks are performed by seasoned artisans, young artisans, and women part-timers alike. A celebration of work identity may even more strongly assert claims to a superiority (maturity) based on skill, precisely because that "superiority" is under siege. Ironically, Ohara-san may fear that his very claims to superiority on the basis of artisanal spirit will one day acquire the status of quaint "traditionalism," particularly if members of the younger generation do indeed identify themselves as "company employees," not "artisans." Ohara-san's story reveals a final irony. He himself has apparently abandoned one important motif in this collective story, for he no longer talks about a desire to strike out on his own, to open his own shop. He has opted for a secure position in a stable company, where security outweighs desires for independence and mobility. In more ways than one, Ohara-san, too, has become an Organization Man.

Artisanal identity is thus no global totality, a unitary "self." On the contrary, Ohara-san's narrative of self-construction revealed not a single "self," but multiple selves, alive with complexities and deeply felt, subtly nuanced, often contradictory emotions. Investigations of selfhood's cultural meaning or workers' identities must begin to sensitively explore the multiplicity of selves and the fragility of those identities.[12]

NOTES

This essay initially appeared as a chapter of *Crafting Selves: Power, Gender, and Discourses of Identity in a Japanese Workplace*, University of Chicago Press, 1990. My appreciation to the University of Chicago Press for permission to reprint. Funds from the Rockefeller Foundation supported a year at the Institute for Advanced Study in 1987–8, when this essay was initially written. Many thanks to Nancy Rosenberger for her support and her critical comments. Participants in the "Gender Seminar," under Joan W. Scott's direction at the Institute for Advanced Study, also provided indispensable readings and provocative insights. Accordingly, thanks to Joan Scott, Judith Butler, Donna Haraway, Rayna Rapp, Evelyn Fox Keller, Carroll Smith-Rosenberg, Louise Tilly, Lila Abu-Lughod, Yasmine Ergas, Julie Tayler, Elliott Shore, David Gordon, Istvan Hont, Jerrold Seigel.

1 The exceptions, not surprisingly, include studies by feminist anthropologists who link definitions of gendered persons with larger systems of power relations – though it is still true that the symbolic and psychological anthropologists often subscribe to a rhetoric accenting the essential over mutable, contextual constructions of selfhood and power.

2 Sewell (1980) is perhaps the quintessential example. For a critical assessment of his argument, see Hunt and Sheridan (1986).

3 My usage differs here from Geertz (1968) who defines force as "the thoroughness with which such a pattern is internalized in the personalities of individuals who adopt it, its centrality or marginality in their lives" (p. 111). I use it here to refer to its distribution within a social field.

4 In speaking of a collective story, I threaten to reintroduce language almost as general, abstract, and totalizing as the accounts I criticize in the introduction. This is not satisfactory to me, but until I find a voice that does justice to variation and multiplicity, simply let the reader be assured that my generalizations are based on countless conversations and interviews with informants.

5 I never interviewed anyone who had actually experienced such deprivation, though many people claimed to "know someone" who did.

6 An analogous form of pedagogy, emphasizing self-realization through the learning of an art, can be found in the Zen master arts: tea ceremony, flower arranging, and the like. Even if one pays for lessons in these arts, students may have to begin – at least on occasion – with cleaning the classroom.

7 Sake shops also sell staples like soy sauce.

8 Bachnik (1978) describes the pervasiveness of this interconnection in everyday Japanese life. Moeran (1984) also refers to the tendency for the potters he studied to discuss their creations in terms of larger social relations, though he never elaborates on this tantalizing insight.

9 The only male part-timer was a retired worker in his sixties, whose duty it was to bring the finished sweets across the alleyway to the shop.

10 In fact, he did end up quitting his job at the Satos, and eventually found another, more lucrative job in a subcontract to Mitsubishi Heavy Industry. I examine his experiences – and specifically, a day he came back to boast about his new job – in another essay.

11 To put this statement in perspective, it is highly unlikely that all "artisans" or

members of any occupation at any point in history were all highly identified with their work. Even this artisanal ideal could not be expected to hold true for all artisans at any point in history; as I have argued, such aesthetics of work are by definition exclusionary.

12 For one such exemplary investigation, see Lynn Hunt and George Sheridan (1986).

REFERENCES

Bachnik, Jane. 1978. Inside and Outside the Japanese Household: A Contextual Approach to Japanese Social Organization. Ph.D. dissertation, Harvard University.

Berg, Maxine. 1987. Women's Work, Mechanisation and the Early Phases of Industrialisation in England. *The Historical Meanings of Work* (P. Joyce, ed.), Cambridge: Cambridge University Press.

Braverman, Harry. 1974. *Labor and Monopoly Capital.* New York: Monthly Review Press.

Geertz, Clifford. 1968. *Islam Observed.* Chicago: University of Chicago Press.

Gordon, Andrew. 1985. *The Evolution of Labor Relations in Japan: Heavy Industry, 1853–1955.* Cambridge, Mass.: Council on East Asian Studies, Harvard.

Gray, Robert. 1987. The Languages of Factory Reform in Britain, c. 1830–1860. *The Historical Meanings of Work* (P. Joyce, ed.), Cambridge: Cambridge University Press.

Hamabata, Matthews. 1981. Unpublished field notes.

Hunt, Lynn and Sheridan, George. 1986. Corporatism, Association, and the Language of Labor in France, 1750–1850. *Journal of Modern History* 58 (4): 813–44.

Kondo, Dorinne. 1987. Creating an Ideal Self: Theories of Selfhood and Pedagogy at a Japanese Ethics Retreat. *Ethos* 15: 241–72.

Lebra, Takie Sugiyama. 1976. *Japanese Patterns of Behavior.* Honolulu: University of Hawaii Press.

Marcus, George and Fischer, Michael. 1986. *Anthropology as Cultural Critique.* Chicago: University of Chicago Press.

Mauss, Marcel. 1968. Une Catégorie de l'esprit humain: la notion de personne, celle de "moi." *Sociologie et anthropologie*, Paris: Presses Universitaires de France.

Moeran, Brian. 1984. *Lost Innocence: Folk Craft Potters of Onta, Japan.* Berkeley: University of California Press.

Phillips, Anne and Taylor, Barbara. 1980. Sex and Skill: Notes towards a Feminist Economics. *Feminist Review* 6: 79–88.

Piore, Michael and Sabel, Charles. 1984. *The Second Industrial Divide.* New York: Basic Books.

Prothero, Iowerth. 1979. *Artisans and Politics in Early Nineteenth-Century London.* London: Dawson.

Rancière, Jacques. 1986. The Myth of the Artisan: Critical Reflection on a Category of Social History. *Work in France: Representations, Meaning, Organization and Practice* (S. Kaplan and C. Kaepp, eds.), Ithaca, N.Y.: Cornell University Press.

Rule, John. 1987. The Property of Skill in the Period of Manufacture. *The Historical Meanings of Work* (P. Joyce, ed.), Cambridge: Cambridge University Press.

Scott, Joan. 1974. *The Glassworkers of Carmaux*. Cambridge, Mass.: Harvard University Press.

Sewell, William. 1980. *Work and the Revolution in France*. Cambridge: Cambridge University Press.

Stark, David. 1982. Class Struggle and the Transformation of the Labour Process: A Relational Approach. *Classes, Power and Conflict* (A. Giddens and D. Held, eds.), Berkeley: University of California Press.

Thompson, Edward Palmer. 1964. *The Making of the English Working Class*. New York: Pantheon Books.

4   Tree in summer, tree in winter: movement of self in Japan

Nancy R. Rosenberger

In this essay, I explore the complexity of self both as constituted by and as constituting its cultural and social world. These explorations are possible only through the affirmation of self as an embodied intersection of various facets of its world – personal experiences, relationships and group contexts, political and economic ideologies, cultural ideas about universal energy, and so on.

Through relationship and language, self originates and develops by means of its socio-cultural world. Emotionally invested in its world through action and language, self reconstitutes that world, albeit with various personal reinterpretations. Self is born and reborn through positioning in various sets of cultural ideas and practice. In short, self is not transcendental with an ultimate meaning within itself. Self's meaning derives from its position in relation to other meanings – meanings of other selves, other relationships, other groups, and so on – and from its movement among these positions (Henriques et al. 1984, Smith 1988, Weedon 1987).

The graphic representation that best shows Japanese self presented in this essay is a three-dimensional checker game with three layers of movement that interconnect both horizontally and vertically. In the first part of the essay, I discuss three dimensions of life that intersect to constitute self in Japan: movements in psycho-spiritual energy, known as *ki*; movements in relationship through the taking and giving of indulgence (*amae*); and movements in context between formality and informality.

When viewed as a whole at any point in time, the checker game forms a certain pattern made up of these three dimensions. These larger patterns shift as moves in psycho-spiritual energy, relationship, or context are made on the three boards. In the second part of the essay, I propose that in Japan these larger patterns relate to transformations of sacred power or universal energy. Studies of two hierarchical Malayo-Polynesian societies indicate that concepts of universal energy can be entwined with notions of selfhood. In Japanese Shinto concepts, sacred power or universal energy goes through transformations that are understood through the seasonal

67

cycles of nature and through gender differences. These transformations in sacred power or universal energy parallel the movements mentioned above in psycho-spiritual energy, relationship, and context.

The complex dimensions of self threaten to spill off the checker boards. If self is considered as a social phenomenon, gender, age, and status are not incidental aspects, but important dimensions of self. The checker pieces' beginning positions and subsequent moves are influenced by these social attributes.

Finally, current economic and political ideologies are dimensions of self that are inescapable when self is situated and its specifics spun out. Ideologies become natural and right by fitting into the positions and movements of the self in this multidimensional checker game.

After outlining these intersecting dimensions that make up self, I proceed to a lengthy narrative by Hosoi-san, a middle-aged Japanese woman who has reinterpreted various parts of her life in conversations with the author. In the last section, I interpret specific dimensions, positions, and movements of Hosoi-san's experiences in order to understand self as embedded in a historically complex world.

Three-dimensional movement of self

In this section, I explain the movement of self in the dimensions of psycho-spiritual energy, relationship, and context. The discussion is brief because they have been discussed at length in other essays (Rosenberger 1989, in press).

The first dimension of self occurs through the movement of *ki*, currently used to refer to a vague psycho-spiritual energy that occurs within every person, but that fits neither psyche nor emotion in translation. In East Asian medical thought, *ki* is a universal energy which courses through people's bodies and connects them with the *ki* energies of the universe, but in colloquial use, these connections have been lost (Lock 1980). Contemporary Japanese no longer make these connections, but they do believe that *ki* is held in common with others. Thus, *ki* energy can meld with other people's *ki* energy or with the general atmosphere of the situation or environment.

At this level of the checker game, moves occur as *ki* energy shifts positions between inner and outer orientation and between spontaneity and discipline. *Ki* is an energy that can carry the inner feelings of the heart (*kokoro*) or the outer feelings of the group or situation. The movement requires the ability to loosen and tighten the *ki*. The more *ki* energy is loosened or allowed to wander, the more inner feelings (*kimochi*) are expressed. The more *ki* energy is tightened or made to stand up straight, the more one has the strength (*kiryoku* or *seishin*) to fulfill responsibilities as the group demands (cf. Rohlen 1976). Although all people have *ki* energy, their control over it varies. The mature person should be able to loosen and tighten *ki*, moving in and out without ever losing control.

A second dimension of self occurs through movements in dyadic relationship. Positions shift between the give and take of indulgence. On one side of the relationship, one gives indulgence (*amayakasu*), allowing another person to be spontaneous and free. On the other side of the relationship, one receives indulgence (*amaeru*), presuming on another's benevolence to act spontaneously. This is epitomized in the mother–child relationship in which the mother indulges the child's free expression of will (Doi 1977). Indulgence may also act in relation to authority, so that the indulger gives an indulgee the right to authority.

Because it assumes ongoing relationship, the *amae* relationship does not end with the receiving of indulgence. The person who enjoys the indulgence incurs a debt to the person who allows the indulgence. The mother may request indulgence of her adult child by becoming sick at points when she wants to impress her opinion on the child. In sum, the sympathies of another person frame any enactment of free will so that present positions of freedom imply movement toward positions of responsibility later.

A third dimension of self is played out through positioning within different contexts, signified by related sets of terms such as outer/inner (*soto/uchi*), front/back (*omote/ura*), and on-stage meaning/off-stage meaning (*tatemae/honne*) (Lebra 1976, Doi 1986, Bachnik 1987). Contexts are more outer (*soto*) if they are organized according to rules agreed upon by the group and if social hierarchy is emphasized. These are more public situations in which people affirm the formal or stage meanings of their groups, often in relation to other groups. Adult males, or in their absence, older females have marked authority. Such contexts are formal and deference is marked. Examples would be a morning meeting at the workplace for all employees or a meeting between households considering marriage.

Contexts are more inner (*uchi*) if they are organized to encourage emotionally expressed harmony and intimate relations. Here people affirm their informal, backstage relations with others, forming an inner group of people. These people share relaxation and (as intimacy increases) inner feelings or emotions. Expressions of social hierarchy and deference are muted. An example would be evenings at home watching TV and snacking, or parties of small groups of workers after hours.

All groups are considered to need both on-stage and off-stage contexts. Selves help to constitute these group contexts with movements in their *ki* energies and relations of indulgence, and in turn selves are given positions within these group contexts.

In summary, self moves horizontally through these three dimensions: *ki* energy tightens and loosens, moving in toward heart and out toward others; dyadic relationships shift as people take different positions in giving and receiving indulgence; and group contexts move between the diversity of formal hierarchy and the unity of informal intimacy.

Vertical relations also exist between the three playing boards. As group contexts shift to inner modes, for example, indulgence of spontaneity increases and people loosen *ki* energies. Likewise, loosening of *ki* energies and indulging of free will would shift the group context toward inner, informal modes. Contradictions exist, however, as those giving indulgence do not relax *ki* energies to the extent of indulgees. A similar correspondence occurs between outer modes of group context, indulgence of authority, and tightening of *ki* energies. Contradiction can also exist there, as those receiving indulgence of their authority have looser *ki* energy than those allowing the indulgence.

The general point is that self is constituted by movement at all of these layers, and self carves experience out of these interacting layers. The interplay will come across more clearly later in the essay in the specifics of Mrs. Hosoi's life.

Universal energy: hints from elsewhere

Both in common sense and academic theory, self is an area which most Americans approach as individualistic and essential, apart from society. In exploring Japanese self, it is helpful to decenter such concepts by pursuing the study from the perspective of societies which acknowledge hierarchy and context as important aspects of self. I have chosen two Malayo-Polynesian societies which indeed may have some cultural links with Japan in the shrouded past of prehistory (Befu 1971). Among the American Samoans (Shore 1982) and the Javanese (Keeler 1987), self is constituted by movements in spirit, relationship, and group context similar to those mentioned in the previous section for Japan. They even resemble the Japanese self in their movements between discipline and spontaneity, deference and intimacy.

These studies suggest a further dimension of self that Japan scholars have not considered. They imply that movements of self intersect with transformations of universal energy, as conceived by these cultures. These studies also show that gender and status differences are important markers in enacting these transformations of universal energy.

In Samoa, multiple dimensions of self move between two modes (Shore

1982). One mode is formal and static (*amio*); people conform to rules in a marked hierarchy of complementary relationships (sister/brother). The other mode is active and utilitarian (*aga*); people act impulsively in competitive relationships (brother/brother) or even chaotically outside the villages. Shore explains these aspects of life as transformations of *mana*, a power of the gods which people appropriate and harness for human needs (1986). The formal, static mode is *mana* tightly bound through ritual for human use. It is bound with both the material (as in clothes and ropes) and the immaterial (actions of etiquette and status). In contrast, the active, utilitarian mode is *mana* loosely bound, literally with less bodily wrappings and figuratively with less deference and status difference. This mode is recognized for both its life-giving generativity and its threatening pollution.

For example, more tightly bound sisters, as well as the "sister" side of the village, exhibit formal, static power whereas more loosely bound brothers or "brother" side of the village enact more fierce, utilitarian power. Yet depending on the contrastive meanings at play, the same people can enact different meanings of universal energy or power. A woman as a sister expresses aloof, quiet power that brings respect, while a woman as a wife signifies wild, fecund power that draws others toward generativity but also toward chaos. Likewise, the sister/brother relationship expresses static ordering power, but the husband/wife relationship embodies generative but chaotic aspects of power. In short, Shore proposes that in everyday life, people use the universal energy of *mana* by binding people and relationships quite tightly to gain its ordering aspects and loosely to increase its generative aspects.

Moving to Java, dimensions of self again embody aspects of power, one more sacred and static, the other more mundane and active (Keeler 1987). Here spiritual power is bound tightly into human use through the renunciation of selfish desires by means of ascetic practices such as fasting, sleeplessness, or silence. The ascetic increasingly acquires the power to command respect from others in hierarchical interaction. Men of higher status are almost always the ones with this kind of potency, stemming from the immaterial world (*batin*). As in Samoa, the binding of spiritual power connects closely with the binding of hierarchy.

In contrast, women, children, and lower-status people are associated with mundane powers of the material world (*lair*). This domain of life is full of chaotic emotions and material needs such as food and money. If people get cheated in the marketplace, "a man would be ashamed to protest, whereas a woman would be ashamed to let herself be cheated" (Keeler 1987: 54). In her ability to be a vessel through which spirits speak or in her ability to bear children, woman is valued as a channel of power.

She paves the way for men's harnessing of immaterial power by protecting husbands from family conflicts or daily concerns. Thought of in another way, women, like the Javanese shadow plays, enact a chaotic but generative world that tests the male equilibrium.

In these examples from Samoa and Java, self embodies aspects of universal energy, often through differences in gender and status. Here, people are not accumulations of experiences and achievements in a linear line of progression toward self-fulfillment as Americans prefer to think. Rather they start as social beings, already situated by status and gender in society, and indeed in the universe (as it is conceived by that culture). Self moves, but always relative to one's own gender, age, and status as it compares to the gender, age, and status of others present. Movement is cyclical and it is this cyclical movement, pausing in patterns of relationship and context, that creates multiple aspects of universal energy.

Back to Japan

Although Japan anthropologists often discuss energies of the individualized spirit (*ki*, *seishin*), they ignore connections to universal energy or sacred power, assuming that Japanese do not have religious beliefs. However, lack of belief and participation in systematized religion does not rule out enactment of ideas about universal energy in everyday life. Indeed, parallels among the aspects of Shinto sacred power and dimensions of Japanese self described above suggest that these exist in relation to each other, and even constitute each other.

In early Japan, there was a belief in the sacrality of the total cosmos so that all animate and inanimate beings participated in a common sacred nature, often called *tama* (Herbert 1967: 60, Kitagawa 1987: 120).[1] Shinto writings and thought show that *tama* or sacred power reveals itself in various transformations. When described by the most enlightened, the power of *tama* can be considered under four different aspects: (1) the raw power of outer manifestation which is empowered to have authority over unruly areas of life (*arimitama*); (2) the mild power of inner essence which leads to consolidation and harmony (*nigimitama*); (3) the power to differentiate, split, or analyze (*kushimitama*); and (4) the power to penetrate and centralize (*sakimitama*) (Herbert 1967: 61–2, Kitagawa 1987: 121).

Thus, Shinto meditations reveal two axes: the first, represented by (1) and (2), runs between outer manifestation and inner essence, or again between authority and harmonious consolidation. The second, represented by (3) and (4), runs between differentiation and centralization. These axes form two poles: one of immaterial unity through inner consolidation and centralization and one of material diversity through outer authority and differentiation (Herbert 1967).

Shinto teachers clarify and ground these differences by using a metaphor of cycles of growth in nature. They explain the powers of outer authority and differentiation as the yearly above-ground development of the tree, manifesting itself in trunk, branches, flowers, and leaves – each with its own place and function. They envision the universal powers of inner harmony and penetrating centralization as the tree's yearly growth below ground – consolidating its energy in its roots, returning to its inner essence for generativity.[2]

Shinto teachers also link these transformations of power with gender differences. Men contain the power of the tree in summer: outer, differentiating, and authoritative. Women contain the power of the tree in winter: inner, harmonizing, and consolidating (Herbert 1967).

In both nature and gender metaphors, an integral relationship between these two aspects of power is represented in Shinto by a circle with three commas in it: one representing the dynamic of outer differentiation, the tree in the full bloom of summer; one indicating the dynamic of inner consolidation, the tree closed in on itself during winter. The third refers to the bringing together of all powers into the full cycle of growth, a process called *musubi*, literally tying together, as in a knot (Herbert 1967: 67–8). Thus, growth moves along a road (*michi*), a "cosmic vitalizing continuum" (p. 32), but in a cyclical pattern of movement between tightly bound material diversity and loosely bound immaterial unity.

Shinto concepts and practices appear to fit Shore's definition of Polynesian religion as "appropriating and harnessing generative and ordering powers from gods in the service of human needs . . ." (1986: 53). Indeed, in Japan symbols of binding abound, as in the ropes binding powerful parts of nature such as rocks along the coast, large pine trees, mountain peaks, or champion sumo wrestlers. As in Java, Shinto ascetic practices bind selfish desires through cold water ablutions, pilgrimages, or walking a hundred times in front of a shrine.

Shinto transformations of universal energy parallel movements in dimensions of self and thus constitute everyday practices and ideas (as well as being constituted by them). Consider the dimension of self constituted in shifting contexts of outer (*soto*) and inner (*uchi*). In outer contexts, hierarchical and disciplined, people are bound much like the tree in summer in an outer show of authoritatively bound diversity. The very differentiation of form and function in hierarchy binds people into complementary relationships of authority and productivity. This is the order with which groups face the outer world. Tight binding is obvious in such contexts. People are bound by differential language of respect and humbleness, and by differential levels of bowing and seating. *Ki*, the psycho-spiritual energy, is tightly bound in self-discipline. When indulgence occurs, it is highly bound people with authority who are indulged. People are visibly bound in such formal contexts with tightly wrapped kimono, or well-buttoned Western wear – the higher the status, the tighter the wrap – although even manual workers wrap themselves round the head and stomach to bind in their powers. Even objects that grace such contexts are tightly bound: formally arranged flowers, tied and knotted money envelopes, wrapped gifts, food in boxes, and symbolically wrapped chopsticks.

While this tight binding affects both men and women, men seem to be most tightly bound into continual hierarchy, from household to school to workplace. As they ascend in the hierarchy, they increasingly manifest the ordering powers of the tree in summer: outer authority over diversity in the material world. Their place in a pattern of diverse statuses does not just show dominance and subordination; the configuration embodies the ordering aspects of universal energy. As men rise in the hierarchy, especially with age, they are in charge of contexts in which ordering aspects of power are passed on to others (women and younger males) through rituals, statuses, and tasks. Older women also can signify such ordering power especially to younger women, but the idea that men are "by nature" identified with aspects of power that are authoritative, outer, and differentiated makes it seem quite proper that men should presently be tied to companies and the financial support of their families.

In contrast, in inner contexts (*uchi*) of spontaneity and intimacy, people are loosely bound much like the tree in winter – in an inner-oriented nest that penetrates people's hearts, centralizing them as a group into intangible unity. Shore suggests that this aspect of universal energy is generative. In relaxed evenings at home or in parties after work, the bounds of hierarchy and status gradually decrease. People loosen almost everything: their *ki* energies, their clothes, and their seating arrangements. Language becomes more informal and childlike with shorter endings, more direct expressions, and onomatopeias. Objects are again an important part of this: noodles, shared finger food, unwrapped rice crackers and oranges, and, of course, the sacred but generative sake. The loosening is relative, however, as people "bind" their hearts with words, song, laughter, and sake. Only at gatherings with closest friends would strong complaints surface, but even these remain bound by context. Group members can be just free enough to meld in heart-felt unity.

If older, higher-status males excel in outer, authoritative aspects of universal energy, women, particularly young or lower-status women, exude generative power of consolidation and centralization. Generally people who are less bound because they are on the margins of productive hierarchy, or between hierarchies, channel this kind of power. Children and unmarried fertile women are particularly effective, but any women, low-status men, and old people help. These people are in charge of establishing contexts of rejuvenation and harmony. The presence and actions of women especially indulge groups in intimate, emotional expression. They help to loosen up the hierarchy of the group by joking, pouring sake, and emitting sexual appeal.

Women and generative aspects of universal energy

The aspects of universal energy attributed to women – the power of the tree in winter – is complex. Women's fecundity is positive if bound by human groups and rituals, generative if loosely bound, but dangerous if the binding loosens too much. As a result, women are closely controlled, but to varying degrees and purposes as their fecundity waxes and wanes.

Women who are fecund but unmarried are used to bring a relatively unbound but generative form of universal energy into the human community. In the past, as shamans and Shinto maidens, they enabled people to communicate with the gods. Gradually, many of these women shifted to entertainment and/or prostitution, thereby enhancing communication among men or bringing rejuvenating energies to them. The "play" (*asobi*) of dance and song to the gods became the "play" (*asobi*) to entertain men. Thus, men's "play" with women still resonates with the channeling of generative powers from the universe.[3] These women could become threatening to the ordering of life, but their generative power has been bound and kept apart throughout history in shrines, in quarters, in special houses, and now in bars and restaurants. Those of lower status are less bound in by clothes, food, and ritual than those of higher status.

Today, not only hostesses or companions in bars, but OL (office ladies) in companies also offer men relatively unbound generative aspects of power – rejuvenating and consolidating. These enduring ideas about the power of unbound fecundity make it seem very natural that companies want to employ women who are young but unmarried or again, that husbands spend time in bars away from their well-bound wives.

Women's fecundity is brought into human use for reproduction by binding women tightly into the hierarchy of households by language, tasks, and indulging of others – those of higher status more tightly than those of lower status. Households protect themselves from women's generative power at its strongest and most uncontrollable points of menstruation and especially childbirth.[4] If women's fecund powers need to be bound into a household to be safely used, then it seems right that women are at home supporting future, present, and past workers in present-day Japanese society. Women in nuclear households with men away at work and children at school are not so tightly bound by hierarchy. The "feeling" that such women's generativity should be curtailed in tasks and hierarchy dovetails nicely with the economic imperative for part-time workers and active consumers.

Postmenopausal women who have graduated to the status of mother-in-law, especially in households that have higher status within the local community, become enforcers of the hierarchy, expressing ordering aspects of power and binding the generative powers of the daughter-in-law.[5] Also women who rise in the hierarchy of professions embody and share a more authoritative aspect of power. Note the women outside of hierarchy in folktales, however; the old woman of the mountains (*yama-baba*) threatens passers-by, even coming into households to eat children (Dorson 1962).

A specific self: Hosoi-san's interpretation

In this section we turn to the world of Hosoi-san, a fifty-year-old woman of a northeastern provincial city. We first met when I was a teaching colleague of her husband on my first stay in Japan. She is a mother and wife at an age of transition between "womanhood" and "grandmother-hood," as she says. As the wife of a teacher and also a part-time teacher herself, she is on the upper side of middle-class status in the provincial city where she lives.

I concentrate on one person in order to ground the previous discussion in historical and social experience. I have chosen Hosoi-san in part because she is a longtime friend who has told me much about her life. As a woman, she gives insight into gender as an important though complex dimension of self. She is middle-aged, a product of both prewar and postwar Japan, and she shows clearly that changing political and economic ideologies entwine with movements of self, constituting another dimension of self. Changing and multiple ideologies offer Hosoi-san multiple positions for self in the historical flow of events. These seem natural because they coincide with positions in the seemingly ahistorical movements of self in relationship, context, and so on.[6]

The narrative takes the form of dialogue because this is material that Hosoi-san spun out for the inquiring friend and anthropologist. This is a compilation of many taped and untaped conversations between her and me, and at times with family members or friends. My responses reflect not only typical responses of praise and self-deprecation used among Japanese women, but the fact that my own opinions as an American were part of the situation. Hosoi-san interprets her life with me in mind. As a mother with two young children, I was a younger person to advise and caution, yet as a graduate student doing research and preparing for a career, I was a representative of a new way for women to live their lives. Both of these positions have meaning for Hosoi-san in her own life.

Hosoi-san's interpretation of her life

I was sitting on a pillow on Hosoi-san's floor, my legs tucked under the blanket that covered the low heated table between us – a treasured warmth in this cold northern city. While periodically refilling our tea cups with green tea and offering a rice cracker now and then, Hosoi-san told me bits and pieces of her life that she thought were important to help me understand her present situation. It was a relaxed time for talking – her husband had not yet returned from the high school where he taught, her younger son was out with his university friends (her older son lived in a different city), and it was not yet time to begin dinner preparations. We were in a small room off the kitchen that had been built as a Western-style room, but carpeted over for more relaxing floor-sitting – the couch pushed against one wall as a backrest.

N.R.: I brought some goodies that somebody gave me yesterday. I don't know if they're any good.
H-SAN: Oh, well, let's put them out. They always say that if you don't eat some of what you brought, you won't know the way back. (laughing) Sit on this pillow here. You're still of childbearing age, so you need a soft place.

Hosoi-san was dressed in a sweater and slacks. Seated comfortably on a pillow with legs bent to the side, she reached for the small teapot and filled it with tea and hot water from the thermos sitting beside her.

N.R.: How are your sons doing these days?
H-SAN: Oh, they're no good. Regrets, regrets – that's all I have with them.
N.R.: But they're doing so well.
H-SAN: Maybe it looks like that from the outside, but we have nothing but trouble. The younger one spends all his time with his friends and his motorcycle and never studies as he should. He won't get a good teaching position at this rate. Now he wants to live in his own apartment. We're not sure whether to let him or not. What do you think?
N.R.: Well, I suppose if you give him some freedom now, he'll come back later.
H-SAN: You think so? I worry so about them. The older one wants to get a job in Tokyo. We had hoped that he would stay here. What if he goes off to Tokyo and finds a citified girl that I couldn't get along with? Yet if we don't let him go, he might always be unhappy.
Actually I think all this worry is part of the reason for my menopausal symptoms. I know I shouldn't worry so, but I can't help it. I don't have good

control over these boys because I wasn't close enough to them when I was young. In home economics, I teach girls that mothers should be close to their children – lots of contact, both affection and punishing. I wish that I had been able to have that and I tell my niece who is about your age that she shouldn't even think about working. Just be grateful that you are able to have the time with your children, I tell her. I have so many regrets about my boys – and you will, too, if you aren't careful. You better not stay here too late today. Your children are waiting.

N.R.: Yes, I can't stay too long. But, tell me, did you work when your boys were young?

H-SAN: I did. I did. I taught school every day. I didn't want to continue working, but my mother-in-law gave me no choice. She said we needed the income. So she and my sister-in-law, who was still single then, cared for my children. I remember crying in my room at night. The problem was that they were too easy with them. So if I would scold them, they would just go crying to their grandmother and she'd let them off. I remember how she let them draw on the walls in the front hall of the old farmhouse.

N.R.: I have the opposite problem. I'm not strict enough with my children.

H-SAN: You'll be okay because you are really raising your children. My children didn't even know I was their mother. When we finally moved away from the farm and for the first time were living just the four of us in a house in the city, my elder son – he was in third or fourth grade then – asked why I was taking him away from the mother who bore him. That's right. And when their grandmother was here in the city at the hospital, my sons would say they had to go to school early and sneak over there to see her on the way.

N.R.: Really? That must have been hard. Were you working then?

H-SAN: No. I taught there in that country school for ten years or so, and then when my husband got transferred to the school where you and he taught together, I took that as an excuse to stay home. I did it all backwards, you see. I should have been home with the kids when they were young and then gone back to work when they were in junior high.

Now, here I am with nothing that I'm intensely interested in outside of the house. That's bad, you know. The doctors say that menopausal symptoms are a luxury disease. Women get all these aches and pains because after the kids are grown, they lie around too much at home doing nothing. If you go to the doctor they brush you off, and tell you to go get a hobby or go back to work. If you come back, they want to give you hormone shots. They think you're just being soft on yourself and have no strength of spirit. But I know I have strength of spirit. I couldn't have made it through that time with my mother-in-law making me work all the time and my sister-in-law always talking meanly of me if I hadn't developed a strong spirit. The closer I got with my husband, the more they talked about me.

N.R.: But you don't lie around the home – don't you work part-time?

H-SAN: That's right. I teach one day a week – home economics to nursing students. My husband encouraged me to go back and teach a bit. He thought it would be good for me to get out of the house and brace my spirit in the outside world. Well, it is strange. On the days when I teach, I feel quite good. I never get sick. Maybe I am soft on myself. My husband said I was just indulging myself the other day when I asked him to tie my apron strings because my arm hurt. Well, I'm not a hypochondriac. I have control over my "self-part" (*jibun*). It's just that when I have stress, my body takes advantage of the opportunity to rule my inner feelings. I suppose there is a psychological side to it ... I always get sick whenever my sister-in-law wants to visit! (laughing) She always talked ill of me. Just when I would feel mother-in-law accepting me a bit, she'd step in between us. But I'm not soft on myself. I know how to endure (*gaman*) the pain.

N.R.: You can endure well; your friends always say that. But if you don't get sick when you teach, would you like to teach more?

H-SAN: No. The teaching isn't really very enjoyable, not when you're part-time like me and have no chance of becoming full-time. You don't get close with the students. Sometimes my old students from the country come to visit me or they invite me to class reunions. That kind of close teacher–student relationship is wonderful, but I can't get close to these girls.

N.R.: Did you always want to be a teacher?

H-SAN: I never thought of it until the war ended. Right then I was in junior high school – the old type that was really like high school now. Everything changed completely. There was a lot of talk about freedom – doing things according to your own will. The teachers started talking about equality between boys and girls. They talked about girls getting jobs out in society and marrying whom they loved instead of whom their parents chose. They talked about democracy. We all thought it meant do-as-you-like-ism. (laughing) But we were very impressed by these ideas – we were just at that age when we were starting to think and question. Well, I started talking about taking the test to go on to school to be a teacher, but my father was of the prewar generation and he wouldn't hear of it. So I studied for the test in secret and took it without telling him. When I passed and got the scholarship to go, he couldn't say anything. (laughing)

N.R.: You really had to make an effort to get out into society!

H-SAN: You couldn't even imagine it these days. But, listen, it made me feel ashamed of myself the other day when I heard on television the accomplishments of those who had received the same scholarship that I received to go to junior college. I really have wasted that opportunity. I wish I had something to devote myself to. And look at you and what you're doing. You won't get to my age and have nothing to do.

N.R.: I'll have the stress of too much to do. But you do flower arranging, too, don't you?

H-SAN: I do – once a week. Actually, we would rather be out making good money than doing hobbies. But what can we do? Clean somebody's house or wash dishes in a restaurant? Just part-time work for little pay. So that's why we do hobbies.

Of course, I do enjoy it. The teacher is very good. She has taught flower lessons for years and has a high-level certificate. After the lessons, we all sit around and drink tea together. We laugh and talk and let our feelings relax. It helps to find out that your problems are the same as everybody else's. That's the best part. It really helps to be with friends. Sometimes when I'm not feeling well, my old friends come over. I can relax my *ki* energy when I'm around them, so it helps if they come over; they just serve us both a cup of tea while I lie under the warming table. Sometimes when I feel good, we go shopping together or out to lunch. We just go to the grocery store, or every once in a while to the department store. Of course I've had to buy a lot of new things for this new house we built, so sometimes they help me go look for those things.

N.R.:   That sounds like fun. My friends in Tokyo like to go to hot springs together. Do you ever do that?

H-SAN: Oh, I love to go to hot springs. They cure your aches and pains as if they never existed. My husband and I go sometimes, but usually I can't get away to go with friends. My husband or the boys need me. My flower group is planning a night at a hot springs. I would like to go, but that is the very weekend when my younger son is taking his test for a teacher's license. I need to be here then.

N.R.:   But can't you go anyway? He'll do all right.

H-SAN: No, I really can't. He has to work so hard, the least I can do is to give him some warm noodles late at night. If he flunked, and I had gone on that trip, everyone would blame me. They always look at the woman of the house if things go wrong. Though they never praise her when things go well! (laughing)

N.R.:   The husband gets all the praise?

H-SAN: That's it. (laughing) People always say that I am the strong one at home and my husband is so gentle. But that's not the case at all. He always makes the big decisions.

N.R.:   With your husband's stomach ulcer, you must have had to care for him a lot.

H-SAN: When his stomach was at its worst, I used to take his lunch to school every day. I would grow vegetables and make him soup out of the freshest, youngest shoots. I'd take it to him every day. I really gave my all for him. Now that we're older, I wish that we had a hobby in common. All we do is shop or take a walk together. I would take up his hobby if it were anything but English, but that I can't do. And that is his whole life – it's his work and his hobby.

N.R.:   Well, it won't be long until you can help care for your grandchildren. (laughing)

H-SAN: No way! I want to enjoy myself, not care for my grandchildren. Anyway, they should be raised by their mother. I don't want to live with my children – I want to live close, but I don't want to be stuck together. My husband built the house, though, so we could make a kitchen upstairs and live up there and the elder son could live downstairs with his family. Who knows what will happen? The daughter-in-law may refuse. It's not good to have two women in the same kitchen – you have to use your *ki* energies to always be careful of each other (*kizukau*). The way it is now I can let my *ki* go when I'm home alone. On days when I don't feel well, I just drink Chinese medicinal tea and put on the medicinal compresses that my son picks up for me at the hospital, and sleep here with my legs under the heated table and the blanket over me. I deserve to rest after all these years of caring for others. I don't need to be out pulling my *ki* energy together all the time.

An interpretation of Hosoi-san's interpretation

Hosoi-san experienced two differing ideologies in her youth: the wartime ideology of devotion to country and family and the ideology of the immediate postwar, a free-will version of democracy. Both have reverberated through her life, shaping the multiple and sometimes ambiguous positions that she has taken.

The wartime ideology taught her that she should work toward discipline of *ki* energy, forgetting indulgence of self in relationship, and indulging elders and the country's efforts instead. For Hosoi-san, this meant respecting her father's wishes in schooling, work, and marriage. (Her mother had died when she was quite young.) As a girl, it meant that she should be disciplined in her home tasks, caring for her brothers and father so that they in turn could carry out their tasks for country outside the home. She was indulged to the extent that she was allowed to go to a girls' middle school, where she got an education and made good friends. However, the main emphasis was on learning appropriate household skills, and devoting spiritual strength to country by making things for soldiers and doing military exercises. In womanhood, she assumed that she would be expected to give even greater proof of devotion to her husband's household than her natal one, but looked forward to the time when she would have the emotional basis for that devotion with her children. In short, Hosoi-san grew up thinking that positions of strengthening *ki*, indulging others, and participating in formal hierarchy were primary, while positions of relaxing *ki*, being indulged, and sharing intimacy were secondary, framed within the former.

After the war, a new set of ideas influenced Hosoi-san and her friends who saw large parts of textbooks blacked out and teachers' ideas changed almost overnight in accord with the dictates of the postwar state. The women told me of their shock, yet intense interest, in these new ideas of sexual equality, co-education, marriage decided by individuals, and women's rights to work. They remembered one young, male teacher in particular who became very close with them, encouraging and sharing their enthusiasm for a new future. Here was an ideology that in provincial Japan had never had life before, but which turned the old ideology around by favoring free will, indulgence of self, and muted hierarchy. The question was how young women in the provinces like Hosoi-san could make positions for themselves within this new ideology.

Hosoi-san did so by taking the teacher's college test without her father's knowledge and by winning a scholarship, thereby forcing his permission to go to normal school and become a teacher of home economics – this at a time when keeping daughters at home until marriage was a mark of status. Hosoi-san went off to teach and board in a distant village, later moving to another where she met her husband. According to the new ideology, Hosoi-san's actions championed the new sexual equality and do-as-you-like-ism of democracy. It enabled her to carve out a position as independent worker in the outer world. She was now like a man, using her *ki* strength to help form ritual learning contexts at school, and relaxing at the home where she boarded at night (although as a woman, she still had to serve tea at school and help around the house in the evenings).

These positions were ambiguous for they also occurred within the ideas of the old ideology. In this framework, Hosoi-san was indulged by her father who accepted her wish to continue schooling and teach regardless of his ideas of propriety. Thus, acting like a man in society was a position of relaxation and indulgence, assumed to be only a preface to a future position of devotion to her husband's family. Considered in this way, she carried generative aspects of universal energy – free-floating fecundity that threatened the status of her natal household and the morals of young female students and adult male teachers. Encouragement to marry came at her in various forms as magazines and home economics books extolled motherhood and her friends cautioned: "Don't be left behind – get a good one before they all disappear."

Not surprisingly, Hosoi-san taught only a few years before she entered a local agricultural household in an arranged marriage to the eldest son. Work outside and inside the home melded to create her ideological position as a devoted daughter-in-law. Her work acquired new meaning as a source of income for her husband's household. Meanwhile, she was responsible for preparing and serving food and drink to create situations that would indulge the relaxation of others – mother-in-law, father-in-law, sister-in-law, husband, and two sons who were soon born. Although the household was an inner, informal situation for these others, she looks back on it for herself as a somewhat outer situation of deference because of the authority of her in-laws over her and her inability to form close emotional relationships with her sons and husband. Rather than a memory of the energy of inner-oriented consolidation which she created for that group, Hosoi-san is left with the memory of the energy of outer-oriented differentiation created in the relationship with her mother-in-law.

Hosoi-san still harks back to the years spent living with her mother-in-law as the proof of her ability to endure suffering (*gaman*). The proof is not in her work as a teacher, but the general suffering incurred by her mother-in-law's authoritative wishes. Although both unpleasant and

involuntary, she translates her suffering under her mother-in-law's authoritative wishes into the honing of a *ki* spirit which she can now control.
On this basis, Hosoi-san assumes she is not indulging herself in imaginary
aches and pains as her husband and doctor suggest.

These ascetic practices toward selflessness under mother-in-law are now
the basis for her powers of outer authority and position of status as she
ages. She, too, will become a mother-in-law, carrying energies of outward
authority and hierarchical differentiation. Hosoi-san does not want to
domineer her prospective daughter-in-law too closely. Yet by living quite
near to a locally bred daughter-in-law who understands the value of self-
discipline, Hosoi-san wants to share such ordering potency with the
younger woman.

Hosoi-san's relations with her sister-in-law are not an experience that
she would care to repeat. When young, their relationship was ambiguous
and competitive. Hosoi-san had higher status as an in-married, permanent
member of the household, but the sister-in-law had status as a resident, inborn member of the household (Bachnik 1983). Later, the two competed
resentfully over divisions in caring for Hosoi-san's mother-in-law when
she was in the hospital dying of cancer. Shore locates this type of
relationship on the generative side of potency (1986: 118). Indeed Japanese often view competition as contributing to the strength of will in boys
and men. But during menopause, Hosoi-san feels that her control over self
and others is weakened by bodily pain. She avoids her sister-in-law
because their relationship threatens her mind/body stability with loosely
bound aspects of power.

In relation to her own children when young, Hosoi-san resented her
female in-laws binding the children to themselves through overindulgence.
Postwar home economics books had convinced Hosoi-san that a mother,
not a grandmother, should raise the children. Had she herself been the one
to give the children both indulgence and strictness when they were young,
she feels she would have more control over them now. Hosoi-san feels
denied of a process by which the power of inner consolidation with her
children at young ages could lead to the power of outer authority over
them later.[7]

Once her sons were in elementary school, Hosoi-san was quite happy to
leave the agricultural household and establish a nuclear household in her
natal provincial city. She felt her job had already been subsumed within
her responsibilities to her in-laws' household and she welcomed the chance
to leave and establish a new situation as a full-time housewife and mother.
Postwar ideologies legitimated positions for women as independent
workers, as mothers, and as wives of loving, preferably self-chosen
husbands, but not as daughters-in-law or mothers-in-law; the latter were

outside the definition of democracy as it was communicated in the early years after the war. The move gave her higher social status as a wife who did not have to work or care for mother-in-law, but could devote herself to mothering and housewifery.

Now free from in-laws, she thought she could establish herself as family nurturer in contrast to her husband, the disciplinarian – just as the home economics books suggested. He would be the source of more authoritative aspects of power in the family, especially as the children faced problems in the outer world, and she would be the source of more consolidating aspects of power within the home. This ordering of different aspects of power within the nuclear household by gender differences naturalized the "typical" economic arrangement of the time in which the husband worked outside to support the family and the wife stayed home.

Today Hosoi-san is left in an ambiguous position: at home without any visible household hierarchy, her generative powers rather loosely bound. On the one hand, she views the nuclear household as her main group of membership – her main center for hierarchy, discipline, and obligations. She views herself in a hierarchy where her husband makes all the major decisions and where her status rises and falls with his and her sons' successes and failures. She feels that she still must tauten her *ki* energies to fulfill obligations for everyday home maintenance, for relating with other households, for furnishing the house, and soon for finding brides for her sons. Further, she is still responsible for providing the generative power of inner consolidation for her family; for example, she stayed home from the hot springs to help her son study. She continues to cook a special diet for her husband's weak stomach and now for her son's as well. The house is a place where she binds in her energies every day when she ties her apron around her.

On the other hand, in contrast with her in-laws' household, she understands her present nuclear household context as relaxed, a place where she can receive some indulgence and mutual relaxation. If feeling terrible, she needs to do little more than push the button on the rice cooker. Her son will go to the hospital and buy her medicinal compresses for her aching shoulders and her husband will tie her apron strings, though not without comment. In a rare praising of her husband in public, Hosoi-san once said to a friend and me, "I felt so awful last night. I thought, what would I do if I had a husband who didn't give me understanding now and then?" In line with prevalent ideals of husband as interested partner and affectionate companion, Hosoi-san wishes that they could have a hobby in common – despite her husband's insistence that because his mother picked her to enter their household as daughter-in-law, she should have no such expectation of their marriage!

When husband and sons are absent, objects and friends provide consolidating powers of rejuvenation. One can almost envision the tree concentrating all its power for growth back in its roots when Hosoi-san is home alone with no responsibilities, able to lie down with her body half under the warming table. She drinks tea brewed from East Asian medical herbs that revive and balance natural energy, and eats fresh vegetables brought by her country aunts. (They brought them with laughter one day – long, thin, obviously phallic vegetables like carrots and *daikon* to give her the male strength she lacked in menopause.) The warm, safe, undemanding atmosphere of this innermost sphere of home allows her *ki* energy to be very inner-oriented and spontaneous.

By virtue of her womanhood, Hosoi-san creates generative power. But in menopause, she feels her natural power waning. Indeed, pracitioners of East Asian medicine comment that a woman loses her natural strength at menopause, and other women report that men often turn to premenopausal women with sharper generative powers, at least for sex. Although Hosoi-san thinks she has control of her *ki* energies, she also realizes her control can fail if threatened from all sides, by both physical symptoms and societal stress.

Hosoi-san was glad to accept the advice of biomedical doctor, husband, and women to rejuvenate her *ki* energies by meeting with women friends. She preferred women friends of the same status or a little below with whom rank and status were not an issue: a neighbor of slightly lower status that she'd known for years, a woman of the same age whose family she had boarded with when she was a young teacher, and a woman with whom she had gone to junior college, slightly higher in status as she now taught at the junior college and her husband was already a vice-principal. Hosoi-san's energies seemed to especially relax when the neighbor of slightly lower status was there. With unbound *ki* energies and hierarchy muted, these groups of nearly homogeneous women signified generative aspects of power as they complained about husband, children, part-time work, and mothers-in-law.

Hosoi-san also enjoyed flower arranging when she felt up to it. Through arranging the flowers, Hosoi-san brought the generative powers of nature into her own sphere and transformed them into a more ordered aspect of power, ordering herself simultaneously. Her teacher was a woman neighbor of slightly higher economic status, trained as a teacher in flower arrangement. Arranging the flowers with care, both speaking politely and quietly, they created a context that signified ordering aspects of power through disciplined *ki*, hierarchy, and task orientation. Through the teacher's gentle authority, Hosoi-san indulged herself in the stability and self-control that an inferior can gain from a status relationship. In addition, the fact that these comparatively high-status, well-educated women stay home seems natural when tied to these ideas of powers acquired in artistic hobbies.

After the lessons, Hosoi-san and her friends again constructed an intimate context with informal language, mundane concerns, gales of laughter, and lots of food. The relative chaos of this situation marked the centralizing but loosely bound energies of the universe – just controlled enough to reach the peak of warm harmony.

Other days she met with these or other friends to go shopping – a leisured enjoyment that signifies relaxed *ki* energies, indulged freedom, and intimate relationships for women. Higher-status husbands of meno-pausal-aged women often laugh indulgingly at their wives' shopping expeditions, feeling that this is a good way for them to get out of the house and regain vitality. (Lower-status men prefer that their wives work.) The economic task of consumption – increasingly necessary to the Japanese economy and even urged by the American government for the Japanese – seems very natural when understood in terms of rejuvenating generative aspects of power. In addition, because shopping for house items is a housewife's responsibility, shopping fits into a larger frame of household obligations. The outcome is that positions of free will in the new ideology (as consumers in this case) are safely framed within positions of obligation in the old ideology (as housewives).

In middle age, Hosoi-san's work has different meanings than it did when she was young, but they are no less full of ambiguities. They reflect contradictions and complexities in the state's expectations of women and in the positions women themselves create in response. On one side, her husband and doctor both encourage Hosoi-san to work. The doctor expresses his advice in terms of strengthening the *ki* energies that are weak at menopause because women often have weak personalities, especially if they have some extra money. Her husband thinks that she is *amai* (literally, too sweet) – too dependent on others and indulgent of self. Work's hierarchy and tasks would make her *ki* stand up straight. In these familiar and convincing terms, Hosoi-san's husband and doctor help to convey – however unwittingly – the needs of the state and the economy for the labor of middle-aged women as cheap, flexible part-time workers.

On the other side, neither husband nor doctor thinks that she should work to the extent that her upkeep of the house and family members suffer. Status must be preserved. Her husband says, "Work only if you can keep the household going." Her doctor says, "Make sure that your weak *ki* is not causing the problems at home that contribute to your stress." In this sense, they are legitimating the needs of the state to have someone available to care for sick or troubled children, workers, and elders.

The situation is no less ambiguous from Hosoi-san's point of view. Given the aches of menopause, Hosoi-san does see work as a drain on her energies to give to the household. On the other hand, Hosoi-san admits that work stretches her *ki* and helps her ward off bodily aches. After all, as a teacher in a relatively hierarchical classroom, she is the sign and enforcer of authority and her *ki* energy stands up straight.

However, she is also clear on a point that doctors and husband do not mention. Part-time work does not build her *ki* in a way that is satisfactory to her. She can contribute little to the household economically and she has little lasting influence on students nor status with fellow faculty. She realizes that having quit once, it would be almost impossible for her to get another well-paying job with status. The world of work as presently constructed denies the ideals of her received postwar ideology. If she is a devoted mother, she cannot easily return to be a devoted, economically independent worker.

Indeed, given its small economic benefit to middle-class life in the provinces, part-time work can be seen as indulgence of will. For some this spells status; articles in magazines targeting middle-aged women insist a woman would work only for a "meaning in living" or as an expression of the inner heart (Rosenberger 1991: 19). Hosoi-san enjoys the status, but would prefer a well-paying job with no question of indulgence.

In spite of her insights on the nature of part-time work, Hosoi-san chastises herself because she is not using her education to the extent of other past scholarship winners. She still blames her lack of *ki* energy control on her inadequate devotion to a pursuit outside of the household. In spite of her best efforts, society's unspoken expectations of women in both household and workplace and her own corresponding actions have embedded her in the old ideology that the woman's principal group of membership and devotion should be the household.

In contrast to part-time teaching, Hosoi-san looks back to her days of full-time teaching as full of meaning for her and her students. As a teacher, she contributed energies of a differentiated, outer-oriented nature to her students through her hierarchical, disciplined relations to them. She taught the girls the actions of hierarchy: greetings to elders, superiors, and family members and the appropriateness of marrying and giving up work when having children. As her doctor and husband did with her, through advice on personal maturity, she connected the students with roles they should play in the political and economic order.

From past students whom she taught full-time, she still receives gifts, visits, and entertainment at parties. As a high-status person in this context, she has the privilege of being dependent on these younger women's generative energy and their attempts to foster harmony. Her authority is not understood as dominance, but as a potent force that does not conflict with her dependency on her students in a more intimate context. Hosoi-san receives their powers of generativity and consolidation, in return for having given them a chance to develop and learn the powers associated with the status system.

In short, Hosoi-san and her friends, students, and relatives together create experiences of ordering and generative powers, giving and receiving as they move through and signify multiple positions in various contexts and relationships. Various combinations of gender, age, and status are important in making these meaningful patterns. Ideologies specify the current positions people take but are often clearest for men, constructed as they are from a male point of view. For women, positions are often greater in number than for men, but also greater in complexity. Women make double interpretations of many situations, one from a male point of view, and one from a woman's point of view (Rosenberger, in press).

Conclusion

I have rendered Hosoi-san's interpretations of her life so as to convey to Western readers a picture of "self" that is qualitatively different from the idea of a linear accumulation of experience and achievements that stands alone. In Hosoi-san's way of understanding, "self" is a cyclical process that takes form and meaning from its position in relation to other people within changing contexts, groups, and ideologies.

In summary, movements of *ki* energy between tautness and looseness occur in correspondence with changes in contexts between formal hierarchy and informal intimacy, and in association with relationships that vary in indulgence. The movements of all of these layers signify aspects of universal energies, more or less bound for human use. Multiple positions in current economic and political ideologies gain meaning by association with these movements of self that change only slowly over many generations.

This is not a perception that action in one domain *causes* action in another, but rather a perception that actions in one domain are significant and proper because they cycle in tandem with actions in other domains. These different dimensions create and constitute each other in an active metaphorical relationship.

Such explanations do not sit easily with Americans who tend to search for cause and effect reasoning, and therefore I turn to a musical explanation in summary. In musical terms, *ki* energy might be the alto line, dyadic relationships of indulgence the soprano line, group the tenor line and context the bass line. In a Japanese context, the chorus, flute, drum, and vocal calls of the Noh drama will do equally well. The tune in one line does not *cause* a change in the tune of another line, but the whole sound would not make sense unless the lines changed in relation to each other. The movement of each line changes the general situation and therefore other lines move to keep apace of the song.

One's *ki* energy line receives its tone from such characteristics as age, status, and gender. Although its range is somewhat limited, its exact tone is determined in relation to other lines. An adult woman strikes a different harmony with an older man than with a young woman, her son, or with a woman her age. They make a certain sound, or in social terms, context, but they also may have to blend their sound with the sound of the larger context played in the bass line.

The song as a whole moves among keys and harmonies, creating different patterns and moods. These are like the different aspects of sacred power or universal energies that are implicated in tight and loose bindings even in modern Japanese life. The patterns of the song, like social arrangements, create moods and energies that people feel and participate in, but never fully verbalize. Their vagueness makes them easy to ignore or to write off as aesthetics, but they connect people and groups to culturally perceived cycles of nature and the universe.

Lastly, the song changes through time and place. Through documented Japanese history, the song may always cycle through similar key changes – between disciplined formality and spontaneous intimacy or between ordering and generative aspects of power. But the lyrics vary with dominant political and economic ideas. As I have pointed out through the text, such contemporary capitalistic divisions as company and household or production and consumption, underwritten by gender, age, and status, are played to the "same old song" of movements in *ki* energy, indulgence, context, and universal energies. It is very easy for people to sing along. They soon are creating these divisions themselves while still singing a song that sounds much like that of their ancestors.

The musical metaphor cannot be overdrawn, but I think it helps us to understand the idea of interconnected movement as the basis for self-understanding. For Hosoi-san, even the Westernized individualism of leisure and consumption gets worked into these cycling patterns – generative but framed in differentiated order. At times, as when she stays home from the flower group trip to help her son, Hosoi-san's tune may be rather off-key with the song sung in more contemporary terms by her friends.

I do not intend to suggest that Japanese understanding of selfhood is at all unique. My references to other societies imply that this is an ideology of selfhood that is found in many other societies, perhaps particularly in those which value hierarchy and context as meaningful markers. The American reader should not conclude that Americans and Japanese are hopelessly different: Americans individualized and Japanese interconnected. My suspicion is that self as a social phenomenon moving with multiple dimensions of life is as important to our everyday understandings of self and other as it is to that of Japanese. We usually choose to explain self in terms of separateness, but our ideology does not necessarily fit everyday experience.

NOTES

Thanks to the Women's Writing Group at Oregon State University, particularly Joan Gross, for help on the manuscript and to Clint Morrison for editing.

1 Various words are used to refer to this sacred nature or soul such as *mono* in animals, *kokoro* in humans, *kotodama* in words, and *tama* or *kami* in the universe and gods (Kitagawa 1987: 36, 121, Herbert 1967: 22). Both Befu (1971: 108) and Norbeck (1977: 71) have proposed that the power represented in the *kami* gods or in the Emperor and at the opposite extreme in women or the low-caste Burakumin was an impersonal power loosely likened to *mana* of Polynesia.

2 These formulations suggest the concepts of Yin and Yang, and are no doubt influenced by them, but words and concepts of *tama* are indigenous.

3 *Asobi* also means play among children or leisure among adults. It has come to be used widely, but comes from the song and dance in Shinto worship. This bespeaks the shift of shrine shamans to itineracy and to areas near the shrine when government was Sinified in the seventh century. While continuing as shamans, they often became entertainers and prostitutes as well, and later the sacred function of "play" was lost to the entertainment function.

4 Evidence from the nineteenth century shows that menstruating women were bound into huts or certain areas of the house. After giving birth, women are put into their natal home or even confined to bed for three weeks in some areas. Also note the extra binding (*sarashi*) that is wrapped around the pregnant woman's abdomen.

5 Sons-in-law who marry in are bound into their new household hierarchy in a similar fashion, but are a laughing stock because they do not have the extent of generative power attributed to a woman. A daughter who stays in her own home is freer because she is bound by a continuous hierarchy like a man, and escapes some of the bindings of the daughter-in-law.

6 In fact these values do get reinterpreted through history. According to the place, era, and person, poles of disciplined hierarchy and spontaneous indulgence have different meanings that fit into different political and economic ideas and circumstances. For example, in Heian, around the year 1000, Genji moves between the ritual of court and the indulgence of his lovers. In the Tokugawa, around 1700, Chikamatsu's heroes move between the disciplined hierarchy of merchant households and the spontaneous indulgence of the

pleasure quarters. In contemporary Tokyo, a "salaryman" moves between the productive hierarchy and stress of a company and the relaxing intimacy of home or familiar bar.

7 My impression is that her control is not as incomplete as she imagines. When her first son got a job with a Tokyo company, she visited him there and fell quite ill in the hotel. Although not explicitly connected by Mrs. Hosoi, several years later, her son quit and got a job as a teacher in their home city.

REFERENCES

Bachnik, Jane. 1983. Recruitment and Strategies for Household Succession: Rethinking Japanese Household Organization. *Man* 18: 160–82.

1987. Native Perspectives of Distance and Anthropological Perspectives of Culture. *Anthropological Quarterly* 60: 25–34.

Befu, Harumi. 1971. *Japan: An Anthropological Introduction*. New York: Chandler Press.

Doi, Takeo. 1977. *The Anatomy of Dependence*. Tokyo: Kodansha.

1986. *The Anatomy of Self*. Tokyo: Kodansha.

Dorson, Richard. 1962. *Folk Legends of Japan*. Rutland, Vt.: Charles E. Tuttle.

Henriques, J., Hollway, W., Urwin, C., Venn, C., and Walkerdine, V. 1984. *Changing the Subject*. New York: Methuen.

Herbert, Jean. 1967. *Shinto: The Fountainhead of Japan*. New York: Stein and Day.

Keeler, Ward. 1987. *Javanese Shadow Plays, Javanese Selves*. Princeton, N.J.: Princeton University Press.

Kitagawa, Joseph. 1987. *On Understanding Japanese Religion*. Princeton, N.J.: Princeton University Press.

Lebra, Takie Sugiyama. 1976. *Japanese Patterns of Behavior*. Honolulu: University of Hawaii Press.

Lock, Margaret. 1980. *East Asian Medicine in Urban Japan*. Berkeley: University of California Press.

Norbeck, Edward. 1977. A Sanction for Authority: Etiquette. *The Anthropology of Power* (R. Fogelson and R. Adams, eds.), New York: Academic Press.

Rohlen, Thomas. 1976. Promises of Adulthood in Japanese Spiritualism. *Daedalus* 105: 125–43.

Rosenberger, Nancy R.. 1989. Dialectic Balance in the Polar Model of Self: The Japan Case. *Ethos* 17: 88–113.

1991. Don't Think! There Isn't Time! Media Messages to Japanese Young Women. Paper presented at the Association for Asian Studies, New Orleans, March 15–18.

In press. Reversals in Japanese Gender Relations: Indexing Contexts and Universal Powers. *Inside and Outside: Defining a Situated Social Order in Japan* (J. Bachnik and C. J. Quinn, eds.), Princeton, N.J.: Princeton University Press.

Shore, Bradd. 1982. *Sala'Ilua: A Samoan Mystery*. New York: Columbia University Press.

1986. Polynesian Worldview: A Synthesis. Unpublished MS.

Smith, Paul. 1988. *Discerning the Subject*. Minneapolis: University of Minnesota Press.
Weedon, Chris. 1987. *Feminist Practice and Poststructuralist Theory*. Oxford: Basil Blackwell.

5 Identification of the self in relation to the environment

Augustin Berque

In his *Fūdo* (1935), the famous Japanese philosopher Watsuji Tetsurō provided an account of cultural uniqueness based on the concept of *fūdosei* (climaticity). With this word, Watsuji attempted to coin a spatial equivalent to the temporal concept of historicity (*rekishisei*). More broadly, he wanted to use *fūdosei* as the basis for a phenomenological theory of humankind – the subtitle of his book is 'An Essay in the Study of Man' (*Ningengaku-teki kōsatsu*) – which would complement Heidegger's project *Sein und Seit*.

Watsuji's study provides a useful starting point for the issue considered in this chapter: the relationship between self and environment in Japan. In the first place *Fūdo* exemplifies the difference between Japanese and Western conceptions of self. Whereas in the modern Western view self and environment are opposing terms, in Japan they are seen as interactive; the self melds with the environment by identifying with patterns of nature which are, nonetheless, culturally constructed. As will be seen, Watsuji's emphasis upon the interpenetration of self and environment represents an approach to the issue of self found in many areas of Japanese culture, including *haiku*, landscape painting, and treatises on Japanese uniqueness (*nihonjinron*).

At the same time, however, Watsuji's account of the self–environment interaction has significant shortcomings. His phenomenology of environment deals only with physical environment. Although he presents human existence as both individual and social (*shakaiteki*), he makes no allowance for the social conditioning of collective representations (in the Durkheimian sense), instead relating them directly to nature. This is all the more intriguing since Watsuji devotes several sections of *Fūdo* to human relationships (*aidagara*). The lack of a phenomenology of social environment in *Fūdo* leads to geographical determinism, obscuring the ways in which the self–environment relation is culturally mediated.

It is the process of cultural mediation which is investigated in this discussion. Following the theoretical purpose of *Fūdo*, I suggest that there is a link between the way the Japanese (or, indeed, people of any society) perceive nature and space, and the way they interact with each other: that is, the way Japanese self is defined within its social context. Yet, diverging from Watsuji's deterministic drift, I argue that the main factors in this relational process are not natural. Nature, here, acts only inasmuch as it is historically perceived, interpreted, and transformed by a specific society, while society acts only inasmuch as it exists in relation to nature.

Mediance and trajection

'A Climate' – the usual translation for the title of Watsuji's work – does not express the anthropological aspects of the word *fūdo*, if only because its derived concept of *fūdosei* cannot be correctly rendered by 'climaticity'. Geography (and thus 'geographicity') might seem more appropriate, but still would not do justice to Watsuji's phenomenological stance. For these and other lexical reasons (Berque 1986) I prefer to translate *fūdo* as 'milieu' and to express *fūdosei* through a neologism: *mediance*. Lexically, this word simply derives from the Latin root of *milieu*, and as such it is related to the already existing adjective *medial*. I define milieu as the relationship of a society with space and nature, and I define mediance as the sense of this relationship (with the specific attributes of the French *sens*, suggesting simultaneously a direction or tendency, a feeling, a meaning), which I consider to be a historical process.

The geographically deterministic drift of *Fūdo* – a drift apparently at odds with its phenomenological premises – can be attributed to the fact that Watsuji does not analyze the social and historical construction of medial relations (*fūdo*) and, concomitantly, of mediance (*fūdosei*). The logic of the Japanese medial process, or mediance, tends both to blur the identity of the self and, at the same time, to enhance the identification of the self with what is not the self: environment, both social and natural. These processes involve not only psychological, social, and ecological relations as such (e.g., self and others, self and environment) but, more generally, the relation of the subject with the object. For this reason I prefer to speak inclusively of the Japanese subject rather than exclusively of the Japanese self.

The theoretical grounds for such an interpretation have been presented in two books (Berque 1986, 1990) which draw upon a range of works including Schutz (1932), Berger and Luckman (1966), Gibson (1979), and Bourdieu (1980, 1986). These books show that mediance, by combining historically the ecological and the symbolic, expresses in environmental terms a more general process that is both subjective and objective, physical and phenomenal. Inspired by the old verb *trajecter*, which Montaigne still used in the sense of "to travel, to transport," I call this process *trajection*. The concept of trajection – understood as a historical displacement of the objective toward the subjective, and the reverse – has much to do with Bourdieu's aim of "going beyond the alternative into which social science lets itself be locked up, that between social physics and social phenomenology" (Bourdieu 1980: 234, my translation). For this, Bourdieu makes use of the concept of *habitus*, which he defines as "systems of transposable and durable dispositions, structured structures predisposed to function as structuring structures" (p. 88, my translation). Yet to my mind trajection is a more general process than habitus (a habitus can thus be considered a trajective process). Mediance, while also being a trajective process, has ecological and geographical components (e.g., landscape, territoriality, urban amenity, etc.) which make it specific to the relationship with space and nature. The determination of Watsuji's study results from his failure to clarify the medial process (the way society relates to nature) and the trajective process (the relation between self and environment) as they operate in Japan.

Blurring and decentering the subject

It is now commonly accepted that whereas European culture has tended to give the subject a stable, central, or even transcendental position, Japanese culture (like many other cultures) tends to give the subject a relative position. This has led Tokieda Motoki (1941) to stress the notion of plane (*bamen*) and Nishida Kitarō (1927) that of place (*basho*), and Nakamura Yūjiro (1983, 1989) to explore a logic which would be based on the identity of the predicate and not that of the subject.

Japanese poetry conspicuously displays such a tendency. Take, for example, Oshi's *haiku*:

Fūrin no	(1)	(3) To be under
chiisaki oto no	(2)	(2) the little sound
shita ni iru	(3)	(1) of the wind-bell

This *haiku* does not say anything about the identity of the person (i.e., the subject) who is under the wind-bell. That could indeed be any of the three pronominal persons of the Indo-European languages, singular or plural, feminine or masculine. Identifying the subject here is not relevant. What is important – though not even posed as a grammatical subject – is the sound of the wind-bell; that is, on both a syntactic and axiological plane, the predicate (the ambience) is here presented and defined prior to the subject. Even by translating *iru* with an infinitive in order to conserve the indefinition of the subject – which is already a notable bias, for *iru* should rather be translated with an indicative – my English translation has nevertheless to posit first the existence ("to be") of this subject, whoever it may be; whereas the Japanese poem reveals this existence only with its last word (*iru*).

If an etymological pun may be used to illustrate this difference, let us say that the subject in question is not placed under the wind-bell as a *subjectum* or *hypokeimenon*, that principle which European culture, especially since Descartes, has posited as the underlying condition for the advent of the world, but as a circumstantial element in a contingent scene. The *hypokeimenon* (underlying condition) in the *haiku* is the predicate or the environment rather than the subject.

A point often at issue in this regard is whether the Japanese subject is so depreciated as to be pervaded by the environment, or on the contrary so enhanced as to be diffused into the environment. Given a statement like *samui!* ("I am cold" or "it is cold") where, at least on a grammatical level, it is not clear whether it is the subject or the environment which is or feels cold, ought we to say that the environment (or the predicate) is subjectivized, or that, on the contrary, the subject is, so to speak, "environmentalized" or contextualized?

This alternative may seem tautological. Does not stating that the position of the subject is a relative one settle the problem? And surely such a statement as *samui!* is not ambiguous at all when pronounced in a real situation. According to a set of clues like intonation, gesture, temperature, etc., one immediately knows who or what is cold; the identity of the subject is not problematical, given that the identity of the situation is known. Yet we shall see, later, that this identification of the situation is highly problematical.

The same tendency also expresses itself in the organization of space. The Japanese mediance tends to decenter, or displace, the subject's integrating point of view. It dislikes unitary perspectives and dominant orientations. This can clearly be seen in the form of cities. Geometrical patterns – with general referents like North, South, or rectangular axes – such as are found in Kyoto or Sapporo are imported models. Indigenous tendencies, on the contrary, favor topological and proxemic organizations, as in Edo where the referents were chosen among concrete and particular landmarks such as Mount Fuji (hence the numerous *Fuji-mi*, as place names), all depending on which landmark was actually visible from each particular place. According to a person's movement from one place to another, the point of view also evolved, and the reference changed (for a detailed analysis of this process and related references, see Berque 1982).

Such a decentering of the point of view is quite alien to the centering process which, in modern Europe, was expressed by the discovery of perspective or by the realization of baroque cities like Versailles or Karlsruhe. In such a "legitimate construction" (as Alberti called modern perspective), the subject – be it the observer or the Prince – acts as the sole focus of the world. Indeed perspective, as Panofsky (1927) has shown, symbolically expresses the world-view which founded modernity, and in which the position of the individual subject is so enhanced as to become transcendental (as, for example, in Descartes's *cogito*).

The cycle of *kata*: forming forms (matrices) and formed forms (imprints)

As we have seen, European culture has striven to give the subject a preeminent status. This tendency eventually brought forth modern scientific objectivity, as an abstraction of the subject from an objectified environment. Needless to say, this abstraction is only effective in the special domain of scientific experimentation, and even there it is not absolute. In all other domains, the European subject, as any other subject, is involved in the cycle of a particular mediance. Only pure objectivity, that is, a total abstraction of the subject, could be truly universal; but pure objectivity is only theoretical.

In a very different way, Japanese traditional culture also tried to suppress the interference of the subject in the environment, that is, to rely solely on phenomena: for example, when Ippen said *suteru koto mo sutero* (reject even the fact of rejecting your ego), or when Bashō said *matsu no koto wa matsu ni narahe* (what is a pine, learn it from the pine).

But such a process is, in fact, the opposite of abstracting the subject from the environment. It implies, on the contrary, a dissolution of the individual self in pure concreteness. This is not an abstraction but a projection of the subject; not an objectification, but a subjectification of the environment. Like scientific objectification, this subjectification can only be performed in particular conditions and cannot be absolute. Like pure objectivity, pure subjectivity is only theoretical.

The quotation above from Bashō reveals another fundamental difference between this way of suppressing the self and the positivistic one: the pine in question must be a concrete and particular pine; it cannot be a general, abstract category. Generalization selects some traits among other traits; particularization selects a whole among other wholes. Thus, the link between this whole and other wholes is metaphorical, not deductive.

This, of course, is only a tendency, but this tendency is at work in many respects in the Japanese medial process. As is well known, Japanese culture has paid scrupulous attention to its natural environment, but this was not environment in general: it was a selection of some places (*meisho*), some plants (e.g., *momiji*), some moments of the year (e.g., *jūgoya*), etc., all entangled into certain sets of regular associations. Elements of the objective environment not included into these representational sets might not be considered at all. The white birch (*shirakaba*), for instance, was not appreciated until Meiji. Ordinary coppice (*zōkibayashi*) did not aesthetically exist until Kunikida Doppo discovered its charm in Musashino. Environmental disruption (*kōgai*) was neglected until it became an international concern, and so on.

These examples show that Japanese culture can be at the same time sensible and insensible to its environment, according to which elements of this environment are considered as *the* environment; or, in other words, according to which elements act metonymically as the whole environment.

Such associations evolve, including new symbols and rejecting old ones, but their pattern is relatively stable. This pattern acts as a mould or matrix (*kata*) for shaping new representational forms, extolling what fits the tradition, and blurring what does not fit it. For example, alpinism, which was introduced from Europe, quickly prospered in Japan, because it had aesthetic and ethical antecedents (Saigyō's poetics, Shugendō, Fuji-kō, etc.); but public greenery in cities, though also imitated, did not thrive because greenery was traditionally associated with the private rather than with the public.

What is Japanese here is of course not the existence of these associations as such, but the degree of their codification, as revealed, for instance, by the use of *uta makura* in traditional poetry (that is, poetical pre-texts in which a substantive, e.g., a place name, is desubstantialized into a purely formal link) or, more generally, by the importance of *kata* in various domains. In the process, no clear-cut distinction can be drawn between forming forms and formed forms. Indeed, the word *kata* can mean both. A famous landscape may act as a matrix (a paradigm) for appreciating other landscapes or shaping a garden (this is the process of *mitate*), but these imprints can become matrices in their turn for shaping other gardens or even whole landscapes (this reverse process is called *gyaku-mitate*; Taira no Kiyomori applied it in Itsukushima, for instance). And just as it transcends one-way causative sequences, the schematization of a *kata* transcends simple objectiveness, as well as the distinction between the individual and the collectivity. Environment exists for a subject (whether individual or collective) only inasmuch as it fits the set of perceptual and actional schemata, or *kata*, of the mediance prevailing there and then.

This phenomenon may lead, as we have seen, to ignoring for some time an objective environmental change. The discrepancy which exists between pure objectivity and the reality of a *kata* explains why the Japanese could at the same time love and respect nature and beauty, on the one hand, and on the other hand let their environment become, during the sixties, one of the most polluted and disfigured in the world.

Yet the medial reality of Japanese *kata* has objective grounds too. Sooner or later, environmental changes are interpreted by culture and metabolized into medial changes. They can indeed be then overestimated (from an objective point of view) just as they were underestimated before. As the proverb has it, "once bitten, twice shy." For example, the fuss which is now being made in Japan about urban amenities can be understood as a counter-effect of the previous neglect of urban quality. Still, this is not a purely subjective reaction. Medial changes are directly proportional neither to objective changes on the one hand, nor to subjective changes on the other hand.

Mediance being something in between an ecological and a symbolic process, some environmental problems, acting as substitutes for the whole, may indeed hide the fact that all problems are not being acknowledged. This may lead to a further degradation of the environment in some domains. Such substitutes, as an expression of the regularity of medial cycles, are those elements which tradition has already enhanced. For instance, the emphasis which is currently put on greenery by amenity movements and policies is a direct heir of that taste for vegetation which the Japanese aesthetic tradition displays. This masks the fact that there are today in Japanese cities more specifically urban problems than greenery problems, for example that of public space. The emphasis on greenery is not a pure reproduction of traditional aesthetic schemata, though; it also owes much to the influence of Western urbanistic conceptions. Medial processes, as we have seen, do admit new inputs. They are cyclic, but not circular.

Personal and collective identity

As both phenomenal matrices and physical imprints, the cycles of the Japanese *kata* appear as paradigmatic illustrations of trajective processes. Inasmuch as Japanese culture has institutionalized some of its patterns or *kata* (as in martial arts), this culture has brought to the level of collective consciousness, and systematically used, certain things which cannot be grasped by the individual subject's consciousness, and which individualistic cultures like the modern European one therefore leave in the realm of the unconscious (thus unmanageable). Needless to say, this propensity to institutionalize trajective patterns may have quite positive effects; this is more or less what a Korean saying summarizes: one Korean is stronger than one Japanese, but three Japanese are stronger than three Koreans.

On the other hand, this propensity leads to a relative incapacity to distinguish the individual from the collective, and thus to objectify the milieu. Watsuji Tetsurō's *Fūdo* is a good example of this permeation of the collective into the individual.

Fūdo draws a parallel between climates and cultural traits. But Watsuji's analysis differs from geographical determinism (as practiced by, for example, his contemporary Ellsworth Huntington, 1924), in that he does not intend to establish a *causal* link between these phenomena. He insists, on the contrary, upon the relativeness of milieu (*fūdo*), which must not be confused with environment (*kankyō*): unlike *kankyō*, milieu (*fūdo*) supposes the existence of Man as a subject. Reciprocally, *fūdo* is "the structural occasion of human existence" (*ningen sonzai no kōzō keiki*).

As can be seen, Watsuji's stance is a phenomenological one. The problem is that, in the same book, he slips more than once into a crude geographical determinism, stating for instance that the people of the Southern Seas have not engendered any culture, *because* of the overly mild climate.[1]

Watsuji's methodological inconsistency stems, first, from an evident discrepancy: in *Fūdo*, he places on the same plane the analysis of a milieu (Japan) which he knew well and experienced from the inside, and of milieux (such as Arabia) of which he had only had an external glimpse, knowing very little of their natural environments, and even less of their cultures. Far from penetrating the mediance (*fūdosei*) of these milieux, Watsuji only describes his own subjective impressions of them.

Why then did Watsuji not notice this evident discrepancy? Because of a fundamental lack of differentiation. In *Fūdo*, Watsuji does not distinguish the collective subject *in situ*, which he addresses when speaking about Japan, from the individual subject (*in vitro* to some extent) he was reduced to when, as a traveler, he confronted foreign milieux. Being only partially subjective in the first case (because endowed with what practical objectivity the Japanese mediance may possess), he is totally subjective in the second case (because he keeps the same approach, although severed from the concerned mediance).

In this respect, *Fūdo* involuntarily reveals a potentiality of the collective in the individual which the Japanese propensity to institutionalize trajective patterns displays in its own way. Had Watsuji more consciously objectified, in regard to his own personal identity, his social environment (and therefore his cultural conditioning), he probably would have been more consistent with his own phenomenological premises. He would probably not have so easily confused his own introspection with foreign mediance and subjectivity which he knew little about, and did not try to grasp.

"Man as a subject," in *Fūdo*, is doubly fraught with Japanese mediance:

first, its personal identification does not matter much in regard to that of its environment, and second, the social aspect of this environment is therefore poorly objectified. Thus, the individual subject is led to overestimate the role of the physical and of the natural in that environment, even though he may reject (as Watsuji's phenomenological and hermeneutical stance does) the positivism of the physical sciences.

To be sure, this propensity is still quite alive in Japan, as treatises about Japanese uniqueness (*nihonjinron*) so conspicuously show. Western authors such as Peter Dale (1986) have more than once denounced the delusions of this genre, its error of fact and its methodological incoherence. In this respect, Watsuji's *Fūdo* could be considered as just one treatise about Japanese uniqueness among well over a thousand ones published since Meiji, were it not for the philosophical premises which have made it a universal classic.

Yet most of the critics fail to catch the mythological essence of the *nihonjinron*. Indeed, in a strictly anthropological sense, the *nihonjinron* share two fundamental characters with myth: the abolition of time (history), and the abolition of the subject (the enunciating individual). Across the centuries and across the personality of their authors, the *nihonjinron* stubbornly tend to refer the Japanese to nature (or prehistory), that is, a set of characters untouched by socio-historical change; and these trajective patterns tend to reproduce themselves regularly, though this may be through some metaphorical transformations. An outstanding example is Hamaguchi Eshun's notion of *kanjin* (contextual man), which basically is a mirror-like anagram of Watsuji's conception of *ningen* (human being), but which indeed adds some new input into the process concerned.

I am not saying that the treatises on Japanese-ness (*nihonjinron*) do not reflect reality (which is what Dale, among others, tends to say). On the one hand, as any social process, the vogue of the *nihonjinron* contributes to the construction of reality for the Japanese. Their trajective patterns partake in making this reality, a reality in between the realness of the thing in itself and the unrealness of representations. What must be seen, on the other hand, is that this logic has little to do with rational inference, or logic in the strict sense. Indeed, one of the interesting features of the *nihonjinron* is precisely that, beyond or beneath the enunciating subject's individual coherence, beyond or beneath the identity of the subject, they illustrate a logic which is founded on the identity of the predicate (Nakamura 1983, 1989), or of place (*basho*) (Nishida 1927), plane (*bamen*) (Tokieda 1941), or milieu (Berque 1986, 1990), in other words, a logic of identification, not of identity, in which sharing a common attribute (e.g., having red hair, or being Japanese, or being in the same situation) entails an intersubjective shift. Such a logic is metaphorical or aesthetic, not rational. Here the subject, identifying itself with other subjects, can *become* what it *is not*, eventually a thing, as the expression *mono no aware* implies. By virtue of this logic, the self can meld with the other.

The logic of mediance is fundamentally a logic of identification, whichever culture *Lebenswelt* concerns; but, according to culture, this logic is diverse. By stressing a logic of identity, the European tradition ultimately produced societies where the self is clearly distinguished from the other. The Japanese tradition not only did not follow that path, but has persistently stressed the necessity of identifying the self with what it is not (or, more precisely, what it is not in the modern Western paradigm), i.e., with nature and the other.

This is, I surmise, approximately what the treatises on Japanese-ness obstinately go on saying with their redundant concepts of indulgence (*amae*) (Doi 1971), extended ego (*kakudai ego*) (Makino 1978), link (*tsunagari*) (Hayasaka 1979), culture of sympathy (*omoiyari no bunka*) (Suzuki 1973), and so on; not to mention Watsuji's interpersonal relationship (*aidagara*).

Consequently, it seems to me tautological – yet, of course, necessary from a scientific or rational point of view – to say that most of the *nihonjinron* exaggerate the Japanese propensity to debase the identity of the self, and by so doing tend to present the Japanese as a uniquely contextual people (*kanjin*) different from the other humans (*ningen*). Being embedded in the medial process of milieu (*fūdosei*) – not abstracted from such a process, as in the Western scientific discourse – the *nihonjinron* illustrate only the Japanese medial process, the identification of the self with its environment. Watsuji's essay on *fūdosei* is itself an excellent example of this cyclical involvement with the environment.

However, analyzing this involvement to understand the quality of the Japanese self requires a double estrangement. First, an estrangement from the cyclical performance of the Japanese self through the Japanese discourse on that very self, i.e. the *nihonjinron*, is needed. Second, an estrangement from the unconscious prerequisites of the modern Western dualistic discourse, i.e., the identity of the individual subject, is required. The first is necessary for objectifying the self and the second for extracting the self from a foundation in identity instead of identification, or in Being instead of Becoming. In other words, objectifying the self – whether Japanese or not – is a cultural *a priori* of the subject; we must put our own medial conditioning in abeyance.

Conclusion

What has been attempted above is an approach to the Japanese self – fundamentally a psycho-sociological question – by way of two complementary problematics: a philosophical one, that of trajection; and a geographical one, that of mediance. The aim is to show that the identity of the self is, both in time and in space, conditioned by a cyclical process tending to schematize reality into certain sets (akin to what the Japanese term *kata*) of forming forms (phenomenal matrices) and formed forms (physical imprints) which resolve into each other. This trajection tends to transcend the individual subject (thus relating it firmly to its physical environment), the more so as trajective processes are institutionalized or codified by culture, which is the case of the Japanese *kata*. In that sense, the Japanese individual self is relatively permeable with its environment (both social and physical); but only inasmuch as this environment has been institutionalized (codified) into what reality is for the Japanese.

A more general or theoretical aim is to show that inasmuch as the trajective process of mediance is related to meaning, it is analogous with language, but only analogous, not homologous: the proper logic of mediance is radically different from that which is based on the identity, or self-consistency, of the enunciating subject, i.e., logic in the strict sense. This is what, for better (the sense of reality) or worse (a low degree of objectification), the Japanese culture has acknowledged, with its distaste for individual reasoning and its enhancement of collective sensibility.

NOTES

1 This is more or less what, from a radically different point of view, Huntington also said (in which he was coherent in his own premises, though these premises were false).

REFERENCES

Berger, Peter and Luckman, Thomas. 1966. *The Social Construction of Reality* (in the French trans.: Paris: Méridiens Klincksieck, 1986).
Berque, Augustin. 1982. *Vivre l'espace au Japon*. Paris: PUF.
    1986. *Le Sauvage et l'artifice. Les Japonais devant la nature*. Paris: Gallimard.
    1990. *Médiance. De milieux en paysages*. Montpellier: Reclus.
Bourdieu, Pierre. 1980. *Le Sens pratique*. Paris: Editions de Minuit.
    1986. *Habitus*, code et codification. *Actes de la recherche en sciences sociales* 64: 40–4.
Dale, Peter. 1986. *The Myth of Japanese Uniqueness*. London and Sydney: Croom Helm and Nissan Institute, Oxford.
Doi, Takeo. 1971. *Amae no kōzō*. Tokyo: Kobundo.

Gibson, James. 1979. *The Ecological Approach to Visual Perception*. Boston, Mass.: Houghton Mifflin.

Hamaguchi, Eshun. 1977. *Nihon-rashisa no sai-hakken* (The rediscovery of Japanese-ness). Tokyo: Nihon Keizai Shinbunsha.

Hayasaka, Tajirō. 1979. *Ningen kankei no shinrigaku* (Psychology of human relations). Tokyo: Kodansha.

Huntington, Ellsworth. 1924. *Civilization and Climate*. New Haven, Conn.: Yale University Press.

Makino, Seiichi. 1978. *Kotoba to kūkan* (Words and space). Tokyo: Tokai Daigaku Shuppan Kyōkai.

Minamoto, Ryōen. 1989. *Kata* (Forms). Tokyo: Shōbunsha.

Nakamura, Yūjirō. 1983. *Nishida Kitarō*. Tokyo: Iwanami Shoten.

—— 1989. *Basho/topos*. Tokyo: Kobundo.

Nishida, Kitarō. 1927. *Hataraku mono kara miru mono e* (From working beings to seeing beings) (discussed in Nakamura 1983).

Panofsky, Erwin. 1927. *Die Perspektive als Symbolische Form* (in the French trans.: Paris: Minuit, 1975).

Schutz, Alfred. 1932. *Der Sinnhafte Aufbau der Sozialen Welt*. Berlin: Springer.

Suzuki, Takao. 1973. *Kotoba to bunka* (Words and culture). Tokyo: Iwanami Shoten.

Tokieda, Motoki. 1941. *Kokugaku genron* (Contemporary theories of Japanese language) (discussed in Nakamura 1983).

Watsuji, Tetsurō. 1935. *Fūdo. Ningengaku-teki kōsatsu* (Climate: an essay in the study of people). Tokyo: Iwanami Shoten.

6   Self in Japanese culture

Takie Sugiyama Lebra

In recent years the concept of "personality" has been discredited in academic discussion, if not in common speech, as too Western-biased, and, particularly in anthropology, as trapped in the tarnished image of the culture-and-personality school. In its stead has emerged the "self" as a more trendy, popular subject of debate involving universalism and relativism, etics and emics (Schweder and Levine 1984, Marsella et al. 1985, White and Kirkpatrick 1985). This essay takes as its point of departure the universalistic thesis on self which is credited to G. H. Mead (1934) and Hallowell (1955). The most essential feature of self, according to these and other scholars, is self-awareness, which is variously worded such as reflexivity, self-objectification, self as an object to itself, self as at once subject and object, "I" and "me," and so on. The same thesis postulates that self-awareness is generated and fostered through self–other interaction on the one hand and the symbolic processing of information on the other. Put another way, self-awareness as a universal feature of self is a product of social participation and cultural representation. To the extent that social and cultural diversity in the human world is inevitable, the quality and content of self-awareness as well as the boundary condition of self are destined to vary from one social-cultural group to the next. The paradox is obvious: universalism and relativism, far from being mutually exclusive, entail each other. A discovery of cultural variations in self-awareness does not disprove but rather confirms the above-stated universalistic thesis on self. My essay is intended, therefore to contribute to understanding the generic features of self by presenting a Japanese variety.[1]

Based upon long years of life as a native Japanese and of research experience as a marginal Japanese, I propose to organize the infinitely variable selves into three dimensions, and these are labeled "the interactional self," "the inner self," and "the boundless self." While defining and elaborating each of these, I attempt to show how one dimension links up to or flows into another.

The interactional self

The interactional self refers to the awareness of self as defined, sustained, enhanced, or blemished through social interaction. This label may sound redundant insofar as all selves are a product of social interaction as stated earlier, and for this reason this dimension of self may be found most commonly across cultural groups. But I am referring here to the particular sense of immediacy of self–other interaction and relationship underlying self-awareness. Self here is "socially contextualized" (Shweder and LeVine 1984), and critically interdependent with others in a high degree of awareness. Of all phases of the interactional self, two polar orientations are singled out here: presentational and empathetic.

The presentational self

The presentational self involves the surface layer of self, metaphorically localized on the person's face, visible or exposed to others either in actuality or imagination. The person's self-awareness is sharpened as the object of attention, inspection, and appraisal by others around. This self-awareness is labeled "kao," "mentsu," "taimen," "menboku," "teisai," "sekentei." These terms might be translated as honor, self-esteem, dignity, reputation, and the like, but such translations do not fully convey the self's sensitivity to interactional immediacy and vulnerability entailed in the Japanese terms.

The presentational self is upheld by the presenter's performance which ranges from routine behavior to status attainment, from enactment of protocols to prominent achievement, from conformity to distinction. What obsesses Japanese today is performance in career making, which is preceded by educational achievements as irrevocably scored by the prestige rank of the school admitted to. The housewife's self is affected by vicarious sharing of her husband's promotion or demotion in his career, or her son's success or failure in entrance examinations.

Self's performance (or appearance) is only a part of the presentational self. Others play an equally indispensable part. First, others are significant as an actual or potential audience, watching self's performance approvingly or disapprovingly. Self here consists of continuous reflexivity between performance by self and sanctions by the audience.

Goffman's (1959) dramaturgical analogy fits in well with the above situation, except that the performance–audience relationship in the Japanese social drama is not limited to face-to-face interaction. While still accompanied by a sense of immediacy, the Japanese self, or face here, is often addressed to the world of audience not in immediate presence here and now. This world of audience is called *seken*, and the face-sensitive self addressed to the *seken* is identified as *sekentei*. The close relationship between the *seken* and face is indicated by common expressions like "unable to face the seken" (*seken ni kao muke ga dekinai*) or "have no face to meet the seken" (*seken ni awaseru kao ga nai*).

The *seken* constituency varies in accordance to where self happens to stand, and in which direction it faces. It may include one's kindred (outside the immediate family), neighbors, schoolmates, colleagues, clientele, or a large, ill-defined aggregate of people, known and unknown to self. In this sense, the *seken–sekentei* relationship offers another example in line with Bachnik's (1986) interpretation of Japanese self and other as indexical (not referential) of spatial/temporal distance with self as the zero point of the coordinates.

While the *seken* has something in common with the Western concept of "reference group" (Inoue 1977), or with "the generalized other" of Mead, I identify it as the generalized audience or jury surrounding the self in an inescapable way. Two features of the *seken* make the self especially vulnerable to its sanction. In parallel with the "face"-focused self, the *seken*-other is equipped with its own "eyes," "ears," and "mouth," watching, hearing, and gossiping about the self. This body metaphor contributes to the sense of immediacy and inescapability of the *seken*'s presence. On the other hand, the *seken* itself is immediately invisible and ill-defined and thus can make the self defenseless.

A person or action is described in relation to the *seken*, such as *seken-nami* (conformative to *seken* standard, or ordinary), *seken-banare* (incongruent with *seken* convention, or eccentric), *seken-shirazu* (unaware of *seken* rules, or naive), and so on. Inoue (1977: 31) speculates that Japanese have traditionally held "seken-nami" as their goal to attain. Even today, my female informants, if unmarried in their late twenties or older, tend to confess that they are eager to marry, not because they really want spouses but because their *sekentei* hurts ("sekentei ga warui"). They wish, in other words, to appear *seken-nami*.

Self as an actor in the social theater needs not only audience but producers, co-actors, and stage staff. Others here play a co-presentional role in protecting or hurting the presentational self. The face-focused self thus depends for its welfare on others' treatment, politeness, hospitality, and so on. A man who takes his presentational self seriously depends upon his wife's cooperation, when the couple are exposed to outsiders, for example, in host–guest interaction, for sustaining his self as the head of the house. The wife may speak respectfully to her husband, appear modest and compliant with him, quite unlike her usual self. Likewise, an organizer of ceremonies like weddings and funerals pays great attention to the proper rank-ordering of attendants in seat arrangements, order of speakers, order of incense burning, etc., so that every face may be sustained or at least no face smeared.

There is a third role to be played by others. The social standing of one's face is rated in comparison with that of another's, and thus two or more faces may become competitive. Under the seniority rule of Japanese bureaucracy, the same-year entrants are expected to be promoted simultaneously as rank peers, but the pyramidal structure of a bureaucracy necessitates some of the peers to outrank others at certain points of their careers. It is this possibility of being passed by one's peers, or worse yet by a junior entrant, that mid-career employees fear most. Paradoxically, the seniority rule, which should function to minimize internal competition, in fact throws peers into ferocious competition and leaves losers totally demoralized. The losers in career competitions are face-losers in the eyes of their families, friends, or *seken* as a whole. Without considering this aspect of work careers, what is known as Japanese workaholism cannot be fully understood. It is for the same reason that the employee, with no prospect of further promotion, is transferred elsewhere or encouraged to retire prematurely and find another job. In short, the presentational self is keenly aware of other as a rival as well.

The presentational self can vary in its expression between two extremes: aggressive and defensive, assertive and inhibited, exhibitive and modest. In private conversation with a congenial other, it is not uncommon for a Japanese speaker, particularly male, to brag about his success and accomplishments, expecting the listener to respond with praise. But under other circumstances, the same speaker is likely to present an inhibited, humble self in reflection of his keen awareness of those others cast in three roles – audience, co-actor or staging personnel, and competitor – at whose mercy his self stands. In public, the Japanese person tends to play up self-effacement and modesty.

The above depiction of Japanese self as presentational reinforces Benedict's (1946) characterization of Japanese in terms of a shame complex, but does so only partially and conditionally. As my analysis unfolds, Benedict's position will be reversed.

The empathetic self

Empirically continuous with, but conceptually distinct from the presentational self is the intimacy-seeking, empathetic self, the second orientation of the interactional self. Involved here is the awareness of self as an insider of a group or network, or as a partner to a relationship. Though not necessarily actualized, the ideal relationship among members is characterized in terms of love, trust, fellowship, support, cooperation, solidarity, interdependence, sociability, and so on. Others surrounding self here are recognized more as *miuchi* (fellow insiders, tied together in actual or figurative kinship) in contrast to *tanin* (outsiders, known and unknown to self, lacking kinship ties). The above-discussed *seken* as the generalized audience for the presentational self is felt to consist largely of *tanin*.

The empathetic self feels attached or bonded to other, as between intimate friends, fellow members of a group, parent and child, leader and follower, master and disciple, patron and client, *sempai* (senior) and *kōhai* (junior), and so on. The ultimate state of this orientation is a feeling of fusion, synergy, or interchangeability of self and other. In the Japanese figures of speech, self–other substitution often appears as in "becoming a surrogate of my mother" (*haha ni narikawaru*), "I apologize as a surrogate of my son" (*musuko ni narikawatte owabi shimasu*).[2] The Japanese idiom, in other words, can load self and other with "surrogate other" and "surrogate self" respectively. It is because of the possibility of such self–other substitution not only in speech but in practice that Japanese often find it necessary to underline the true, non-substitutive self as *honnin* in distinction from *dainin* or *kawari* (surrogate). This aspect of self has been elaborated elsewhere (Lebra 1989).

Empathy is expected to be mutual. Not only does the self feel bonded and empathetic to other but seeks empathy from other. Again in personal conversation, a Japanese speaker reveals reasons for the listener to feel sorry for him, such as being a victim of someone's unfair treatment. Empathy thus ties in with *amae*, the desire for being indulged. The self, in seeking empathy, may stimulate empathetic feelings in others through *amae* behavior, and other in turn may respond with empathetic indulgence, *amayakasu*.

Like the presentational self, the empathetic self, too, is a universal element of self. Difference may lie in the central location of bonding. While middle-class Americans, for example, tend to locate the bonded self within the family, Japanese spread it to wider society, particularly in a group of intimate peers (Salamon 1974) such as former classmates, or an office group within a company (Rohlen 1975). Further, for Americans, sexual bonding seems essential to the well-being of the empathetic self, and therefore, within the family, it is conjugal ties that claim priority. For Japanese, sexuality plays a less crucial role, and the strongest bond within the family is that of parent, mother in particular, and child. Thus, conjugal estrangement does not necessarily result in a family break-up as it would in America. It may be hypothesized, then, that intimacy seeking among Americans is more concentrated within a family, and further condensed in a sexual pair, whereas it is more dispersed and generalized among

Japanese. Insofar as intimacy translates into bodily touching, Barnlund's (1975) finding is interesting in this context.

Based upon the responses from samples of college students, Barnlund found out that more American students touch their parents in more areas of the body than the Japanese. Further, in touching a friend, the American respondents showed a stark contrast between the same-sex and opposite-sex friend as target persons, the latter being much more touchable in all regions of the body. The Japanese did not reveal so much difference between the two kinds of friends. This finding, however, should not be taken as evidence of Japanese being more isolated than Americans are: intimacy or solidarity can take many forms, e.g., co-drinking, co-dining, without necessarily touching, and Japanese are likely, as stated above, to disperse intimate feelings over wider circles which are not included in Barnlund's research.

The bonded self does not always come into awareness as something positive. To the extent that a social bond is sustained by each participant's share of dedication or responsibility, the emotional, social, or economic cost may be felt to outweigh the benefit. In a reciprocal relationship usually involved in such tight consociation, a sense of obligatory *giri* may come to override that of sentimental attachment, *ninjō*. Nevertheless, the intimacy-seeking self is not easily abandoned partly because isolation is a worse alternative but also because it is locked with the presentational self, as will be explained below.

The presentational and empathetic dimensions of self are in opposition in that the former presupposes social or psychological distance between self and other to the point of self-defense and other-avoidance while the latter minimizes such distance. The main commodity in self-presentation is esteem but empathetic ties are constructed on the basis of mutual attachment. If the faulty self-presentation brings shame, the loss of the empathetic self means loneliness. All these differences notwithstanding, the empathetic self flows into the presentational self. Being isolated, being excluded from a group, lacking a friend whose support one can count on or who counts on one's support – all these can result in one's loss of face vis-à-vis the ubiquitous audience. Some of my elderly informants expect to be looked after by their daughters or daughters-in-law, however unwillingly on both sides. The family care of the aged, which superficially may indicate a strong bonding between generations, in fact turns out to involve the presentational self to be kept up in good standing: the elderly "abandoned" into a nursing home, as well as the children abandoning them, would have their *sekentei* damaged. This is why some Japanese, including my informants, consider the childless elderly more fortunate since they are shame-free to enter care homes. Giving and receiving a gift as a symbol of friendship may be also in the same bind in that giving is a performance to live up to one's reputation as much as receiving is a proof of one's honor being sustained. I speculate that the self-presentational function makes gift exchange so compulsive.

The above examples presuppose a triad: self (e.g., gift-giver), other in direct interaction with self (gift-receiver), and a third as audience (*seken*). But the last two are not always distinct. The self–other distance may decrease and increase between the same partners to interaction. One and the same other moves over toward self to create an empathetic rapport, and moves away from self to become an audience, stage manipulator, or even rival confronting the presentational self. A group of inseparable neighbor women usually support one another but also, behind the scenes, may compete with one another over their husbands' promising or faltering careers, and their children's school performances. Co-workers who work side by side every day and spend after-work hours together at a bar, may not be free from rivalry and jealousy. Father and son, co-residing, may feel close to each other until a flood of end-of-year gifts (*seibo*) are delivered home, as in a story taken from a TV home drama series, "Jikan desu yo." All the gifts turn out to be addressed to the son, a section chief of a company, from his subordinates, but none to the senior man and head of the house who is a family shop operator. The father's crushed presentational self is now stimulated and held at distance from the son as well as other members of the family.

The inner self

The interactional self is what occupies Japanese most of the time, and yet they are aware of its basically precarious, vulnerable, relative, unfixed nature. The relativity of the interactional self is best illustrated by the Japanese terms for self and other. The Japanese speaker either uses no term for self or other ("zero form" [Fischer 1964]), or selects certain terms from among many possible ones that are appropriate to the given relationship at a certain time between self and other. In addressing a child, for example, an adult male stranger is likely to call himself "uncle," just as children do in addressing male adults. Likewise, a schoolteacher, speaking to students, calls him/herself "teacher." This speech behavior, called by Suzuki (1986) "empathetic identification," reflects the lack of the exact equivalent of "I" which would serve as the fixed point of self. As long as one stays in the interactional world, multiple and variable self-identification seems necessary. A multiple and variable self like this ultimately boils down to "non-self" as symbolized by the zero form. Self saturated in the interactional world is therefore negatively described by

as *jibun ga nai* (devoid of self), and is advised to retrieve itself,
orimodosu.

ore stable self, something like "I," more immune from social
ty, is sought inwardly. The socially, outwardly[3] oriented inter-
al self is thus compensated for by the inner self. Japanese do
divide self into the outer part and inner part. As much as the social world
is divided into outside and inside (*soto* versus *uchi*), or front and back
(*omote* versus *ura*), and others into outsiders and insiders, so is self divided
into the outwardly (socially) involved and the inwardly oriented realms.
The two realms make complementary or compensatory oppositions or
juxtapositions.[4] It is the inner self that provides a fixed core for self-
identity and subjectivity, and forms a potential basis of autonomy from
the ever-insatiable demands from the social world. The inner self is also
identified as the residence (shrine) of a god that each person is endowed
with.

The inner self is symbolically localized in the chest or belly (though the
latter will appear more in the third dimension of self to be discussed
below), whereas the outer self is focused on the face and mouth which are
socially addressed. At the center of the inner self is the *kokoro* which
stands for heart, sentiment, spirit, will, or mind. While the outer self is
socially circumscribed, the *kokoro* can be free, spontaneous, and even
asocial. Further, the *kokoro* claims moral superiority over the outer self in
that it is a reservoir of truthfulness and purity, uncontaminated by
circumspections and contrivances to which the outer self is subject. This
association of the *kokoro* (or inner self) with truthfulness gives rise to the
paradoxical notion that the "real" truth is inexpressible. Thus words and
speech as means of expression are often regarded as potentially deceptive
and false, and silence as indicative of the true *kokoro* (Lebra 1987).

The moral superiority of the inner self partially accounts for the
ambivalence the Japanese actor holds towards the interactional self. The
face-conscious presentational self, for example, carries a negative tone,
and sensitivity to shame is taken as something to be surmounted. Self-
revival through religious conversion oftentimes involves a deliberate self-
exposure to shame in order to become free from shame sensitivity.
Instead, the "true" feelings of guilt stemming from the bottom of the
"heart" are elevated in the hierarchy of moral values. Shame and guilt are
not a dichotomy as conceived by Benedict, but rather, when applied to
Japanese, they occupy different ranks in the moral hierarchy within a
culture, guilt outranking shame (Lebra 1983).

The centrality of the inner self in Japanese self-awareness is further
indicated by the sentence-completion-test result obtained from urban
samples from Korea, Hong Kong, and Japan (Lebra 1986). Japanese

respondents, compared with Chinese and Korean counterparts, were found consistently to pay more attention to their state of mind, feeling, and *kokoro*. To complete the sentence fragment "If you are kind to others," nearly half of the Japanese sample referred to the inner satisfaction of joy of the kind actor whereas similar responses were given by about a quarter of the Korean sample, and only 4 percent of the Chinese.

The Japanese inner–outer division of self seems to resemble the Javanese "bifurcate conception of the self, half ungestured feeling and half unfelt gesture" (Geertz 1984: 128). Indeed, the inner part, when coupled with the socially contextualized presentational self, tends to be encapsulated and remain uncommunicated or "ungestured." In this context it is not surprising that Japanese college students, compared with their American counterparts, were found to hold a larger "private" self which is not shared in communication with others, in proportion to the "public" self that is shared (Barnlund 1975).

Communicational inhibition is only one of the possible manifestations, however. The inner–outer division of self is channeled in the following directions as well. First, while this division may be detrimental to communication, Japanese also believe that the inner self, the *kokoro* in particular, is what makes communication possible and complete. One's heart, if strong, pure, and persistent enough, will eventually remove the communication barrier and reach another's heart (*kokoro ga tsūji au*). The truly empathetic self thus emerges in heart-to-heart communication. While the presentational interaction is at the opposite pole from the inner self, the empathetic communication merges with the latter.

Second, the inner self, when dissociated from the outer self, may be directed as an asocial obsession with self-expression or self-actualization through work or sheer perseverance. We find single-minded craftsmen, artists, and other professionals entirely immersed in their own world of work and performance in indifference to their social surroundings. The products of such inner concentration are often described as "loaded with *kokoro*" (*kokoro no komotta*).

Third, the moral emphasis upon the interiority of self leads to "spiritualism" aiming at the triumph of the spirit over the material world, of mind over matter, the heart over technology. It was this spiritualism that was mobilized in wartime Japan to overcome its material and technological handicaps against its Western adversaries. The inner self was a fountain of strength, energy, and perseverance independent of external resources. Today's version of spiritualism functions differently: economically affluent and technologically advanced, Japanese warn themselves against losing the *kokoro* in the midst of material abundance. Products of the most advanced computer technology are advertised in terms of *kokoro*. As noted by Moeran (1986: 73), "the word *kokoro* was the most commonly used word in advertising in Japan during the 1970s." Very recently, an automatic bread maker was invented to become available to house-wives, which must have thrown all the professional bakers into identity crisis. A baker, interviewed by a TV reporter, looked unperturbed, saying, "I am not upset, because what counts after all is one's *kokoro*." He meant that his *kokoro* would produce the kind of bread that no machine could. Here, the *kokoro* is meant to counter not only techno-materialism but to preserve individual identity against mechanical standardization.

Lastly, when one is under cross-pressures from inside and outside of self, the inner self may assert itself insofar as its moral superiority is recognized. The imperative of conforming to interactional norms thus may give way to fidelity to one's inner self. "Be faithful to yourself" (*jibun ni chūjitsu ni*) becomes a final verdict. Spontaneous, emotional, impulsive acts are thus tolerated, and even illicit love affairs or other deviant acts, if proved to stem from the center of the inner self, are considered to have to take their "natural" courses to a final consummation. The overloaded "private self" thus has a way of releasing itself into public self.

The boundless self

The inner self thus comes to join hands with autonomy and freedom from the external world, whether material, social, or cultural. To the extent that it is free from cultural regulations, it is closer to nature than is the interactional self. And yet we have also noted that the inner self is a locus of spiritualism to transcend the natural basis of existence, and in this sense it is purely cultural. The bipolarity of the inner self along the nature–culture continuum is a corollary of the fact that the inner self is contained within the self boundary. Further, the *kokoro* is believed to manifest itself in *katachi* (outer form), and the latter in turn to shape the former. Freedom associated with the inner self is not without a ceiling. In order to attain unlimited freedom, one must be free from the self boundary itself and become a boundless self, the third dimension of self.

The notion of the boundless self, though this is my term, is embedded in the Buddhist version of transcendentalism. It is tapped from time to time particularly when one faces a need of fundamental self-reorientation. The boundless self entails disengagements from the shackling world of dicho-tomies, dichotomies between subject and object, self and other, inner and outer realms, existence and non-existence, life and death, sacred and profane, good and bad, and so on. The self as the subject or imposer of such dichotomies through thinking, willing, feeling, or evaluating, then, must be overcome. Self-awareness must be freed from the subject–object differentiation.[5]

With no resistance, self is supposed to merge with the rest of the world. Merging means a twofold process: on the one hand, self becomes part of the objective world or nature; and on the other, self absorbs the outer world into itself. These processes are two aspects of the same coin. Suzuki, in his popular writings (1955), finds the essence of all religions, including Christianity, in the absolute "passivity" or non-resistance without which nothing really can enter the self. With passivity, self becomes an unlimited receptor or reflector of the "true" nature.

In self–other relationship, we have characterized the interactional self as relative, multiple, and variable in accordance to where and how self stands vis-à-vis other; a less relative, more stable, fixed self is captured in the encapsulated inner self – the world of pure subjectivity. Now, in the boundless self, relativity is overcome by the mutual embracement of self and other, subject and object. Far from being actively assertive, self is supposed to be absolutely passive and receptive, and passivity entails the state of being empty. The ultimate self then is equated, paradoxically, with the empty self, non-self, non-thinking, mindless, or nothingness (*muga*, *mushin*, *mu*, etc.). Self-awareness itself is to be transcended.

As for body symbolism, the boundless self centers around the belly, *hara* (Lebra 1976), while the center of the inner self is the heart, *kokoro*, although *hara* and *kokoro* are also used interchangeably to mean the inner self. "Having a *hara*" (*hara ga aru*), or "having one's *hara* well-settled" (*hara no suwatta*), refers to the mental stability not upset by small matters. "Having a big *hara*" (*hara ga ōkii*) implies a mental capacity for absorbing all kinds of troubles instead of being upset and obsessed with them. The *hara* capacity thus seems to correspond to the degree of autonomy from the boundary of self.

To transcend dichotomies involves a negation of order. The world of religion is that in which "you can hit anybody when you want to, kick anybody if you want to, or conversely, you just let yourself fall down when kicked by someone or even let yourself die – it is the world of lawlessness (*muchakucha*). That kind of world, if there could be one, must be recognized as one of indiscretion, one that transcends good and bad" (Suzuki 1955: 27–8). If order is a cultural product, the Buddhist universe is pure nature where chaos predominates. The boundless self, merging with such a universe, represents entropy, so to speak. When applied to time, entropy is translated into *mujō* (evanescence) in which everything in existence is believed to change or perish.

All these ideas around the boundless self may represent a symbolic license of exaggeration which cannot be actualized. Concepts like non-self

self, and entropic self may sound simply absurd. Nevertheless, the boundless self, thus conceived, offers an alternative goal or strategy that can be mobilized to disengage one from the socially or inwardly obsessed, or entrapped self.

Still, chaos is an overstatement in need of correction. There is a universal order running through the seeming chaos, and that is the idea of predestination which is expressed in the vernacular as *innen, en, inga, shukumei, unmei*. Self is no free agent to determine its own course of action, but is destined to act this way and that way. The "boundless" self is thus surrendered to this fundamental universal law. In order to become free from this chain of destiny, one must "understand" and accept it. Further, since the boundless self does not recognize the dichotomies of subject and object, good and bad, etc., it does not reject the social order. There seems to be a correspondence between a "Zen person" and a secular (social) person with respect to the significance of relationality (Kasulis 1981). The boundless self does not really "replace" the socially bounded relative self.

Conclusion

Three dimensions of self have been examined. These three are by no means mutually exclusive but partially overlapping layers of self which are activated as alternative strategies for self-orientations and reorientations. They are mutually compensatory, complementary, or reinforcing.

Illustrative of the dynamic interrelationship between different dimensions of self are two therapies developed in Japan, well known among medical anthropologists as well as Japan specialists. One is Naikan ("inward-looking") therapy which reorients the client from the interactional to the inner self through a period of isolated, concentrated self-reflection. Its purpose is to arouse and maximize guilt consciousness by "piercing" the innermost of his/her *kokoro* with a mental drill so that the peak intensity of guilt will serve as a lever for self-transformation. This interiorization does not entail an alienation from the interactional dimension as a whole; rather it means a rededication of self to other through empathetic realization of other's sacrifice for self.

The other is Morita therapy whose motto is "Accept things as they are." The neurotic patient, instead of trying to fight and get rid of his illness, should swallow it as part of self. Here, we can see the therapeutic strategy to lift the self bound by the interactional (presentational in particular) dimension or preoccupied with the inner dimension to the boundless dimension. In this therapy, self and nature or self and illness are to be absorbed into one another. Here, too, social obligations, like other "facts," are to be confronted, accepted, and fulfilled.

The three dimensions are thus interrelated, without excluding one another. Ultimately, these converge in the highest value in Japanese culture, namely, "purity" – a key word embracing a variety of meanings cutting across all the three dimensions. Purity refers to the absence of selfish motives which is positively demonstrated by sacrificial self-dedication to others or causes; single-minded endeavors at some project; emotional commitment in oblivion of calculated interest; honesty, sincerity, truthfulness, openness, and so on. In the boundless self, purity is identical with emptiness, non-self, nothingness, an unlimited receptor, or a reflector likened to a spotless mirror.[6] The seemingly "autonomous" inner self thus merges with the self-less self via purity.

In conclusion, I speculate, if I may, that the three dimensions can be aligned in a value hierarchy, the interactional self as the lowest, the boundless self as the highest, the inner self in the middle. Thus, the empathetic self, as closer to the inner self, ranks higher than the presentational. This hierarchy may be applied to the culture–nature continuum that has appeared in the text. It was pointed out that there is a variation in the degree of cultural "regulation" of self. It is the interactional self that is most regulated, and the boundless self least regulated, whereas the inner self is mixed. If freedom from cultural regulation is equated with the state of nature, we can say there is a culture–nature continuum along which the three selves are located. It follows then that the more cultural, the lower in the value hierarchy of selves; the more natural, the higher.

This odd correlation between culture–nature and lower–higher makes sense for Japanese to the extent that they place things natural above things artificial. After all, the more natural, the purer. Nevertheless, it does not accord with our common sense to place the natural self above the cultural self. After all, what is natural is so defined only through a cultural lens. The problem lies in our definition of culture only as regulative of nature, and of nature as free from regulation. If culture is understood as symbolically mediated "meaning," what appears as natural is profoundly cultural. The inner self is just as cultural as the interactional self in this sense. It is less regulated but more loaded with ideational "meaning." If culture is thus redefined, the above hierarchy must be reversed: the boundless self is the most cultural and the interactional self least so. It may be further conjectured that these two components of culture – regulatory and ideational – are mutually compensatory so that the less socially regulated, the more meaningful the self tends to be. In other words, the above hierarchical proposition should be restated: the lower the self, the heavier in regulation, and the higher the self, the richer in meaning. With this restatement, it may be said that the levels of self correspond to stages of mental maturation.

Returning to the initial statement on universalism and relativism, I can offer nothing more than my hunches: the interactional self is more universal and thus cross-culturally accessible, and the boundless self the least so; the meaning-loaded self is more culture-bound (culture in still another sense) than the socially regulated self.

NOTES

1 The everlasting controversy between universalists and relativists, nomotheists and idiographers, seems now to have reached a boiling point in Japanese studies. Relativists, who have portrayed Japan with emphasis upon differences between national cultures, have dominated Japan area studies, and are now under attack from universalists as creating a stereotype of Japan and thereby hindering international communication. In my view, it is a wrong question to ask whether Japan is unique or no different from other nations. Why should difference and sameness be mutually exclusive, why should we respond with an either–or answer? In fact I do not think that a staunch universalist really believes Japan to be an exact replica of, say, Australia; neither do I find a devout relativist as seeing no speck of similarity between Japan and other countries. The either–or question itself is just another example of logical dichotomy removed from reality. Nevertheless, one must take one stand or another to write about Japan. What stand should be taken is, in my opinion, a pragmatic question. It depends upon the writer's interest or purpose at hand, or upon the kind of audience he/she has in mind. If one's goal is to facilitate international communication, one's approach has to vary depending upon the given audience: addressing the Japanese audience convinced of Japan's uniqueness will have to be quite different from addressing a group of Americans who do not question their way of life as natural and human.

2 Such identity substitution between self and other is greatly played up in some religious sects, as observed in a sect called Gadatsukai. Here "other" may be a god, ancestor, the spirit of the dead, animal spirit, or any other supernatural entity as well as a social other (Lebra 1986).

3 To avoid confusion, it should be noted that Dumont (1985) uses "inward" and "outward" in a sense totally different from the way I use them here. Comparing Western with Indian individualism, Dumont characterizes the former as "inwardly" because Westerners are "individuals-in-the-world," whereas the latter is "outwardly" in that Indians actualize their individualism when out of the world, that is, when they renounce the world. My use of inward is closer, though not identical, to Dumont's outward.

4 The double-sidedness of the Japanese self in terms of *omote* and *ura* (or *tatemae* and *honne* which are used in a sense similar to the other pair of concepts) is analyzed by Doi (1986).

5 Continuity, instead of dichotomy, between self and the object world or mind and matter, is symbolized by common references to external phenomena such as weather in depicting the moods of self. A good, happy, healthy state of self is described as "sunny," "cloudless," while the opposite state is associated with

bad weather like "cloudy," "rainy," and so forth (see Tanaka-Matsumi and Marsella 1976 for word association studies on depression).

6 Out of this assemblage of the meanings of purity emerges another key word describing an ideal character of person, and that is *sunao*. Japanese parents use this term when asked what type of person they want their children to be. *Sunao* is, like purity, an admixture of different attributes: obedient but straightforward, pliable but honest, gentle but truthful to self, and so on (for the therapeutic use of this concept, see Murase 1982).

REFERENCES

Bachnik, Jane. 1986. Time, Space and Person in Japanese Relationships. *Interpreting Japanese Society: Anthropological Approaches*. JASO Occasional Papers no. 5 (J. Hendry and J. Webber, eds.), Oxford: JASO.

Barnlund, Dean C. 1975. *Public and Private Self in Japan and the United States*. Tokyo: Simul Press.

Benedict, Ruth. 1946. *The Chrysanthemum and the Sword: Patterns of Japanese Culture*. Boston, Mass.: Houghton Mifflin.

Doi, Takeo. 1986. *The Anatomy of Self*. Tokyo: Kodansha.

Dumont, Louis. 1985. A Modified View of Our Origins: The Christian Beginnings of Modern Individualism. *The Category of the Person* (M. Carrithers, S. Collins, and S. Lukes, eds.), Cambridge: Cambridge University Press.

Fischer, John L. 1964. Words for Self and Others in Some Japanese Families. *American Anthropologist* 66: 116–26.

Geertz, Clifford. 1984. From the Native's Point of View: On the Nature of Anthropological Understanding. *Culture Theory: Essays on Mind, Self and Emotion* (R. A. Shweder and R. A. LeVine, eds.), Cambridge: Cambridge University Press.

Goffman, Erving. 1959. *The Presentation of Self in Everyday Life*. Garden City, N.Y.: Doubleday.

Hallowell, A. Irving. 1955. *Culture and Experience*. Philadelphia: University of Pennsylvania Press.

Inoue, Tadashi. 1977. *Sekentei no kōzō* (The structure of *seken*). Tokyo: Nihon Hōsō Shuppan Kyōkai.

Kasulis, T. P. 1981. *Zen Action, Zen Person*. Honolulu: University of Hawaii Press.

Lebra, Takie Sugiyama. 1976. *Japanese Patterns of Behavior*. Honolulu: University of Hawaii Press.

1983. Shame and Guilt: A Psychocultural View of the Japanese Self. *Ethos* 11: 192–209.

1986. Compensative Justice and Moral Investment among Japanese, Chinese, and Koreans. *Japanese Culture and Behavior: Selected Readings* (T. S. Lebra and W. P. Lebra, eds.), Honolulu: University of Hawaii Press.

1987. The Cultural Significance of Silence in Japanese Communication. *Multilingua* 6: 343–57.

1989. *Migawari*: The Cultural Idiom of Self–Other Exchange in Japan. Paper presented at the Conference on Perceptions of Self: China, India and Japan,

East–West Center Institute of Culture and Communication, Honolulu, August 14–18.

Marsella, Anthony J., DeVos, George, and Hsu, Francis L. K., eds. 1985. *Culture and Self: Asian and Western Perspectives.* New York: Tavistock.

Mead, George Herbert. 1934. *Mind, Self, and Society.* Chicago: University of Chicago Press.

Moeran, Brian. 1986. Individual, Group and *Seishin*: Japan's Internal Cultural Debate. *Japanese Culture and Behavior* (T. S. Lebra and W. P. Lebra, eds.), Honolulu: University of Hawaii Press.

Murase, Takao. 1982. *Sunao*: A Central Value in Japanese Psychotherapy. *Cultural Conceptions of Mental Health and Therapy* (A. J. Marsella and G. McWhite, eds.), Dordrecht: Reidel.

Rohlen, Thomas. 1975. The Company Work Group. *Modern Japanese Organization and Decision Making* (E. F. Vogel, ed.), Berkeley: University of California Press.

Salamon, Sonya. 1974. In the Intimate Arena: Japanese Women and Their Families. Ph.D. dissertation, University of Illinois.

Shweder, Richard A. and LeVine, Robert A., eds. 1984. *Culture Theory: Essays on Mind, Self and Emotion.* Cambridge: Cambridge University Press.

Suzuki, Daisetsu. 1955. *Mushin to yū koto* (Reflections on *mushin*). Tokyo: Kadokawa.

Suzuki, Takao. 1986. Language and Behavior in Japan: The Conceptualization of Personal Relations. *Japanese Culture and Behavior* (T. S. Lebra and W. P. Lebra, eds.), Honolulu: University of Hawaii Press.

Tanaka-Matsumi, Junko and Marsella, Anthony J. 1976. Cross-cultural Variations in the Phenomenological Experience of Depression: Word Association Studies. *Journal of Cross-Cultural Psychology* 7: 389–96.

White, Geoffrey and Kirkpatrick, John, eds. 1985. *Person, Self, and Experience: Exploring Pacific Ethnographies.* Berkeley: University of California Press.

7   The reference other orientation

Takami Kuwayama

The Japanese self has variously been described as "relational," "inter-actional," "interdependent," "particularistic," "situational," "con-textual," "relative," "collective," "group-oriented," and "sociocentric." Of these labels, group orientation or groupism, as it is often called, has gained the widest currency. In the observation of many writers, the Japanese have such strong group orientation that "[a]n unkind commentator has likened the Japanese to a school of small fish, progressing in orderly fashion in one direction until a pebble dropped into the water breaks this up and sets them off suddenly in the opposite direction, but again in orderly rows" (Reischauer 1988: 136). Indeed, conformity to the group lies at the heart of the stereotyped image of the Japanese.

A moment's reflection on the Japanese pattern of behavior confirms this image. In the 1960s, when Japan was at the height of the so-called "high economic growth" period, pianos became very popular among upper-middle-class families in Tokyo. For those wishing to claim upper-middle-class status, it became almost a tacit rule for one's daughter to receive piano lessons in one's own living room. As a result, many people vied with one another to buy a piano, and the sound of pianos was heard in every exclusive residential area in Tokyo. In the 1970s, expensive consumer products like color television sets, air conditioners, and cars spread among the urban middle class in a similar fashion.

In the summer of 1984, I carried out preliminary research in Niiike, a suburban community located at the northwestern end of Okayama City. When I heard the people of Niiike talk enthusiastically about agricultural machines, it occurred to me that the conspicuous consumption described above had occurred in a different form in Japan's traditionally farming areas. My speculation turned into a conviction when I saw an array of expensive agricultural machines in the storage sheds of Niiike's households in 1986. They included riding tractors (an average cost of about US $13,500 in 1985), combines ($8,800), and rice transplanters ($2,700).

Full-scale mechanization of agriculture began in Japan in the 1950s. Given the fact that rice cultivation, Japan's "cultural core," has been

121

iced over two thousand years without the benefit of modern
1ines, the significance of this change cannot be overstated. The heavy
stment by the people of Niiike in agricultural machines is puzzling,
however, because their agricultural income is quite limited today (approximately 8 percent of the total household income). As a result of dramatic
changes in Japan's industrial structure since the 1950s, the reliance upon
agriculture as the major source of household revenue has rapidly dimin-
ished. Also, the machines are used only during the peak work season and
stand idle at other times. These facts make any large investment in farm
machines risky and unwise. Moreover, people in Niiike often complain
about the enormous cost of purchasing machines and the high maintenance cost, describing themselves as suffering "kikai binbō" ("machine-
induced poverty"). Nevertheless, there is a widespread feeling that they
must buy new machines or models at any cost, and they frequently do,
even at the risk of carrying a great financial burden.

Below, I will analyze this feeling and behavior in terms of the influence
others exert on the self in shaping one's attitudes and self-evaluation. In
doing so, I will demonstrate that the investment in agricultural machines is
a reflection of the interaction pattern of people in the community of
Niiike. They buy machines not merely because they are necessary, but
because they are essential to maintain the people's status as respectable
members of the community. In other words, the machines are symbols of
the personal achievement of the people of Niiike, as well as of their
commitment to community norms. Thus, it is inadequate simply to
describe them as conformists. The issue here is the self–other orientation
or, more generally, the conception of self.

My theoretical focus is on two propositions: (1) that others provide the
self with significant frames of reference for self-appraisal and attitude
formation; and (2) that there are three distinct categories of others in
Japan, *mawari* (people around), *hito* (people at large), and *seken* (society),
which are concentrically related to the self (*jibun*) at the center. The
concept of "reference other orientation," which derives from reference
group theory, is introduced to support the first proposition. The second
proposition is named the "reference other model" and is compared with
the *uchi–soto* or inside–outside model.

The ethnographic background

Niiike is a small community located some 10 kilometers northwest of
central Okayama. It constitutes *buraku*, a small settlement which is the
basic social unit outside urban areas in Japan. Although this word tends
to be avoided in official language today because it is often used to mean

"outcastes" (*burakumin*), it is still commonly used by the people of Niiike to refer to their community. Moreover, *buraku* is recognized by local officials as a de facto administrative unit. *Buraku* is understood here to mean a basic "frame" (*ba*) of life – a locality which provides a group of people with a common basis on which to build their social relationship – which has been passed down from one generation to the next. It is translated here as a "community," instead of a "hamlet," a word sometimes used by students of Japan.

As of 1986, there are 118 people (59 males and 59 females) and 26 households in Niiike. With one exception, these households are divided into two surname groups: Hiramatsu (17 households) and Iwasa (8 households). Both Hiramatsu and Iwasa are divided into independent lineages, the Hiramatsu group consisting of 3 lineages and the Iwasa group 2 lineages. Neither of these surname groups may be considered a clan because they do not have common ancestors who unite the lineages.

Each lineage or *kabuuchi* in Niiike comprises a central parent household (*honke*) and branch households (*bunke*) which are descended patrilineally from the parent household or from earlier branches. *Kabuuchi* is a local variation of *dōzoku* in its broad sense. Opinions differ about whether *dōzoku* is a descent group, but given the significant role kinship plays in *dōzoku*'s membership recruitment, it is understood here as a lineage. However, *kabuuchi* in Niiike lacks the fundamental property of *dōzoku* in its narrow sense: strong hierarchical structure centered on the socio-political, economic, religious, and juridical authority of the parent house-hold over branch households (Nagashima and Tomoeda 1984: 17). Although *kabuuchi* functions as a basic organizing principle of community life, its importance is diminishing today as a result of weakening kinship ties brought about by the industrialization and urbanization which started in the late 1950s. *Kabuuchi*, whose unit of participation is the household, rather than the individual, is concerned today primarily with rituals, such as ancestral memorial services (*hōji*) and weddings.[1]

In contrast to the diminishing importance of kinship-based networks, particularly that of *kabuuchi*, the individual has come to play a central role in establishing social networks both within and outside the community. Relationships formed by individuals who are not genealogically related are informal in that they depend on personal factors such as likes and dislikes, trust, common interests, and so forth. Unlike kinship ties, these relationships – "friendships," if you will – may be severed at any time at the discretion of those who are involved. In this sense, individually centered informal networks are fragile, but they serve as a kind of "glue" for community life in today's highly industrialized Japan.

Despite the often-reported disintegration of the Japanese community,

Niiike continues to function as a viable social unit. Indeed, kinship-based relationships and individually centered relationships are connected by the common community good. The strong solidarity and interests of the community take precedence over those of any other group within the community.

What makes Niiike special is the fact that this small community has been studied intensively by many scholars since the early 1950s. The first large-scale research project was carried out by those affiliated with the Center for Japanese Studies at the University of Michigan. The research results were published as *Village Japan* (1959) by Richard Beardsley, John Hall, and Robert Ward. This book has been evaluated to date as the most comprehensive account of a Japanese community written in English. Since the publication of *Village Japan*, various research projects have been conducted in Niiike. Among the most notable are Okada and Kamiya (1960), Muramatsu (1962), and DeVos (1973). Very few communities in the world have been documented as thoroughly as Niiike.

Agriculture in Niiike in the 1950s and the 1980s

In the early 1950s, Niiike was a small-scale farming community. It is reported in *Village Japan* that during the crop year of 1950–1 net agricultural income occupied 72.6 percent of Niiike's total income. Because Niiike's landholding was small, with an average of 69 ares (about 1.7 acres) per household, double-cropping was practiced in order to maximize production. Rice was the chief summer crop, whereas wheat, barley, and mat rush were the major winter crops. Mat rush, a special product of Okayama, for which there was a large demand as material for *tatami* cover, was particularly important because it was one of the few sources of cash income. Non-agricultural work, on the other hand, provided only 27.4 percent of Niiike's total income; it consisted primarily of salaries from work outside the community and mat rush weaving.

In 1951, there were 128 people and 23 households in Niiike. In 1954, only 16 people (13 males and 3 females) from 12 households were non-agriculturally employed. Although Niiike was relatively affluent for a Japanese farming community in those days, the average annual income per household was only US $387. (The exchange rate at the time was 360 Japanese yen to one US dollar.) Despite the modest life the people of Niiike lived, they called themselves "pure farmers" (Beardsley et al. 1959: 74) and took pride in the traditional place of honor given their occupation.

Niiike today can hardly be described as a farming community. Although 22 out of 26 households are registered as farms, most of them are part-time (*kengyō nōka*). Among 118 residents, 33 (26 males and 7 females) are non-agriculturally employed on a full-time basis, and 6 (3 males and 3 females) work part-time. Together, they represent 67.2 percent of Niiike's workforce (i.e., people between the ages of 18 and 59). All of the men in this age group have salaried jobs, whereas only one-third of women work outside the community. Table 7.1 summarizes Niiike's non-agricultural employment outside the community in the 1950s and 1986.

It is difficult to assess exactly the agricultural income of Niiike, but it is estimated at about 8 percent of the total household income.[2] Thus, agriculture today has become a side business.

Like other Japanese farming communities, farm work is usually left to elderly people in Niiike. Men with salaried jobs work the fields only at weekends during the peak work season. They are seldom seen on weekdays because they leave for work early in the morning and spend much of their time inside the home after they return. Although their contributions to farm work cannot be overlooked – they are the only people able to operate large agricultural machines – their allegiance is primarily to their salaried jobs. Thus, they play only a secondary role in farm work. As one Niiike man aptly remarked, they are "Sunday farmers."

The scale of agriculture in Niiike remains as small as ever. If anything, landholding has slightly decreased from the previous average of 69 ares because some households converted their fields into house sites after the 1950s. Reclaiming land is impossible because there is no more arable land left. Mat rush continues to be grown in neighboring communities, but it is no longer cultivated in Niiike today. Weaving mat rush, a symbol of the harsh living conditions which prevailed until recently, remains only in the memory of elderly women. Agriculture constitutes only a small portion of total household income. As in much of the rest of Japan today, it is no longer the basis of life in Niiike.

This decline in agriculture was brought about by the dramatic change Japanese society underwent after World War II and may be summarized as the shift from primary to tertiary industry. In 1950, five years after the end of the war, the percentages of people engaged in agriculture and those engaged in service industry were, respectively, 48.5 percent and 29.6 percent for the nation, and 56.0 percent and 23.9 percent for Okayama. By 1985, the trend had been reversed; the percentages of primary and tertiary industry were 9.3 percent and 57.5 percent for the nation, and 11.7 percent and 51.9 percent for Okayama (Sōmuchō Tōkeikyoku 1986, 1987). In Niiike, this change in industrial structure is best expressed symbolically by the fact that the site on which a cowshed stood in the 1950s at one

Table 7.1. *Non-agricultural employment in Niiike in the 1950s and 1986*

| | Population (Males/Females) | Households | Non-agricultural employment | | | |
			Workforce (Males/Females)	Full-time (Males/Females)	Part-time (Males/Females)	Total (Males/Females)
1950s	128 (57/71)	23	84 (34/50)	15 (12/3)	1 (1/0)	16 (13/3)
1986	118 (59/59)	26	58 (29/29)	33 (26/7)	6 (3/3)	39 (29/10)

Note: Workforce refers here to people between 18 and 59 years of age. Population, household numbers, and workforce in the 1950s and employment in the 1950s utilize statistics for 1951 and 1954, respectively.

Source: Beardsley et al. 1959: 62, 180.

Table 7.2. *Ownership of agricultural machines*

Area	Year	Motor cultivator	Tractor	Rice transplanter	Binder	Thresher	Combine	Dryer	Huller	Sprayer	Brush cutter	Pump	Total
Niiike	1986	45.5	77.3	68.2	45.5	40.9	54.5	63.6	54.5	90.9	100	95.5	66.9
Okayama	1985	66.8	42.9	49.4	42.1	—	29.2	43.3	—	54.9	—	—	46.9
Japan	1986	59.0	42.3	48.4	(34.7)	—	26.6	(33.7)	—	(49.2)	—	—	42.0

Note: Parentheses indicate statistics for 1985.
Sources: Nōrinsuisanshō Tōkei Jōhōbu 1987: 149, Chūgoku Shikoku Nōseikyoku Tōkei Jōhōbu 1986.

Hiramatsu house is used today for a beauty parlor managed by the housewife.

Mechanization of agriculture since the 1950s

Nevertheless, agriculture in Niiike has attained a remarkable degree of mechanization in the past few decades. As Table 7.2 shows, the average ownership of 11 kinds of machines I surveyed in 1986 is 66.9 percent. With regard to 7 kinds of machines for which national and regional statistics are available, the average ownership is 42.0 percent for the nation, 46.9 percent for Okayama, and 63.6 percent for Niiike. Niiike's average is about one-and-a-half times higher than the national average. It is clear from this casual comparison that the people of Niiike have invested heavily in agricultural machines.[3] A comparison of Table 7.2 and Table 7.3 reveals how rapidly agriculture has been mechanized in Niiike since the 1950s.

Many factors are involved in this increase in the mechanization of agriculture. The general financial support provided by the Asia Foundation in 1955 needs to be considered first. After the Michigan research was completed, Niiike agreed to cooperate with the Foundation's project for examining the socio-economic effects of mechanization on Japanese agriculture and received some $92,000 of support for planned mechanization. This was an extraordinary amount of money at that time and gave a strong incentive to mechanization.

Another major factor which exercised a lasting influence is Niiike's proximity to central Okayama and Kurashiki City located about 15 kilometers west of Okayama. Like most other Japanese farming communities, Niiike suffered from surplus labor or "concealed unemployment"

Table 7.3. *Major agricultural machines owned in Niiike in 1954*

Machine	Number	Percentage of ownership
Kerosene motor	11	45.8
Mat rush loom	23	95.8
Thresher	14	58.3
Winnower	20	83.3
Huller	4	16.7
Polisher	12	50.0
Field pump	13	54.2
Motor cultivator	1	4.2

Source: Beardsley et al. 1959: 174.

even before mechanization began. This concept refers to the condition of household members who are ostensibly at work on the farm but are not needed for their labor (Beardsley et al. 1959: 214). Land shortage is the primary cause of concealed unemployment. Niiike was fortunate to have two solutions to this problem: weaving *tatami* covers with mat rush, and working outside the community. The second solution was possible because Niiike is located within commutable distance from central Okayama and Kurashiki. Thus, Niiike's proximity to two major cities made possible the effective use of surplus labor to obtain extra cash income, which in turn was converted into a large investment in machinery.

There are also historical factors which affected Japanese farmers across the nation (Okada and Kamiya 1960: 3–25). Among them is the land reform which took place after World War II, bringing about an increase in independent farmers and reductions in farm rents. In this context, and given the premiums attached to agricultural products in times of food shortage after the war, farm households prospered temporarily and could afford to purchase expensive machines. In addition, large-scale land improvement projects were carried out in many parts of Japan, which facilitated improvements in agricultural techniques, including the growing use of machines. Significantly, Okayama has long been recognized as a pioneer in the production of farm machines. Extensive use of machines in newly reclaimed land along Kojima Bay to the south of central Okayama commanded attention from various quarters. It is not clear to what extent Niiike was influenced by this development, but it is unlikely that Niiike was completely unaffected. Finally, a low property tax rate on farm land, as well as the Food Control Law of 1942 by which the government purchases major crops at prices favorable for farmers, encouraged farmers to invest in agricultural machines.

Considering the fact that mechanization is the desire of farmers all over the world, the achievement of the people of Niiike is spectacular. However, we need to ask one important question: why do they make such a considerable investment in farm machines even though agriculture is no longer the basis of life? This proves even more puzzling if we consider their balance of payments. For example, the average ownership of combines in Niiike is 54.5 percent (72.7 percent if co-ownership is calculated accurately), and a standard combine costs as much as $8,800. (This amount is calculated at the 1985 exchange rate of 200 yen to one US dollar.) However, the use of combines is limited to the harvesting season. They stand idle at other times. Moreover, considerable space is necessary to store them, so people often convert part of their house or field into storage. Despite such efforts, agricultural income in Niiike is estimated at only about 8 percent of the total household income. It is clear that such machines are not worth the financial investment.

People in Niiike are well aware of this, but there is complete agreement that they *must* own machines individually because their salaried jobs force them to concentrate farm work at weekends, which makes it impossible to share machines. In the words of a man who has recently retired, "We can't ask others to work for us because all of us have salaried jobs and are busy on the same day. That's why we buy machines even if they are too much for our purse." Thus, they buy machines because they work, and they work to buy machines. This vicious circle is commonly observed in many Japanese farming communities today and is known as *kikai binbō* (machine-induced poverty).

The Niiike community's view should certainly be respected. Indeed, it is the most reasonable answer to my question concerning the heavy investment in farm machines. As I spoke with many people in Niiike on this subject, however, I noticed that there is a hidden, yet powerful, motivation working behind the scene: the psychology of "keeping up with the Joneses." The following comment is illuminating:

If others buy machines, I want to buy one for myself. It makes me feel good to have machines others don't. But it really makes me mad to see others work with machines I don't have. Suppose my neighbor comes after me and finishes his work earlier because he has a new machine, whether it's a tractor or a combine. I say to myself, "Damn you! I'll get a better one." I think other people would feel the same way. Otherwise, we wouldn't buy machines one after another to this extent.

I propose to designate this psychology as the "reference other orientation" and to analyze mechanization of agriculture in Niiike from this perspective.

The reference other orientation: a theoretical overview

The concept of reference other orientation derives from reference group theory (Schmitt 1972). This theory is based on the recognition that people often orient themselves to groups other than their own in shaping their attitudes and evaluations. As Herbert Hyman (1968: 4) remarks, "The fact that men may shape their attitudes by reference to groups other than their own and their self-evaluations by the choice of unusual points of social comparison is perhaps the most distinctive contribution of reference group theory." Thus, reference group theory is concerned with subjective perception centered on orientation to non-membership groups. It has been widely used by sociological social psychologists (Hyman and Singer 1968). Although it was only in the early 1940s that the theory of reference groups emerged, the concept itself is undoubtedly old, finding immediate precursors in the works of William James (1950 [1890]) on the "social self," Charles H. Cooley (1983 [1902]) on the "looking-glass self," George H. Mead (1934) on the "generalized other," and those of other scholars associated with the early school of symbolic interactionism. Also, the psychiatrist Harry Stack Sullivan's notion of the "significant other" (1945, 1970) is closely related to this school's orientation.

The concept of reference group was originally formulated in opposition to that of membership group, but the two often overlap in actual contexts. For example, most families are both membership and reference groups for younger members of the family. Similarly, people in Niiike who own agricultural machines may serve as a reference group for those who do not, even though they both belong to the same community. Thus, what distinguishes a reference group from a membership group is not so much whether or not one has a formal membership in a particular group as whether or not one refers oneself to that group, either positively or negatively, in shaping one's attitudes and evaluations.

Basic to the theory of reference groups is the distinction between "normative" and "comparative" reference groups, as well as their attendant functions (Kelley 1968). "Normative reference groups" refers to groups which set and enforce norms for a person who wishes to gain acceptance or membership in those groups, whereas "comparative reference groups" refers to groups which provide standards of comparison for appraising the self or others. In the words of Harold Kelley (1968: 80–1):

A group functions as a normative reference group for a person to the extent that its evaluations of him are based upon the degree of his conformity to certain standards of behavior or attitude and to the extent that the delivery of rewards or punishments is conditional upon these evaluations ... A group functions as a comparison reference group for an individual to the extent that the behavior, attitudes, circumstances, or other characteristics of its members represent standards or comparison points which he uses in making judgments and evaluations.

Conceptually, it is possible to draw a clear line between these two types of groups, but they are actually interrelated. It is therefore important to examine the reference group phenomenon from both perspectives.

In investigating the process by which reference groups are selected, we need to consider whether or not there are similarities between one's self and one's reference group. As Robert Merton and Alice Rossi (1968: 42) state, "some similarity in status attributes between the individual and the reference group must be perceived or imagined, in order for the comparison to occur at all." This proposition is known as the "principle of similarity" or the "principle of relevance." It is important to note here that this similarity is basically a matter of perception and that no objectively definable similarities need to exist at all. Thus, reference groups provide ample room for "autistic perception" (Hyman 1968: 17). When comparative reference groups are concerned, groups of higher social status than one's own tend to be selected.

It is often argued that reference group behavior is a distinctive characteristic of open societies, such as the United States, where there is a high rate of mobility, and that it seldom occurs in rigidly structured societies. This view is open to question. For example, even in India, which has one of the most elaborate caste systems in the world, it is reported that people often emulate the attributes and behavior of those who belong to a caste higher than their own. This is widely known as "Sanskritization." This movement is usually carried out on a group basis (Berreman 1966: 290), yet someone must always initiate it. Thus, the explanation is neither one of social structure nor one of group action. Also, the widely supported view that the reference group phenomenon is observed only in mass societies (e.g., Shibutani 1968) overlooks the complexity of life in small-scale societies.

The term "reference others" will be substituted in this essay for reference groups because the former can comprise more categories of people and entities than the latter. Moreover, the new term is convenient in that it is not constrained by such distinctions as "reference groups" versus "reference individuals." Also, it has an additional advantage of being able to make clear the contrast between the self and others, as well as interactions of the two. Accordingly, the phenomenon in which people refer themselves to others in shaping their attitudes and evaluations will be called the "reference other orientation." I owe this terminology to Raymond Schmitt (1972).

The reference other orientation is aligned with the perspective used by such scholars as Robert Smith (1983) and David Plath (1980), who emphasize the importance of the interaction of the self with others for understanding the Japanese self. Smith (1983: 73), for example, has this to say:

In the West we are taught the central importance of nourishing and developing our individuality. Social conformity is defined as a positive evil when carried beyond a very low threshold of behavior. It is hardly surprising that foreign observers find the Japanese to be collectivity-oriented, too likely to submerge the self in the group, and possessed of weak ego boundaries that are all too permeable. In short, we find that the Japanese are apparently willing to forgo growth as individual human beings, and lack the kind of self-reliance we deem essential to self-realization. What this view causes us to miss is that the Japanese assign a high priority to the growth of human beings as social persons.

Criticizing the essentially individualistic approach that has been used in the study of Japanese personality, character, personhood, sense of the self, and so forth, Smith (1983: 74) further states:

It is not mere idle speculation to suggest that our understanding of these matters would be very different today if over the past thirty-five years research had been conducted in the framework of the interactionist social psychology of figures like George Herbert Mead and Henry Stack Sullivan [*sic*], rather than the individual psychology of Freud and others who provided the framework that was in fact employed. Had the intellectual influences been different, we should long since have had an eminently plausible picture of the Japanese conception of the self.

Reference group theory is particularly useful in applying this insight to the investigation of human relationships in Japan.

Below, I will analyze how the reference other orientation has developed among the people of Niiike and how it has contributed to mechanization of agriculture in their community. The analysis will focus on the two major functions of reference others: comparative and normative. Particular attention will also be paid to ecological, social, and psychological levels of cultural analysis.

Analysis

Crowding is the major characteristic of Niiike's ecological setting. Most households in Niiike are clustered at the foot of a small hill about 400 meters long. This hill is densely covered with bamboo and pine trees, but it is so low that it takes no more than a few minutes to reach the top. Houses are built almost side by side, with one row of houses lying upon another along the steep hillside. As we go through the alleys in the inhabited area, we can see what is going on inside the houses, particularly those of the traditional style, because they are built in such a way as to allow people to do farm work in the dooryard, receive visitors at the front door (*genkan*), chat, read, or bask in the sun on the porch (*engawa*), do small jobs in the outbuilding (*hanare*), and so on. Unless people shut up their homes on cold days, their behavior is generally observable. It is reported that the average distance between two household centers was only 10.3 meters in the middle 1950s (Okada and Kamiya 1960: 289). Although the inhabited area has expanded a little since then, the size of Niiike remains so small that people unfamiliar with the local area can drive through without noticing its existence.

There are no clear boundaries between Niiike and its adjacent communities, but most of the landholding of Niiike is concentrated around the hill. The longstanding tradition in rural Japan of managing irrigation systems with the community as a unit makes it difficult for outsiders to obtain land in this area. In contrast, land is fragmented into tiny pieces within Niiike's territory. Excluding dry fields and wood lots on the hillside, I could identify as many as 198 fields (excluding 3 fields owned by non-farms) within the 1,660 ares of Niiike's territory. This means that each of the 22 farm households in Niiike owns an average of 9.0 fields. Considering the small size of landholding, about 69 ares per household, we can easily understand how land has become fragmented in Niiike. Furthermore, each household's fields are widely separated, so that people must move back and forth carrying their agricultural machines between their fields, which are often located at opposite ends of Niiike's territory. Each household's fields are scattered over the whole irrigated area and interlock with those of others. What at first sight seems a single stretch of farm land is actually divided into numerous tiny fields, which indicates that the rights and interests of the people of Niiike are intertwined in a complex way.

Crowding in Japanese farming communities is a result of land shortage and is deeply related to the form of agriculture practiced in Japan. Japanese agriculture is "intensive" in that it aims at maximum production per unit of land, rather than per unit of labor. Because land is limited, people can only expect to increase production by lavish expenditure of human energy. As Beardsley and his associates (1959: 114–15) point out, intensive agriculture imposes two major conditions on the society it supports. First, its high yield stimulates dense population. Second, its heavy requirements of manpower in turn depend on dense population.

A strong sense of being observed arises from this ecological setting. In an environment with severe spatial limitations like Niiike, virtually every social behavior is visible, and this makes people vulnerable to the scrutiny of others. It is, for example, a common experience for young women who have recently married into Niiike to be exposed to personal, often embarrassing, questions and comments, such as "I saw you take a three o'clock bus yesterday. Where did you go?" and "The bride of that house went out in a flashy dress." Even middle-aged women who have been in Niiike for years complain about the inquisitiveness of their neighbors, particularly elderly women. It should be noted, however, that they observe others just as carefully as they are observed. Thus, crowding gives rise to what may be called "a mechanism of mutual observation," which exposes people constantly to the prying eyes of others.

Because each household's land is fragmented and dispersed in Niiike, people can easily observe how others work their fields. For example, when Hiramatsu Setsuo transplanted rice seedlings into one of his paddy fields in early June before anyone else in Niiike had done so, he was observed throughout by Iwasa Takashi at very close range. Takashi owns a tiny dry field (less than 2 ares) next to Setsuo's field, and the two men's fields are separated by a narrow pathway about 2 meters wide. Takashi, of course, did not intend to "inspect" Setsuo; Takashi was there to cultivate his own field, but he could not help observing Setsuo because they were working so close to one another. It is difficult to feign indifference to that which comes into one's view. Because most of the fields in Niiike are in similar proximity, information concerning others' performance, as well as one's own, spreads very quickly throughout the community. Indeed, it is no exaggeration to say that who cultivates which field in what way is common knowledge because the whole process of land cultivation – plowing the ground, applying fertilizer, letting water into or out of the fields, transplanting rice seedlings, managing the fields during a slack work season, and finally harvesting crops – is visible.

Peformance is not the only thing that is visible; productivity of one's land is also part of the community's common knowledge. As some elderly men in Niiike told me, it is the "inborn nature" of farmers to take great pride in their fields if they yield more crops than those of others even though such a difference may be negligible. Because productivity of land is one of the major concerns for farmers as it affects their life significantly, they will make a secret of it as much as possible. The irony is that in a community like Niiike where much of life is carried on in full view of one's neighbors, even such a vital matter as productivity of one's land is subject to the scrutiny of others. Indeed, this is one major reason why it is extremely difficult to exchange land in order to create contiguous boundaries: very few people are willing to exchange a fertile field for a less fertile one even if the latter may be more conveniently located.

Comparative reference others, shame, and achievement

This kind of situation is particularly conducive to two patterns of thought. First, people constantly evaluate one another and determine each person's worth by relative standards of excellence. Certainly, one's performance is judged only in relation to that of others because there is no such thing as an absolute standard of excellence. The point is, however, that in a place like Niiike with high social visibility, one is constantly exposed to stimuli coming from others, and this intensive exposure makes one sensitive to disparities that may exist between oneself and the others. Thus, if others have machines which one does not, one feels isolated, as well as ashamed, and is motivated to work hard to catch up with the others. What counts here is not the balance of payment itself, but keeping pace with others so that one may not disgrace oneself. This desire to maintain one's self-

Table 7.4. *Landholding and dates of purchase of agricultural machines in Niiike*

Household number	Landholding (ares)			Dates of purchase		
	Paddy	Dry	Total	Transplanter	Tractor	Combine
1	109	12	121	?	1982	1976
2	108	8	116	1975	1975	1975
3	70	30	100	[1976]	1982	[1978]
4	85	15	100	?	1980	1975
5	63	17	80	[1974]	[1980]	[1985]
6	50	20	70	1970	[1981]	[1982]
7	63	7	70	?	*1985	[1980]
8	53	15	68	none	1981	none
9	50	13	63	1970	1983	none
10	53	8	61	1970	*1984	1984
11	54	6	60	1978	1977	none
12	36	12	48	none	*1984	*1981
13	40	7	47	[1972]	[1984]	1978
14	40	4	44	[1976]	1978	[1978]
15	41	2	43	1975	1977	1975
16	40	0	40	[1974]	[1980]	[1985]
17	20	8	28	none	[1981]	[1982]
18	23	5	28	[1972]	[1984]	none

Note: Brackets indicate co-ownership. Asterisks indicate used machines at the time of purchase.

esteem even at the risk of carrying a financial burden is clearly reflected in the words of Iwasa Takashi:

These days, agriculture doesn't pay, but I feel I must continue to cultivate my land. Farmers would do anything to keep their land intact. We can't sell what has been handed down from our ancestors in our generation. That's farmers' spirit. I don't know how young people feel about it, but they will change after they are forty or fifty years old. But the problem is that we need machines to farm, and they cost a lot. We could get more agricultural income if we worked without machines like we did before, but people would laugh at us. That's why we must buy machines. We don't want to be humiliated by others. I got my riding tractor sometime around 1978 before most people in Niiike did. Soon after that, everyone else bought a tractor, and Niiike was packed with tractors in less than two years. It's better to buy a new model early because we must buy one sooner or later.

On closer examination, the actual pattern of machine ownership proves to be far more complex than Takashi's statement implies. Table 7.4 shows the landholdings of 18 farm households in Niiike and the dates of purchase of three major farm machines that became popular after 1970:

rice transplanter, riding tractor, and combine. Four households on which sufficient data could not be obtained are excluded. As is clear from Table 7.4, it took almost a decade, not just a few years as Takashi said, for each of the machines to be in common use in Niiike.

With a few exceptions, the dates of purchase given in Table 7.4 are approximate. Most people in Niiike did not remember exactly when they had bought their machines. There were even some who gave me completely different dates although they shared the same machines. Nevertheless, Table 7.4 reveals some interesting facts about agriculture in Niiike.

First, there is no clear correlation between landholding and the pattern of ownership of agricultural machines. For example, it was not households with more than 100 ares of land, but those whose land size is about Niiike's average (69 ares), that introduced rice transplanters first. Similarly, some small-scale households purchased tractors and combines earlier than others. Probably, a major socio-economic factor in this irregularity is the difference in manpower: households which are short of hands need to buy machines irrespective of their landholdings.

Second, households with small landholdings tend to share agricultural machines to a greater extent than those with large landholdings. Five out of seven households with less than 50 ares of land co-own machines with their lineage members. Thus, despite the strong tendency towards individual ownership, balance of payment is an important consideration in purchasing machines. However, there is no alternative but to buy one's own if one has no appropriate partner.

Third, compared with tractors and combines, rice transplanters became popular very quickly. Within about five years after they were first introduced in Niiike in 1970, the majority of the households had bought one. This popularity derives from two facts: (1) transplanters are relatively inexpensive (an average cost of US $2,729 in 1985); and (2) they are an invaluable asset for farmers because transplanting by hand is laborious and back-breaking work.

Despite these objective observations, however, Iwasa Takashi's assertion that riding tractors spread throughout Niiike in a very short time is suggestive for investigating the motivational basis for the readiness of the people of Niiike to go into debt in order to purchase expensive farm machines. As Takashi suggested, it is not merely a problem of rationalizing labor or increasing productivity that is at issue. From the psychological point of view, it is basically a problem of self-esteem: nothing is more humiliating and injures one's pride more seriously than not to have machines that others have. This sense of humiliation is all the more intense in Niiike because these others are not just people to whom one is remotely related. They are one's peers – those who were born and raised in the same community, went to the same schools, share much of life in adulthood, and will spend their afterlife in the community cemetery. They are, in other words, "significant others." Thus, it is not objective facts concerning who bought what and when that count in the minds of the people of Niiike. Rather, it is their subjective perception or judgment of whether or not they are keeping pace with the significant others that is important. This is best summarized in the words of a seventy-four-year-old man: when I asked him when he had bought his agricultural machines, he could not remember the exact dates. After a short silence, he smiled and said, "At about the same time as others" (*Minna to onaji koro*).

This attitude, which is observed in many other farming communities in Japan, has been interpreted by administrators as the "vanity of farmers," and a formal warning was issued as early as 1958. The Agricultural Cooperative Association in Okayama Prefecture adopted the following resolution at its seventh convention (Okada and Kamiya 1960: 41, my translation):

Resolution concerning Promotion of Cooperative Use of Major Agricultural Machines

Major agricultural machines, such as motor cultivators, are commonly used today as a result of farmers' efforts to improve farm management by mechanization. However, because of the manufacturers' skillful advertisements and the vanity of farmers, many of these machines are owned individually. This has not only brought about an excessive investment in machinery and ineffective use of surplus labor. It is also a major factor in the recent increase in the cost of production as well. We shall, therefore, dispel the widespread notion that it is difficult to share agricultural machines, formulate and carry out definite policies in order to promote cooperative use of major agricultural machines, and help to improve agricultural productivity, as well as the economic condition of farmers, by reducing the cost of management. We hereby agree to adopt this resolution.

October 21, 1958

The point is, however, not so much vanity as a feeling of shame, mortification, chagrin, or a complex of these feelings caused when one realizes that one is left behind in a competition with others. Having assimilated the norms, values, sentiments, and standards of one's peers, one employs these as a frame of reference for self-appraisal. If one finds oneself comparatively lacking, one is compelled to restore one's self-esteem. The sense of deprivation and personal inadequacy which arises from comparison with the achievements of significant others is often so intense that the failure to reduce disparities one perceives to exist between oneself and the others would affect one's whole existence. Thus, the act of purchasing agricultural machines at any cost may be understood as a reflection of one's desire to remove oneself from an inferior position.[4]

In terms of reference group theory, we may reformulate this proposition as follows: To be without a machine which others have constitutes a typical case of "relative deprivation," which is broadly defined as a situation in which "(1) [a person] does not have X, (2) he sees some other person or persons, which may include himself at some previous or imagined time, as having X (whether or not they do have X), and (3) he wants X (whether or not it is feasible that he should have X)" (Runciman 1968: 70). Deprivation is not simply a sense of lack; it is a lack of that which is a means of comparison and self-evaluation. Put another way, it is when one realizes that one has not yet attained standards of excellence set by reference others that one feels a sense of personal inadequacy. Shame is a typical emotional response to this painful experience. Yet, shame will eventually relieve one from the predicament because, as Piers and Singer (1971 [1953]) contend, shame arises out of a tension between the ego and the ego ideal and demands achievement of a positive goal.[5] Thus, the comparative function of reference others, shame, and achievement are significantly related.

Normative reference others, guilt, and conformity

There is yet another pattern of thought which typically develops in a small community like Niiike where people are constantly observed by their neighbors: they will learn to conform to the dominant norms and values, or at least pretend to do so, out of concern for their image and reputation. For example, once reaping with combines has become the norm, it is difficult to keep to one's own way and continue to reap with sickles. To deviate from community norms and expectations would not only invite strong disapproval and ridicule from others, but also instill a deep sense of guilt in the self. This is such a strong sanction that people will eventually shape their attitudes in conformity with those of others and behave accordingly.

It is a well-known fact that the community exerted rigid control over the individual in traditional Japan. Each household was held collectively responsible for the improper conduct of its members, and in extreme cases, the whole household was ostracized from the community (*mura hachibu*). Although such a strong measure was seldom taken, and although the community is not as closely knit as it used to be as a result of the change in industrial structure after World War II, evidence suggests that the behavior of the people of Niiike continues to be influenced by community norms. For example, there is a tacit agreement in Niiike that one's farm land is a precious property which has been inherited from one's ancestors and that one may sell one's land only in extreme financial difficulties. For this reason, strong, yet invisible, sanctions are applied to casual attempts to trade land within the community. An elderly man who was adopted by one of the most influential men in Niiike as his successor eloquently explained this situation:

There is little profit in agriculture today, but I must continue to cultivate my land because it is there. I am emotionally attached to it. It has been handed down to my family from generation to generation. But my attachment to the land cannot be compared with the attachment my deceased parents-in-law and my wife had. After all, I came here from outside. I was adopted. Should I sell my family's land, people in this community would denounce me saying, "That guy sold his land because he's an adopted son. No real son would ever do that."

As has been suggested, much of the strength of community norms, values, and expectations derives from the ecological setting in which the people of Niiike and, certainly, the majority of Japanese farmers are placed. The following remark by the critic Ōmura Ryō is informative:

While I worked as a peddler for four years, I traveled widely throughout farming communities [in northeastern Japan] and visited thousands of farm households. Through this experience, I realized that farmers completely lack independence of mind. They do not set their own standards of behavior. Their behavior is guided by their imagination of how they would look to others if they did such and such. This applies not only when they choose their clothes, but also when they decide what time to get up.

When I visited a farmer's family shortly after the New Year holidays, I asked them what time they arose. "Four in the morning," they said. But it is pitch dark at four o'clock in January. What keeps them so busy in midwinter, I thought. Their answer surprised me. They said that they had nothing to do but that they must get up early because their neighbors opened the shutters at about that time. So, I suggested that they take a rest after they opened the shutters. They then told me that they would be found out if the chimney was not smoking. (Quoted in Araki 1973: 61, my translation)

Ōmura's criticism that the farm family's attitude reflects the "lack [of] independence of mind" of Japanese farmers is not completely misdirected. However, the problem is not one of individualism or conformity. Rather, the point is that in a crowded environment, people often become excessively sensitive to the observation of others and that their behavior and attitudes are regulated by what I have called the "mechanism of mutual observation."

The nature of agricultural work should also be considered. Rice cultivation, in particular, is heavily dependent on irrigation, and managing irrigation systems demands concerted efforts among community members. Thus, the failure of one individual to comply with rules may affect the whole community. Put another way, conformity to group norms is required for individual survival. This is demonstrated by the fact that all households in Niiike, whether farms or not, *must* participate in ditch clearing, which takes place shortly before the rice transplanting period. Clearing irrigation ditches is exhausting work because it is done under the scorching sun of early summer. No one, however, dares to escape this obligation. As an elderly Niiike man said,

We farmers need to maintain a good balance with our neighbors. For example, we must let water into our paddies in the arranged order, so we can't allow one individual to be late or early. It's also important to transplant rice seedlings at about the same time others do. We will give them trouble if we don't. Likewise, if we don't weed, we will have many insects which will annoy all of us. So, we must keep pace with other people. Agriculture needs cooperation with others. Isn't this the same with farmers all over the world?

Under such circumstances, it is understandable that the people of Niiike purchase agricultural machines one after another. Once someone has set a new norm by introducing a new machine or model, and his action is followed by a few innovative others, the rest of the people feel compelled to follow suit in order to maintain their status within the community. Failure to do so may result in withdrawal of the respect due to full-fledged members. The community, then, constitutes a normative reference group for its individual members.

On the basis of these observations, we may propose that the comparative function of reference others, which arouses a sense of shame in individuals if they have not yet attained the standards set by these others, is positively related to achievement, while the normative function, which arouses guilt when norms set by the reference others are transgressed, prevents deviance and compels conformity.[6] Thus, mechanization of agriculture in Niiike may be understood both as an achievement *and* as conformity.

Two cautionary remarks are necessary here. First, there are some social factors peculiar to Niiike that strengthen the reference other orientation of its people. Among the most important is the fact that there has been no single powerful figure in the history of Niiike. It is known that Niiike's origin dates to sometime around 1670, when the completion of certain reclamation projects along a nearby river occasioned the migration of the first settlers to this community. This history is reflected in the very name of Niiike, which means a "new pond." Considering the severe limitations imposed on reclamation in the area where Niiike is situated, it may safely be inferred that no large landlords or politically powerful villagers arose

(Beardsley et al. 1959: 54–5). Thus, unlike many other communities, particularly in northeastern Japan, where strong landlord–tenant relationships prevailed, Niiike has remained egalitarian. Strong competition among the villagers has resulted from this fact.

Another factor in the strong reference other orientation of people in Niiike is their well-developed kinship network. As was mentioned earlier, there are only two major surname groups in Niiike: Hiramatsu and Iwasa. Each of these surname groups is divided into two or three lineages, whose members periodically visit one another's homes when important rituals, such as memorial services for their common ancestors and wedding ceremonies, are held. This gives rise to a rapid flow of information among households, which greatly increases social visibility in Niiike.

Closely related to the well-developed kinship network is the low rate of mobility. In contrast to American communities, where there is a constant flux of people, Niiike is inhabited by a group of people who have known one another for generations. Harmony with one's neighbors is respected in such a community. Considering these social factors is essential because, although ecology may provide a basic framework within which human beings live, there is no simple causality between ecology and psychology.

The second cautionary note is concerned with intra-community differences in the reference other orientation. So far, our discussion has taken the community as a basic unit of analysis, paying particular attention to the inner feelings of its individual members. It is obvious, however, that different people orient themselves to different reference others in different degrees. As I will mention below, *hito* (people at large) serve as the most abstractly conceived category of reference others. But a question remains as to what kinds of people are most positively or negatively oriented to these others. Although data on this point are scanty, three general comments may be made. First, as far as purchasing agricultural machines is concerned, men are more seriously concerned than women. This gender difference is probably related to men's pride as household heads. Second, parent households tend to take the initiative in setting new standards of excellence or norms. Household 2 in Table 7.4, which purchased machines much earlier than did others, is the parent household of the largest Hiramatsu lineage. Third, there are a small number of "deviants." Deviants are of two opposite types. The first type consists of "reclusive" people who withdraw into their own world and do not socialize. The second type comprises people who are "hyperactive," that is, those who are too ambitious to confine themselves to the narrow framework of community life. They are represented by people who emigrated to the United States hoping to make a fortune.

Categories of reference others: toward a native theory of the self

The foregoing discussion shows that others exert great influence on the self and often provide frames of reference for self-appraisal and attitude formation. The question to be asked at this point is: who are these others? More specifically, are there any categories of people who serve as a point of reference for the Japanese self? If so, what are they?

In carefully reviewing the interview materials from Niiike, paying special attention to the words and phrases actually used, I discovered that the Japanese relationship between the self and others is expressed systematically as *jibun* (I) versus *mawari* (people around), *hito* (people at large), and *seken* (society). The following statement by a fifty-five-year-old man in Niiike was instrumental in this discovery:

Jibun (I) must work because *mawari* (people around me) work. I worked hard and saved money to buy a television because my neighbors bought theirs. We must work if we want to live like others (*hito nami*). But the idea of "hito nami" (just like other people) also prevents us from doing bad things. I am satisfied if I can live without being ridiculed by *hito* (others) and keep pace with them. So, if *hito* (others) have such appliances as televisions and washing machines, *jibun* (I) must also have them. If *mawari* (people around) do farm work with sickles, *jibun* (I) don't mind using them, but if *hito* (others) use combines, *jibun* (I) want to use one myself.

In this statement, the self is labeled as *jibun*, and others are categorized into two groups, *mawari* and *hito*, depending on the distance between the self and others.

Jibun is a reflexive pronoun which is often used to indicate the self, especially in opposition to *hito*. *Hito* is the most generally used word to mean a "person" or "people." (Japanese has no strict distinction between singular and plural except some personal pronouns.) *Mawari* is a noun which refers to things or people that surround a person or an object. In this sense, *mawari* is more immediate than *hito*. To this list of words may be added *seken*, a Japanese equivalent to "society," which represents a group of *hito*. Comments made by the people of Niiike, such as "We live in a rural place, so we are sensitive to *seken-tei* (what people in society think of us)," would be an example.

Thus, we get three distinct categories of others which are concentrically related to the self as the center: *mawari*, *hito*, and *seken*. Although the importance of *jibun* and *seken* for Japanese human relationships has been pointed out by some scholars (e.g., Doi 1977, Inoue 1977), it has not yet been noted that the Japanese self is related systematically to these categories of others. In accordance with their proximity to the self (*jibun*), and in view of the fact that they provide the self with important points of

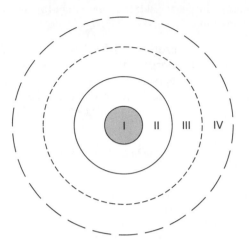

I   *jibun* (self)

II   *mawari* (immediate reference others)

III *hito* (generalized reference others)

IV   *seken* (reference society)

Figure 7.1. The reference other model. Boundaries indicate the degree of actual acquaintance of the self and others.

reference, I propose to call them "immediate reference others," "generalized reference others," and "reference society," respectively (Figure 7.1). I have named this model the "reference other model."

The significance of this model may be demonstrated by clarifying the nature of *hito*, which is the most comprehensive of the three categories of reference others. First, linguistic evidence shows that *hito* serves as an agent of socialization. As expressions like *hito ni warawareru* (to be laughed at by *hito*) illustrate, Japanese parents often appeal to the imagined reactions of *hito* in order to sensitize their children to the opinions and feelings of others (Clancy 1986: 236). In Japanese, *hito* is the most abstractly conceived category of persons. It does not indicate any specific individual: it may mean parents, teachers, peers, colleagues, or anyone else, depending on the context. This referential ambiguity makes *hito* function as a powerful source of sanctions across diverse situations. Indeed, the use of *hito* as a third person is a distinctive feature of Japanese socialization. As Takie Lebra (1976: 153) observes:

The mother tells the child that he will be laughed at or ridiculed by neighbors, his playmates, his relatives, or anyone whose opinion the child values most ... The third person thus plays a significant role in sensitizing the child to shame and embarrassment. The mother uses the third person not only as a verbal reference but as an audience present on the scene. The child learns the difference between the dyadic situation (with only himself and his caretaker) and the triadic situation (with a third person present as audience) in terms of freedom: he feels completely free in the dyad, inhibited in the triad. This may result in sensitizing the child more to outsiders' opinions than to those of intimate insiders, to the extent that his own family may not be able to discipline him.

Second, *hito* may be considered the prototype of other categories of reference others. Two examples help clarify this point. First, as the expression *seken ni warawareru* (to be laughed at by *seken*) shows, *hito* is easily extended to *seken*. One of the first to note the importance of *seken* as an agent of socialization in Japan was Ruth Benedict (1946: 287–8) who stated:

> One striking continuity connects the earlier and the later period of the child's life: the great importance of being accepted by his fellows . . . [T]he promised reward is that he will be approved and accepted by "the world." The punishment is that "the world" will laugh at him. This is of course a sanction invoked in child training in most cultures, but it is exceptionally heavy in Japan. Rejection by "the world" has been dramatized for the child by his parents' teasing when they threatened to get rid of him. All his life ostracism is more dreaded than violence.

There is little doubt that the term "the world" in this quotation is an English translation of *seken*.[7]

The second example centers on *nami*, a word which means the average or standard. People familiar with Japanese can easily understand that such popular expressions as *seken nami* (just like society) and *ōbei nami* (just like Europe and America) are extensions of *hito nami* (just like other people). Significantly, the *ōbei nami* orientation has contributed greatly to Japan's modernization in the form of "ōbei ni oitsuke oikose" ("Catch up with and excel the West") – Japan's national slogan since the Meiji era (1868–1911). Europe and America have served as Japan's "reference civilization" in modern times. Interestingly, this role was played by China during the nation-building period of Japan. As is exemplified by the large number of students, monks, and officials who were dispatched to the Sui and the Tang dynasties for study from the seventh through the ninth centuries A.D., absorption of China's superior civilization was Japan's major goal in its early history.[8]

Finally, the fact that *hito* and *jibun* are interchangeable in Japanese illuminates the nature of *hito*. Although this semantic interchange applies only under certain circumstances, as when the speaker attempts to create a distance from the addressee (Suzuki 1976), it remains that words for the self and for others may be used interchangeably in Japanese. It is precisely because of this interchangeability that the perspectives of others are readily assumed by the Japanese self, which blurs the boundary between the two.

The reference other model differs from the *uchi–soto* or inside–outside model (Figure 7.2), which has been used extensively in Japanese studies, in

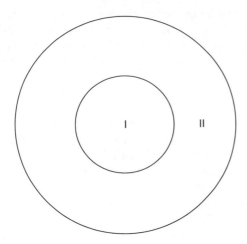

I   *uchi* (inside)

II *soto* (outside)

Figure 7.2. The *uchi–soto* model

two significant respects. First, whereas the place of the self is ambiguous in the *uchi–soto* model, it is clearly indicated by the term *jibun* in the reference other model. One weakness of *uchi–soto* is that the self tends to be submerged into *uchi*: the self is undifferentiated from an unspecified category of "insiders" and is given no formal recognition. This is unfortunate because, even though the Japanese self is relational, as the occasional interchangeability of *jibun* and *hito* shows, the self has an identity of its own. Paradoxical as it may sound, it is only by acknowledging the existence of a self, whatever form it may assume, that we can discuss relationships of the self and others. Where there is no self, there are no others, and therefore, no true relationships.

Doi Takeo, in his book *The Anatomy of Dependence*, clarifies this point when he writes that "a man who has a *jibun* is capable of checking *amae*, while a man who is at the mercy of *amae* has no *jibun*" (Doi 1977: 19). He further contends that self-awareness emerges only when a person can maintain independence from his group. As Doi (1977: 134) states: "If the individual is submersed completely in the group, he has no *jibun*. But even where he is not completely submersed in the group ... he does not necessarily have a *jibun* ... [A]n individual is said to have a *jibun* when he can maintain an independent self that is never negated by membership of the group."

Second, the reference other model can show the interaction of the self and others in more concrete terms than the *uchi–soto* model. Others are classified into three categories in accordance with their proximity to the self, instead of the two opposing categories of the inside and the outside. Certainly, as with *uchi* and *soto*, there are overlaps among these classificatory categories. What is *mawari* in one situation is *hito* in another. And there is no clear dividing line between *hito* and *seken* which sets off one from the other across diverse situations. However, this referential ambiguity is not so much a weakness as a reflection of the ever-changing social contexts in which the self and others are situated.

This is not to say that the *uchi–soto* model has no significance. On the contrary, as other essays in this volume show, it is a very useful model in the analysis of Japanese behavior and mentality. In fact, the Japanese themselves often emphasize this same distinction. What is not clear, however, is whether *uchi–soto* is uniquely Japanese. It may be universal, as is suggested by William Sumner's classic distinction between "in-group" and "we-group," on the one hand, and "out-group" and "others-group," on the other (Sumner 1979).[9] Thus, the reference other model is presented here not as a substitute for *uchi–soto*, but rather as an alternative.

Summary and conclusions

Niiike was a self-contained farming community in the early 1950s. As a result of the sweeping changes that occurred throughout Japan beginning after World War II, it has been transformed into a suburban community where agriculture is practiced only on a part-time basis. Yet, despite the diminishing importance of agriculture as a means of livelihood today, Niiike has attained a remarkable degree of agricultural mechanization in only a few decades. Many factors are responsible for this change. Among the most important are the generous financial support for planned mechanization received from the Asia Foundation, Niiike's proximity to central Okayama and Kurashiki, and a set of historical changes that had enormous impact on Japanese farmers throughout the nation.

From the psychological point of view, a somewhat different picture emerges. The people of Niiike have purchased seldom-used and expensive farming machines because they are essential to maintain the people's status as respectable members of the community. Purchasing agricultural machines in Niiike is a reflection of the way they relate to others in the community. In other words, the machines are symbols of the people's achieved status, as well as of their compliance with the community norms, values, and expectations. The reference other model was introduced to explain this attitude.

I conclude with two general comments. First, reference group theory has great potential for the anthropological study of the self, particularly the changing consciousness of the self in times of social and cultural change. It is no coincidence that this concept has been used implicitly, though seldom explicitly, by many anthropologists interested in acculturation. Examples include the notions of "out society" and "model society."[10] Also, the reference other model is a valuable contribution to the interactionist approach in the study of the self.

Second, although this essay has examined Niiike's mechanization of agriculture in terms of the influence others exert on the self, there is an opposite dimension to this problem: the individuality of the people of Niiike. Indeed, we may reverse the whole argument and say that they are so "individualistic" and even "egoistic" – we might describe this as "competitive conformity" (Lebra 1987) – that they cannot share machines. In my earlier work, I discussed this problem in relation to the difficulties of sharing machines and, also, of exchanging farm fields to create contiguous boundaries (Kuwayama 1989: 282–339). I present this as a reminder because the relationality of the Japanese has often been emphasized at the expense of their individuality.

NOTES

1 In addition to surname groups and *kabuuchi*, there is another category of kinship-based groups in Niiike: *shinseki*. *Shinseki* is the closest Japanese analogue of kindred that is formed primarily through marriage. Because the community is usually the largest exogamous unit in rural Japan, *shinseki* members are found outside the community. In Niiike, there is a clear distinction between *kabuuchi* and *shinseki*, but confusion occasionally occurs among members of an exceptional household whose founder married a woman from his own lineage.

2 Because reliable statistical data could not be obtained, the following method was used to calculate Niiike's agricultural income. In 1985, the national average (excluding Hokkaido) of agricultural income was 10.4 percent of the total household income for farms with 50 to 99 ares of land (Nōrinsuisanshō Tōkei Jōhōbu 1987: 142). Niiike's average has been estimated at about 8 percent because its rice production in the same year was approximately 20 percent less than the national average.

3 The percentage of ownership indicated here is calculated using the total number of machines, rather than the total number of farms which own machines either individually or collectively, which is then divided by the total number of farm households. This is the method used by the Ministry of Agriculture, Forestry, and Fishery of Japan. Thus, co-ownership is not reflected accurately in the figures presented in Table 7.2.

4 I was influenced by William James' discussion of the self, particularly his "law of self-esteem," in this argument. As James (1950 [1890]: 310) noted:

I, who for the time have staked my all on being a psychologist, am mortified if others know much more psychology than I. But I am contented to wallow in the grossest ignorance of Greek. My deficiencies there give no sense of personal humiliation at all. Had I "pretentions" to be a linguist, it would have been just the reverse. So we have the paradox of a man shamed to death because he is only the second pugilist or the second oarsman in the world. That he is able to beat the whole population of the globe minus one is nothing; he has "pitted" himself to beat that one; and as long as he doesn't do that nothing else counts. He is to his own regard as if he were not, indeed he *is* not.

Yonder puny fellow, however, whom every one can beat, suffers no chagrin about it, for he has long ago abandoned the attempt to "carry that line," as the merchants say, of self at all. With no attempt there can be no failure; with no failure no humiliation. So our self-feeling in this world depends entirely on what we *back* ourselves to be and do. It is determined by the ratio of our actualities to our supposed potentialities; a fraction of which our pretensions are the denominator and the numerator our success; thus,

$$\text{Self-esteem} = \frac{\text{Success}}{\text{Pretensions}}$$

5 Although different scholars define shame differently, there seems to be agreement on the following two propositions: (1) that shame presupposes the existence of the other; and (2) that shame arises when sensitive, intimate, and vulnerable aspects of the self are exposed to the eyes of the other. This other would not necessarily be a person who actually exists or with whom one has personal contacts. It can be an imaginary person or an imaginary category of people or even the objectified self. See Erikson (1950: 251–4), Lynd (1958), and Sakuta (1967).

6 I owe this observation to Inoue Tadashi (1977: 129), who relates the distinction between shame and guilt to that between the comparative and the normative functions of reference groups. Inoue has this to say:

> The normative function of reference groups is concerned with the moral standard by which the degree of the actor's conformity to the norms of his reference group is judged, whereas the comparative function of reference groups is concerned with the standard of excellence by which the actor's performance is evaluated against that of others in his reference group. In other words, the normative function and the comparative function of reference groups are based on the superego and the ego ideal, respectively ... We may postulate that the former is related to guilt, whereas the latter is related to shame. (My translation)

In addition to Inoue's work, the proposed relationship between the comparative function of reference groups, shame, and achievement, on the one hand, and the normative function of reference groups, guilt, and conformity, on the other, is based on the observation of Gerhart Piers and Milton Singer (1971 [1953]). They maintain that shame is a reaction to the ego ideal, which demands achievement of a positive goal, whereas guilt is a reaction to the superego, which inhibits and condemns transgression. For the view that Japanese achievement is related to guilt, rather than shame, see DeVos (1973).

7 Either the term *seken* or *seken no hitobito* (people in *seken*) is used for "the world" in Hasegawa Matsuji's Japanese translation of *The Chrysanthemum and the Sword* (*Kiku to katana*, pp. 333–4, Tokyo: Shakai Shisōsha).

8 By the same token, we may hypothesize that Japanese-Americans rapidly assimilated into American society because the white middle class represented *hito* or *seken* in their minds. For an analysis of culture change in terms of "reference culture," see Charles Hughes (1958: 27), particularly his comments on the experience of Japanese immigrants to the United States.

9 For the relationship between *uchi–soto* and *omote–ura* (front–back), see Ishida Takeshi (1984).

10 Among the anthropological studies which explicitly used the reference group concept are Hughes (1957), Hughes (1958), and Berreman (1964).

REFERENCES

Araki, Hiroyuki. 1973. *Nihonjin no kōdō yōshiki* (Patterns of Japanese behavior). Tokyo: Kodansha.

Beardsley, Richard, Hall, John, and Ward, Robert. 1959. *Village Japan*. Chicago: University of Chicago Press.

Benedict, Ruth. 1946. *The Chrysanthemum and the Sword: Patterns of Japanese Culture*. Boston, Mass.: Houghton Mifflin.

Berreman, Gerald. 1964. Aleut Reference Group Alienation, Mobility, and Acculturation. *American Anthropologist* 66: 231–50.

  1966. Structure and Function of Caste Systems. *Japan's Invisible Race: Caste in Culture and Personality* (G. DeVos and H. Wagatsuma, eds.), Berkeley: University of California Press.

Chūgoku Shikoku Nōseikyoku Tōkei Jōhōbu. 1986. *Chūgoku shikoku nōrin suisan tōkei* (Statistics on agriculture, forestry, and fishery in the Chūgoku-Shikoku area), Okayama: Chūgoku Shikoku Nōseikyoku Tōkei Jōhōbu.

Clancy, Nancy. 1986. The Acquisition of Communicative Style in Japanese. *Language Socialization Across Cultures* (B. Schieffelin and E. Ochs, eds.), Cambridge: Cambridge University Press.

Cooley, Charles. 1983 (1902). *Human Nature and the Social Order*. New Brunswick, N.J.: Transaction Books.

DeVos, George. 1973. *Socialization for Achievement: Essays on the Cultural Psychology of the Japanese*. Berkeley: University of California Press.

Doi, Takeo. 1977. *The Anatomy of Dependence*. Tokyo: Kodansha.

Erikson, Erik. 1950. *Childhood and Society*. New York: Norton.

Hughes, Charles. 1957. Reference Group Concepts in the Study of a Changing Eskimo Culture. *Cultural Stability and Cultural Change: Proceedings of the 1957 Annual Spring Meeting of the American Ethnological Society* (V. Ray, ed.), Seattle: American Ethnological Society.

  1958. The Patterning of Recent Cultural Change in a Siberian Eskimo Village. *Journal of Social Issues* 14 (4): 25–35.

Hyman, Herbert. 1968. Introduction. *Readings in Reference Group Theory and Research* (H. Hyman and E. Singer, eds.), New York: Free Press.

Hyman, Herbert and Singer, Eleanor, eds. 1968. *Readings in Reference Group Theory and Research*. New York: Free Press.

Inoue, Tadashi. 1977. *Sekentei no kōzō* (The structure of *seken*). Tokyo: Nihon Hōsō Shuppan Kyōkai.

Ishida, Takeshi. 1984. Conflict and Its Accommodation: Omote–Ura and Uchi–Soto Relations. *Conflict in Japan* (E. Krauss, T. Rohlen, and P. G. Steinhoff, eds.), Honolulu: University of Hawaii Press.

James, William. 1950 (1890). *The Principles of Psychology*, Vol. I. New York: Dover.

Kelley, Harold. 1968. Two Functions of Reference Groups. *Readings in Reference Group Theory and Research* (H. Hyman and E. Singer, eds.), New York: Free Press.

Kuwayama, Takami. 1989. The Japanese Conception of the Self: The Dynamics of Autonomy and Heteronomy. Ph.D. dissertation, University of California, Los Angeles.

Lebra, Takie Sugiyama. 1976. *Japanese Patterns of Behavior*. Honolulu: University of Hawaii Press.

——— 1987. Comments made on the panel "Japanese Self: Creating and Receiving Culture" at the 86th annual meeting of the American Anthropological Association, Chicago.

Lynd, Helen. 1958. *On Shame and the Search for Identity*. New York: Harcourt, Brace.

Mead, George Herbert. 1934. *Mind, Self, and Society*. Chicago: University of Chicago Press.

Merton, Robert and Rossi, Alice. 1968. Contributions to the Theory of Reference Groups. *Readings in Reference Group Theory and Research* (H. Hyman and E. Singer, eds.), New York: Free Press.

Muramatsu, Tsuneo, ed. 1962. *Nihonjin: Bunka to pāsonaliti no jisshōteki kenkyū* (The Japanese: An empirical study of their culture and personality). Nagoya: Reimei Shobō.

Nagashima, Nobuhiro and Tomoeda, Hiroyasu, eds. 1984. *Regional Differences in Japanese Rural Culture*. Senri Ethnological Studies 14. Osaka: National Museum of Ethnology.

Nōrinsuisanshō Tōkei Jōhōbu. 1987. *Poketto nōrinsuisan tōkei 1987* (Statistics on agriculture, forestry, and fishery, 1987). Abridged edn. Tokyo: Nōrin Tōkei Kyōkai.

Okada, Yuzuru and Kamiya, Keiji. 1960. *Nihon nōgyō kikaika no bunseki* (An analysis of mechanization of agriculture in Japan). Tokyo: Shōbunsha.

Piers, Gerhart and Singer, Milton. 1971 (1953). *Shame and Guilt: A Psychoanalytic and a Cultural Study*. New York: Norton.

Plath, David. 1980. *Long Engagements: Maturity in Modern Japan*. Stanford, Calif.: Stanford University Press.

Reischauer, Edwin. 1988. *The Japanese Today*. Cambridge, Mass.: Harvard University Press.

Runciman, W. G. 1968. Problems of Research on Relative Deprivation. *Readings in Reference Group Theory and Research* (H. Hyman and E. Singer, eds.), New York: Free Press.

Sakuta, Keiichi. 1967. *Haji no bunka saikō* (Shame culture reconsidered). Tokyo: Chikuma Shobō.

Schmitt, Raymond. 1972. *The Reference Other Orientation: An Extension of the Reference Group Concept.* Carbondale and Edwardsville: Southern Illinois University Press.

Shibutani, Tamotsu. 1968. Reference Groups as Perspectives. *Readings in Reference Group Theory and Research* (H. Hyman and E. Singer, eds.), New York: Free Press.

Smith, Robert. 1983. *Japanese Society: Tradition, Self and the Social Order.* Cambridge: Cambridge University Press.

Sōmuchō Tōkeikyoku. 1986. *Wagakuni jinkō no gaikan* (Major aspects of population of Japan). Tokyo: Nippon Tōkei Kyōkai.

1987. *Okayama-ken no jinkō* (Population of Okayama). Tokyo: Nippon Tōkei Kyōkai.

Sullivan, Harry Stack. 1945. *Conceptions of Modern Psychiatry.* New York: Norton.

1970. Self as Concept and Illusion. *Social Psychology through Symbolic Interaction* (G. Stone and H. Farberman, eds.), Waltham, Mass.: Xerox College Publication.

Sumner, William. 1979. *Folkways and Mores.* New York: Schocken.

Suzuki, Takao. 1976. Jishōshi to shite no hito (*Hito* as a self-specifier). *Bulletin of the Institute for the Study of Languages and Culture at Keio University* 8: 43–58.

8   *Kejime*: defining a shifting self in multiple organizational modes

Jane Bachnik

Ruth Benedict's early characterization of the Japanese by the simultaneous representation of both "sword" and "chrysanthemum" sets the stage for understanding a more modern Japanese sense of self as well. By "sword" and "chrysanthemum" Benedict meant not simply categories, but "assumptions about the conduct of life" (1946: 13). Two different and contrasting sets of such assumptions have since been defined, involving contrasts between discipline/distance, and spontaneity/intimacy (Rosenberger 1989, Lebra 1976, Doi 1973, 1986). Yet, to the extent that *both* self-discipline and self-gratification are considered desirable by the Japanese, they raise a series of issues, both theoretical and practical.[1] The essays in this volume – particularly those of Tobin, Kondo, Rosenberger, and Lebra – make it clear that Japanese choose appropriate behavior situationally, from among a range of possibilities, resulting in depictions of the Japanese self as "shifting" or "relational." But how do Japanese manage to link behavior appropriately to situations and on what do they base their frequent shifts of context?

The essays in this volume all develop complementary perspectives on the Japanese self which attempt to encompass these multiple, contrasting dimensions, and, in doing so, clearly transcend a unitary, abstract model of "self." They also move well beyond the model of G. H. Mead's social or interactional self, which is still grounded in self/society dichotomies. Their discussions of shifts between situations also raise further issues of human consciousness, agency, and context – all of which seem highly relevant to the organization of self in Japan. In this essay I will focus on further defining the process of shifting, for which a native term, *kejime*, has already been introduced (Tobin, this volume). The paper will involve two levels: it will discuss shifting within a sustained ethnographic situation, in order to develop a theoretical focus which can deal with the issues of multiple organizational modes raised by the "shifting" self.

Dynamic polar tensions and the organization of self

The contrasts between discipline/distance and spontaneity/intimacy discussed above are commonly expressed in the Japanese language as paired
sets of terms, which include *omote* "in front; surface appearance" versus
ura "in-back, what is kept hidden from others" (Doi 1986, Lebra 1976:
112–13); *soto* "outside" versus *uchi* "inside" (Wetzel 1984, Lebra 1976:
112–13); *giri* "social obligation" versus *ninjō* "the world of personal
feelings" (Hamabata 1983: 22, Doi 1973: 33, Benedict 1946); *tatemae* "the
surface reality" versus *honne* "the motives or opinions distinct from
[*tatemae*] . . . [held] in its background" (Doi 1986: 37). This list is not
exhaustive.

Two sets of polar meanings are implicit in these terms: first, a series of
meanings specifying self and society; second, a series of directional
coordinates ("inside" and "outside"; "in-front" and "in-back"). The
meanings for self include personal feelings (*ninjō*), inner feelings (*honne*),
and what is hidden from others (*ura*); meanings for society include social
obligations (*giri*), the surface reality (*tatemae*), and appearance (*omote*).
Doi finds the meanings of these sets of terms to be related, so that aspects
of self cluster at one pole (*ninjō, honne, ura, uchi*); while aspects of social
life cluster at the other (*giri, tatemae, omote, soto*) (1973, 1986). The
directional coordinates can thus be linked to a set of organizational
coordinates for self and society, such that outward-looking forms are
juxtaposed to inward-looking feelings. Doi's argument that these sets of
polar terms are related is crucial, since it means that aspects of self and
society are linked directionally to degrees of inside- and outside-ness.[2]

These double coordinates are pervasive in Japanese social life, appear-
ing in virtually every sphere. For example, linguists define a double axis of
address or distance (Ikuta 1980) and reference or direction (Wetzel 1984, in
press), which corresponds to the spontaneity/discipline and inside/outside
coordinates (Bachnik and Quinn, in press). The double coordinates also
appear in discussions of political hierarchy (Ishida 1984), large and small
enterprise organization (Gerlach 1992, Kondo 1990), household/family
organization (Bachnik 1992b, Hamabata 1990), marriage (Edwards 1989),
gender (Rosenberger, in press, Hamabata 1990), health and illness
(Ohnuki-Tierney 1984), religion (Hardacre 1986), and human relationships to technology (Kondo and Kuwayama, this volume). The fact that a
common "thread" cross-cuts all these different spheres indicates not only
that the double coordinates are extremely basic, but that they are basic
organizational coordinates of language and social life, rather than mere
taxonomic categories.[3]

A focus on the organizational nature of the double coordinates of inside/ outside, self/society is a major contribution of this volume. Here Lebra and Rosenberger present self as a dynamic tension between self *and* society, such that self is defined alternately within or juxtaposed to society. Both define these dynamics in relation to inside/outside coordinates, and both use these coordinates to develop relationships between notions of power, and connections with the sacred, or transcendent. Thus inner is related to the spontaneous and even asocial *kokoro* (heart, sentiment, spirit) and outer to *seishin* or social discipline acquired by spiritual strength.[4]

Because it involves adhering to one's social requirements, the disciplined self is widely regarded as having higher value than the spontaneous self (Hamabata 1990, Kondo 1987, Lebra 1976, Smith 1983). This is true, but only from the standpoint of being in, and thus having to interact in the world. From another standpoint Lebra considers the "inner" self to be more highly valued precisely because it provides a means of "anchoring" the interactional self away from the demands of the social world and allowing for a self which can resist, rather than simply mirror the outside world. Thus "shame and guilt are not a dichotomy as conceived by Benedict, but rather . . . they occupy different ranks in the moral hierarchy within a culture, guilt outranking shame" (Lebra, this volume). The idea of a moral hierarchy is of considerable importance in reconciling seemingly contradictory characteristics such as guilt and shame.[5]

Neither Rosenberger's nor Lebra's discussion of various aspects of self should be understood as typological, but rather as a process of continuing movement, which involves constant transformations. These flow in a spiraling circle for Rosenberger and a series of levels (which can be conceptualized as a circle) for Lebra. To put this in Rosenberger's terms, "inner" and "outer" are not dichotomies, but transformations of universal power that are represented in Shinto by a circle with three commas, one the dynamic of outer differentiation (Lebra's "presentational" and "synergistic" selves), the second the dynamic of inner consolidation (Lebra's "inner" self), and the third representing the bringing together of all the powers into a full cycle of growth.[6]

The other essays can be located along the continuum (or spiraling circle) of Lebra and Rosenberger's multiple, transformational portraits of self. Kuwayama's focus on an other-oriented self is but one aspect of these transformations, since the "presentational" self must be grasped in relation to the "synergistic" self, as Buber eloquently noted in similar ways in his juxtaposition of "I and Thou" relationships. Human relationships to technology are also defined not only through competition in "presentational" self situations as Kuwayama discusses. They also provide a way of developing the "inner" self through intense identification with work, through *kurō* or suffering, as both Lebra and Kondo note.

Thus Kondo's discussion of a mature artisan depicts a man who crafts a finer self, in the process of crafting fine objects (as *shokunin katagi*). The machines here can be considered extensions of human beings so that polishing the machines is equated with polishing one's *kokoro* (Hamabata, in Kondo, this volume).[7] Berque's focus on relationships of self to environment also complements the self/society focus developed in all the other papers. Thus the cycle of "mediance" in which the subject is "diffused" into the environment complements the presentational or disciplined self. In this mode, rather than a well-defined, or transcendental "I," which is distinguished from the environment, the Japanese subject permeates the environmental scene. We can ask whether the dynamic movement from outer to inner exists in the relationship of self to environment as it does in the relation of self to society.

We can also ask whether terms such as "blurring" and "decentering" of self are overly vague – themselves a product of a tendency toward unified frames of reference, resulting from a polarized focus. A focus which is not polarized but moves *between* poles, such as *omote/ura* and *uchi/soto*, must be organized on a basis of constant transformations. Thus, for example, the dynamics of an interactional self are focused on differentiation; those of a synergistic self on consolidation and centralization. The defining factor here is movement, since the same "other" can be defined by different movements for synergic and presentational aspects of self. The crucial question for defining self here is to look away from "fixing" a unified typology of self to the process of "fixing" a series of points along a sliding scale for a self which is defined *by* shifting. If movement between different modes is central to the organization of self, then the question of how movement is initiated and defined at a given "point" along the sliding scale is *the* central organizing factor for the double continuum which defines both self and society. Thus for Japanese, appropriate personal and social behavior is identified, not as a general set of behaviors which transcends situations, but rather as a series of particular situations which generate a kaleidoscope of different behaviors *which are nonetheless ordered and agreed upon.*

Because of this, the ability to *shift* successfully from spontaneous to disciplined behavior, through identification of a particular situation along an "inner" or "outer" axis, is a crucial social skill for Japanese, which must be learned in order for one to function as an adult. It makes sense that this ability to shift – or *kejime* – is also a major pedagogical focus in Japanese education, and that in the first educational experience outside the home – that of preschool – the primary focus of the preschool program is on learning *kejime* (Tobin, this volume).

Kejime thus emerges as a crucial kind of native knowledge about how movement is initiated and defined along the double set of coordinates. If one could grasp how a preschool child actually "knows" *kejime* one could also grasp an essential requirement of mature selfhood for the Japanese, as well as an essential requirement for a "shifting" organization of self and society.

In the remainder of this essay, I will focus on *kejime*, and its usage not by children, but by adults. I will investigate: (1) the kind of knowledge *kejime* represents; (2) how *kejime* is demonstrated in social situations; (3) the relationship between *kejime* and the organization of self and society in Japan; and (4) theoretical implications derived from *kejime* about the definition of self via multiple organizational modes.

Indexing and pragmatic meaning

At the outset *kejime* seems paradoxical to define because it is difficult to identify its meaning. Thus *kejime* refers to "the knowledge needed to shift fluidly back and forth between *omote* and *ura*" (Tobin, p. 24 above), or any of the other double sets of terms. This is because *kejime* refers, not to the content of *omote* and *ura*, but rather to a participant's ability to differentiate between them, and is therefore meta-level knowledge – knowledge about knowledge.

To understand what *kejime* means, we must examine *omote/ura, uchi/ soto*, and the other double sets of terms. These terms all share the characteristic of relationality, such that each is defined in relation to the other. Inside is defined in relation to outside; in-front in relation to in-back. By the same token, spontaneity and discipline, consolidation and differentiation, organization and chaos are also defined in relation to one another: "There can be no true expression of spontaneity without the prior experience of restraint, no understanding of informality without an experience of formality" (Tobin, p. 26 above).

All of the directional coordinates above require a contextual locus – or reference point – to be defined. In-front or in-back is defined in relation to something – my body, or the house I live in, for example. Objects such as "this piece of paper" or "that car parked on the street" are in front of me or in front of my house according to these reference points which are here used as physical coordinates. As coordinates of self and social life, in-front or in-back refer to a relationship between appearance (*omote*) and behind-the-scenes secrets (*ura*), that also require a contextual locus – someone who is communicating *omote* versus *ura* to someone else in a particular situation. These participants must decide on the appearance they want to project versus what they also feel but cannot say; or what is going on behind the scenes, which they do not wish to reveal. *Kejime* consists of the decision of how much *omote* versus *ura* one wishes to convey.

The preschool schedule Tobin discusses alternates between periods of organization and apparent chaos; between formality and informality; and distinctions between inner and outer. The point of the organization of the preschool program is not to learn *omote* or *ura* per se, but to learn *kejime*. *Omote* and *ura* themselves are difficult to define concretely, since the meaning of each is defined in relation to the other, and thus seems utterly relativistic.

Kejime is a meta-level concept, which focuses on the relationship of these sets of relationally defined terms. *Kejime* refers to relationships between contexts, and also to the production of an organization which is both highly contextual and a major organizational focus for self and society. But how can a concept so particularly related to context also be a general focus of the preschool program as well as of the organization of self and society? To put this another way, how can *kejime* mean anything general about context if it requires context to mean what it means?

Two ways of perceiving cultural meaning are at issue here. The first kind of meaning is semantic – where the semantic value of a sign has its meaning apart from contextual factors. "A *genuine* symbol is a symbol that has general meaning" (Peirce 1931–5: II, 293). The second kind of meaning is pragmatic – where a sign stipulates the relationship between objects and contexts, detailing spatiotemporal contiguities (such as distance), and thereby relating something to its context. "Both kinds of meanings are essential to language (and to culture), yet we have paid far more attention to semantic (or referential) meaning than to pragmatic meaning in regarding culture. Pragmatic meaning is far less obvious to the English speaker than semantic meaning, although this has nothing to do with the existence or non-existence of indexes" (Bachnik 1989: 241). Instead, inattention to pragmatic meaning has to do with what Silverstein (1979) calls an "ideology" of language, which Crapanzano regards as "going back at least to Aristotle, that gives priority to the naming, referential, denotative function of language (over such other language functions as the indexical)" (1982: 181). The strong tendency to focus on reference (on words like "dog," "woman," and "tree") rather than words like "here," "there," or "I" is linked to a set of assumptions about the nature of language (Silverstein 1979, Crapanzano 1982). These assumptions are also appropriate for culture, making it possible to differentiate pragmatic and semantic meaning here as well.

We can approach the issue of pragmatic meaning through C. S. Peirce's formulation of indexical signs, developed as part of a comprehensive philosophical system which includes both a set of phenomenological categories and an equally comprehensive sign system. For Peirce, indexes held deep importance, because of his concern with escaping the Cartesian legacy of mind/matter and subject/object dualism. Peirce's phenomenological categories and sign systems are based on three irreducible sets of relationships: monads, dyads, and triads, which in turn are related to three kinds of signs: the icon, index, and symbol.

Each of Peirce's three different kinds of signs is characterized by different relations of the sign to its object. Thus the icon is characterized by resemblance in the form of a diagram or image; an index by contiguity so that an indexical sign has a direct relation to its object, as smoke to fire; and the symbol by an association of convention, such as the nouns "dog," "woman," or "tree".[8] It is worth examining the index more carefully here, since this was considered by Peirce to be the most important of the three kinds of signs.

Indexes do not name objects; they are used to identify and measure degrees, magnitudes, and numbers of specific observations.[9] "The [readings measured by the] barometer, plumb line . . . weather vane, pendulum, and photometer are cited by Peirce as respective indices of observed specific pressure, vertical and horizontal directions, wind direction, gravity, and star brightness" (Singer 1980: 490). What makes all of these indexical is the reference point from which they are "gauged" (or "read").

Also relevant to our discussion is the fact that Peirce considered indexes as dyads comprised of "two subjects brought into oneness." Thus indexes are crucial for Peirce because they present possibilities for overcoming the dualities that are widely perceived between self and the external world. Specifically, "These subjects have their modes of being both in themselves and in their connection with each other . . . The dyad is not the subjects, but the relation between them" (Freeman 1937: 18). As indexes, *omote/ura*, *uchi/soto*, and the other dual sets of terms can be seen as indexing (or "gauging") relationships between self and the world.

Indexes in social life are undoubtedly overlooked for the same reasons they are overlooked in language. Here also, an "ideology" of social life gives priority to referential aspects of meaning which relate to "structure" and organizing principles. Yet this focus has undoubtedly contributed to certain theoretical difficulties, including the delineation of structures too often viewed as bifurcated from individual meaning and action; and rules too often removed from situational context (Giddens 1979, 1984).

The importance of indexical signs in *organizing* contexts raises exciting possibilities since "Such indexes as do not contribute to the referential speech event *signal the structure of the speech context*" (emphasis mine)

(Silverstein 1976: 30). Moreover, it seems likely that indexes can also signal the "structure" of a social context, although this would involve considerable rethinking of the concept of "structure." The organizational role of indexes has already been acknowledged in such areas as deference (which is also defined by *kejime*, and must be differentiated in the use of such paired terms as *uchi/soto*, *tatemae/honne*, and *omote/ura*). Here Silverstein states that: "Nonreferential, relatively performative indexes ... [establish] the parameters of the interaction themselves, as in deference forms, which in effect establish overtly the social relations of the individuals in the roles of speaker and hearer, speaker and audience, or speaker and referent" (1976: 36). The relationship between actual interactions and social roles, between speaking and organizing speech, can clearly be approached through pragmatic or indexical meaning. Rather than distinctions which appear as abstracted "products," *kejime* includes the process of *making* distinctions, incorporating both organizational parameters, and the spatial, temporal, and social loci of the person making the distinction.

Omote/ura as indexes

Through a focus on *kejime*, the paired sets of Japanese terms can be approached as indexes, demonstrating that indexes can signal the organization of social as well as language coordinates. More specifically, indexes involve an organization whose content is defined in relation to a reference point. Participants can shift their behavior as they define different reference points in different contexts. From an analytical perspective, indexing thus provides a means of relating constantly shifting behavior. In contrast to normative specifications which focus on *what kind of* behavior or personality characteristic is appropriate, indexing specifies how much (or how little) of the qualities defined by the paired sets of terms is appropriate. In other words, *kejime* can index *how much* discipline, submission of self, or boundedness, and conversely *how little* emotion, self-expression, or spontaneity is appropriate in a given situation.

Obviously contextual parameters are essential to grasping *kejime*, as indexing. Yet the process of *kejime* must also transcend a single context, or it would be impossible to learn *kejime*. It would also be futile to organize a preschool curriculum around *kejime* if the children were unable to relate this to other contexts after they leave preschool. In order to develop a sense of the parameters of *kejime* it is essential to focus on sustained relationships in social contexts. To do this, I will develop three vignettes which took place in a Japanese *ie* (usually translated as "household" or "family"), which I call the Katō family. I lived and conducted research in the Katō house for six years over a twenty-year period, and since I am in the scenes, it is important to know that they occurred when I had known the Katōs for fifteen years. Space constraints also require that I limit my discussion here to the single axis of *omote/ura*, although all the axes can be interrelated, as discussed above. Following this I will develop a set of parameters for "knowing" *kejime*.

The guests: three vignettes

Vignette 1

The setting is the Katō farmhouse in Nagano Prefecture on a warm, August day. The house is large, with a thick thatch roof and a large flower garden which is blooming profusely. It is opened up all along the front (south) side facing the garden, and a group of people are sitting around a low table (*kotatsu*) in a small room at the end of the house – a room which faces only the edge of the garden (see parlor 1, Figure 8.1). The *ojīsan* and *obāsan* (grandfather and grandmother), who live in the house, are surrounded by their second son, his wife and two small children, who have just come to visit from Tokyo. I am a major reason for their visit, for I have come back to see the family after a long absence. The occasion is joyful, for it is the first time I have seen the two children, and there is much to catch up on. We sip tea from the old brown ceramic teapot which I remember from my previous visits to the house – where I lived for several years from the time this son was in high school. We are chatting, catching up on happenings and gossip as the children play on the sidelines. The room is comfortable and lived in, with worn *tatami* mats and a hole cut beneath the *kotatsu* into the floor. We are surrounded by a comfortable clutter; there are holes poked in the paper-covered doors by grandchildren, and magazines lying around. The old TV is in the corner.

We howl with laughter as the *obāsan* tells us the saga of the crotchety neighbor down the road (always creating problems) who has recently decided that the telephone pole in front of his house takes up far too much space. His efforts to remove it have set off a long series of difficulties with his neighbors, the accounts of which regale us in laughter. We begin to catch up on major events in the past few years, punctuated by screams from the children, as they fight over the same toy. We are interrupted by a car pulling into the driveway.

Vignette 2

A young couple and their baby are beckoned through the garden to the last room at the end of the house. They walk up a stone set of steps,

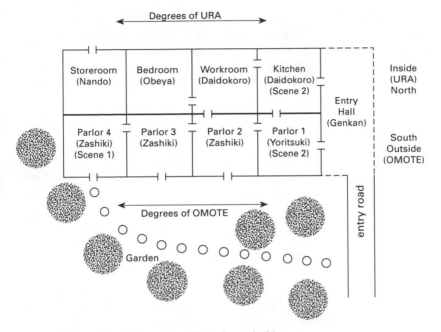

Figure 8.1. House plan, Katō household

remove their shoes, step up to the *tatami* mats, and kneel, bowing so their heads touch the floor, and speak in formal language to the Katōs. The Katōs also kneel and bow just as low in return. The guests present gifts to the Katōs, and are invited by the Katōs to sit around a low table on *zabuton* (cushions).

The guests – a young couple named Itō, and their small baby – are friends of the youngest Katō son, who has accompanied them. The husband works with the son, Nobu, in Tokyo and Nobu has also come back to the house primarily to see me. The *obāsan* serves tea, this time from a porcelain teapot into lacquerware cups, and we are all introduced and sit quietly sipping tea, enjoying the view of the garden, which is best from this room. At the far end from the garden is an alcove which has a flower arrangement – made from flowers in the garden – and a scroll, mounted on silk, which hangs in the alcove. The room has the newest *tatami* mats, and gives a feeling of openness, by its lack of clutter.

While the new guests sip tea, the group which had been relaxing around the *kotatsu* now galvanizes into action: the men begin to chop wood for the bath, while the women begin preparations for dinner. Dinner must be sumptuous, since it is the first time the Itōs have visited the house. The *obāsan* and Michiko (the second son, Yoshi's wife) make *sashimi*, accompanied by special fish for which the area is famous, along with a stir-fried Chinese dish, and rice. This is an accomplishment since the old, dark kitchen is equipped only with two gas burners and a rice cooker. A small hot water heater has been installed, but it is not connected to the main supply of water, and is inconvenient to use.

I am delegated to set up the table, which is in another guest parlor (parlor 2, Figure 8.1) from where the family usually eats. The Itōs are placed at the head of the table; the Katōs and their son's family at the lower end; I am next to them. The Itōs are given a double portion of the *sashimi* and fish, while the Katōs make sure that their glasses are full, and we hold conversation on subjects in which they can participate, since the conversation includes everyone at the table. This means that topics chosen are those which imply no more knowledge than the Itōs have of the Katōs and their house, or *omote* topics. After dinner we sing *karaoke* – using a machine which plays recorded background music minus the main melody, which is filled in by us individually taking turns. Finally, the *obāsan*, Michiko, and I wash the mountain of dishes, and sink into bed, exhausted.

Every day for the next three days this scene repeats itself. Each morning Nobu takes his friends out sightseeing, and each afternoon the *obāsan* and Michiko begin cooking a sumptuous dinner – different every night. I help in setting up the table and ferrying dishes back and forth to the kitchen. During the day the *ojīsan* gets special regional products for the Itōs, like butter from the dairy farm in the nearby mountains. Each night we entertain the guests in a different way – with firecrackers, singing, beer and homemade wine. All our attention is focused on Nobu's guests, rather than ourselves; although nobody actually knows the guests except Nobu. All our conversation is also tailored to the guests, and our time taken with them; we are never able to return to our conversation in the *kotatsu*. I become increasingly frustrated as the time and effort of the family members and myself is virtually taken up by attending to the Itōs, who are incidental to what I thought was the focus of the get-together – my return.

Vignette 3

After three days, the second son, Yoshi, and his family return to Tokyo. Just as they leave, the eldest son, Shigeto (who will later inherit the house, but is now working and living in another part of the prefecture), comes with his eleven-year-old son, and his wife's sister's son. The latter is visiting from the sister's natal homestead, in the Ryūkyū Islands. Shigeto's wife is unable to come because she is taking their daughter to camp. This leaves only the *obāsan* and myself to cook for ten people, and I am admittedly a terrible cook.

For the next two days we continue to have splendid meals of special guest food – *sushi, sukiyaki,* and special fish. But now the eleven-year-old cousin (representing his important affines) is at the head of the table and *he* is the recipient of double portions of the main dish. The Itōs are now seated below the cousin. The Itō wife first begins to help clear the table; then finally enters the kitchen and helps the *obāsan* with the cooking. The Itōs are now deferring to the new head guest, and this arrangement lasts until both the Itōs and Shigeto's guest leave.[10]

Omote/ura: axis of formality/informality

This extended series of vignettes is complex. On one level it depicts a conflict of expectations between the Katōs and me on my first visit after a nine-year absence. My visit was short, and I expected to converse with the Katōs, catching up on interim events, much as we did in the first vignette. Yet ironically, the return of all the Katō sons specifically for the occasion of my visit prevented this kind of communication, since the guests they brought with them created a contextual shift which required us to turn all our attention on them. Providing the guests with sumptuous meals, entertainment, and conversation required us to shift from spontaneity to discipline and from self-expression to self-restraint. The guests became the center of attention, as outsiders, even though they were peripheral to the main reason for the gathering. The original reason for the gathering was in fact subordinated to the new situation created by the arrival of the guests. Yet the guests had not simply appeared; they had been invited by the same family members who came for the occasion of my visit. Hadn't they themselves known of the consequences of bringing these guests? Did it make any difference to them if the situation shifted from self-expression to self-restraint?

The first vignette in parlor 1 is relaxed, spontaneous, and intimate; characterized by the familiarity which an American might expect in such a situation. Both adults and children displayed emotions openly; by joking, laughing, and even conflict – at least among the children. The room was cluttered; we were dressed informally, drinking ordinary tea, speaking in informal language, and slapping each other on the back as we sometimes howled with laughter. We were displaying degrees of *ura*, not paying attention to surface appearance, or form, but to matters of the heart, or emotions (*kokoro*). The room we were in, our informal language and social expression, and even the teapot we were using, were all indexed by our relationships, which were "close" or "inside," since I had known the

Katōs for many years. Our relationship, then, indexed both the form and content of our situation, which was characterized by expression of inner feelings, *kokoro*, and by conflicts (such as the neighbor's antics, and the children's fights). This was a slice of *ura*, of everyday life.

But the slice of life was soon preempted by the arrival of Nobu and the new guests. Their arrival redefined the communication as formal and distant – *for the duration of the visit*. Thus all three of the Katō sons, their families, the *ojīsan* and *obāsan* and myself, focused our attention for the next five days upon the succession of guests. As distant "outsiders" the relationship of household members to the guests took priority over their relationships to one another. The former relationship required a different indexing of the expression of self and social life in that situation, and the much greater distance between the Itōs and Katōs required us to shift rooms, language register, and even teapots.

Because the Itōs were virtual strangers, our focus shifted from content to form; to sumptuous banquets and formal entertainment, accompanied by conversations which were general (and emotionally shallow), but in which the Itōs could participate. Catering to the Itōs required a shift from self-expression to self-restraint; from spontaneity to discipline. This was *omote* – appearance – rather than everyday behavior. The *kejime* decision which created this shift was based on a weighting of the form/content axis acknowledging that formal communication to outsiders took precedence over informal communication among insiders. And by the same token, "distant" ties preempted "close" ones. The *kejime* decision is significant as the catalyst which creates each shift between *omote/ura*. Just as the form/content communication in the first vignette was produced by my entrance into the situation, the shift in the second vignette was produced by the youngest son's entrance with the three guests.

The same dynamics occurred again with the arrival of a new guest, brought by Shigeto. The eleven-year-old cousin from the Ryūkyū Islands now became the central focus of attention, and because this position could be occupied by only one group or person, he replaced the Itōs. In opposition to this new outsider, the Itōs were drawn "inside," because they had already been guests at the house for three days. They moved down to lower places at the table, while the cousin occupied the highest place. And since the second son and his wife had now left, the shortage of women also drew the Itō wife into the inside in another sense. She began helping at the table; then came into the kitchen to help with food preparation. Thus in the space of three days, she shifted from a distant guest who *received* deference, to a helper of the host, who *gave* deference; from outside to inside.

Indexing self and society

The appearance of the Itōs created a two-way directionality in communication: the Katōs *gave* deference, or catered to the guests; the Itōs *received* deference, or were catered to. In such communication one person ordinarily takes the role of facilitator (*amayakasu*), by indulging the other, who is indulged (*amae*) (Lebra 1976: 54, Rosenberger, this volume). The self-discipline of the former facilitates the spontaneity of the person being indulged. However, in formal situations, the guests also refrain from spontaneity through *enryo* (restraint).

This two-way directionality in communication means that there can be only two positions in any particular situation: those catering and those being catered to. The arrival of the Itōs unified all the participants in vignette 1 as "caterers" vis-à-vis the Itōs. The arrival of the young cousin drew all these participants plus the Itōs into the position of "caterers." But the relationships of discipline/spontaneity, inside/outside had to be re-defined as each new person entered the situation. This means that the group boundary is permeable, depending on how social relationships are defined, or depending on *kejime*.

The focus in these scenes was not solely on communication between persons, for each person was also defined via a group anchorpoint.[11] The two-way directionality of inter-group communication, and the fact that there were only two possible communication positions, created a constant shifting between "inside" and "outside," as well as degrees of inside and outsidedness, producing what I have arbitrarily defined as "different" vignettes. As indexes, the paired sets of terms were inversely related, so that, for example, the degree of *presence* of outsidedness, discipline, or *omote* also specified the degree of *absence* of insidedness, spontaneity, or *ura*, and vice versa (Doi 1986: 23, Bachnik 1989).[12] In the second vignette the process of catering to the Itō guests meant that we could not disclose anything of the intimacy of our behind-the-scenes communication to the Itōs (nor they to us). In deferring to the Itōs, our attention was bent toward *them*, and self-expression among ourselves was disregarded for the duration of their stay. The Itōs clearly understood the basis of this *kejime*, for when the next set of guests arrived, and some of the Katōs left, the wife shifted from catered to caterer – a position which brought her access to the physical behind-the-scenes *ura* of the kitchen.

But even in the first vignette distinctions and shifts between inside and outside were being made. The second son, as a non-successor, was an outsider to his natal house, and his wife was even more so.[13] Nor was I a true member of the house. Although the situation could be characterized as highly informal and spontaneous, with little inside/outside distinction, nonetheless communication in this scene was not "free," but was still defined relative to the positions of its participants. Thus a boundary existed between the *ojīsan* and *obāsan* and the other members of the scene, who were all "close" outsiders. The second son and his wife deferred to his parents (the *ojīsan* and *obāsan*) in subtle ways, which made them the center of attention in the discourse. Moreover, the females "catered to" the males, so that the *obāsan* and the second son's wife did all the cooking and serving – even when the number of guests increased greatly. Yet the elder Katō male, the *ojīsan*, did begin to help set and clear the table when the women were most short-handed, during the visit of the second set of guests, at the time the Itō wife also came into the kitchen to help. Thus males could also shift from being catered to, to catering when outsiders appeared, and not enough women were present to cater to them adequately.

Significance of *kejime* and the indexical axis

The priority of developing one's relationship to others over "self"-development is what creates the value-weighting of self-discipline over spontaneity for Japanese. Restraint of self-expression is necessary for the organization of social life; the necessity of relating harmoniously to others, both individually and in a larger context, creates the focus on discipline. Yet this restraint rests upon a moral basis – on development of the "inner" *kokoro*, as Lebra points out. The Japanese acknowledge that every instance of self-expression is possible only through someone else's self-restraint; that disciplining one's self for the greater good of the social "whole" does not destroy, but rather develops the self. The combination of mutually negotiated self-sacrifice and self-expression is what constitutes hierarchy – and here the harmonious negotiation of *kejime* is essential for a smoothly working social life. This does not mean that self-expression is not valued, but simply that spontaneity is inversely linked to self-discipline and to the social sphere. In appropriate situations, such as vignette 1, when no "outside" demands are pressing, spontaneity predominates. One gravitates from greater expression of an inner, spontaneous self in informal social scenes, to greater self-discipline in formal scenes. Here smooth gravitation is a euphemism for adroitly ascertaining *kejime* – by indexing the degree of distance defined between the participants and coordinating the expression of formality/informality to this distance.

Within individual situations Japanese gravitate from *amayakasu* or indulging, to *amaeru* or being indulged; from restraining one's self to allowing another's self-expression through one's own self-restraint. This is a blueprint for indexing the inner/outer axis at the boundary of the self –

depending on the *kejime* appropriate to two-person interactions. Inner/ outer can also be read as an axis for indexing social contexts, by the shifting of group boundaries which constantly occurs because everyone in a scene must be defined as either "outside" or "inside" relative to all the other participants. Such shifts are based on grasping the *kejime* appropriate to an inner/outer social axis.

In retrospect, it did not seem to matter to the Katōs whether we spent our time in the "spontaneous" mode communicating *to* each other, or whether we communicated *with* each other, in the process of doing what was necessary to make the Itōs (or the cousin from the Ryūkyū Islands) feel welcome as guests.[14] The sons did not view the shifts from spontaneity to formal communication the way I did because the spontaneity of the first vignette did not have the same priority for them as it had for me. The formal situations which involved restraint of self-expression, and which to me spelled out an *absence* of self, did not appear that way to the Katōs, since to them the disciplined situations were also permeated with self. The point for them was not in weighting the communication more highly toward "self" (as I tended to do). For them, behaving appropriately toward outsiders took precedence over "inside" behavior among themselves.[15] Moreover, how one defined and shifted appropriately between and within these situations had an even greater importance. Thus "self" is not constituted as an autonomous individual; rather self in the narrow sense is constantly being related beyond one's self, both through the disciplined energy of social participation, and in the larger sense of moving beyond the boundaries of inner and outer to the open, boundless self.

Implications

Process, context, and human agency are all essential to the organization of self *and* society in Japan, and they are also central issues in social theory. All require a shift from assumptions of monolithic unity underlying social reality to an examination of the parameters by which social life can be shared (implying unity) yet still organized dialogically (implying individual intentionality). As Stark puts this, we must grasp how we can do justice to the real integration of the social order and the real independence of the individuals which comprise it (1962: 1).

Kejime, as a meta-index, provides a way to view these issues of organization in practice. *Kejime* reverses the priorities of starting point, so that structure (for example, the parameters of formality/informality) is defined *through* human agency, rather than vice versa. The process of doing *kejime* is agreed-upon, and therefore generalizable, although the contextual expressions of spontaneity/discipline may vary infinitely along the double axis of self/society and inside/outside.

The Japanese case is worth examining for a sustained example of the organizational implications of an indexical axis. For example, *ura* can also be translated as "underlying reality" and *omote* as "surface appearance." The *omote/ura* axis can then be viewed as indexing the similarity versus difference of underlying social reality. The more distance gauged between the Katōs and their guests, the more surface appearance or social form which must be displayed, as in vignette 2. The more closeness, or similarity of underlying reality (*ura*), the greater depth of content, or spontaneous self-expression which can be displayed, as in vignette 1. It is worth noting that no unified social "reality" is presumed to exist here. Difference between self and other is readily acknowledged by householders, and is one of their most common topics of conversation. In fact, degrees of difference (or similarity) based on degrees of shared social reality are constantly acknowledged, and the process of gauging difference is discussed in minute detail.

The difficulties of defining organizations which move beyond monolithic unity may be overcome by including the reference point of the subject in the theoretical frame of reference, which is consistent with the vantage points of relativity theory and quantum mechanics. The distinction between an indexical reference point (which can be generalized beyond the individual) and the individual qua individual provides a means of overcoming longstanding difficulties inherent in subject/object dichotomies. More specifically, a focus like *kejime* facilitates the overcoming of subject/object dichotomies by relating self to society on at least three different levels: on an interactional level between self and other; on an organizational level between self and society (defined as a juxtaposition of spontaneous self-expression versus conformity to social constraint); and on a theoretical level which indexes similarity versus difference of shared social realities. The significance of *kejime* (and the paired sets of terms) in Japanese society thus transcends this particular ethnographic situation, since it constitutes a focus in practice incorporating multiple, shifting, and pluralistic perspectives for the organization of both self and social life.

NOTES

1 This paper is based on a fuller development of ideas discussed in Bachnik 1992b, especially the axes of distance (*omote/ura*) and direction (*uchi/soto*) discussed in chapter 5. Different but related aspects of indexicality are also developed in Bachnik 1989 and 1992a.

2 This relationship is clear in the Japanese title of Doi's recent book on the self, *Omote to Ura* (*Omote* and *ura*), which is translated as *The Anatomy of Self*.

3 The significance of this double axis for the organization of both language and social life is the subject of Bachnik and Quinn, in press.

4 The continuum of spontaneity versus discipline which relates self to society and defines each in terms of the other, is itself part of the broader relationship to "bound" and "unbound" energy that gives larger meaning to self and society. This relationship of spiritual energy to "inner" and "outer" ultimately provides a means for transcending the limitations of both self and society. Thus it allows for different manifestations of self to be evaluated according to a hierarchy of values which index a movement from lower to higher along the same continuum of inside and outside.

5 The existence of contradictory social ideals is not unique to Japan but seems widespread in human societies. For example, Abu-Lughod (1986) contrasts honor and love among the Egyptian Bedouins; Rosaldo (1980) violence versus social control among the Philippine Ilongits; and Shore (1982) natural freedom versus social control among Samoans.

6 Notice that the third "comma" represents a synthesis of the first two, and is thus on a different level. By the same token, Lebra's "boundless self" represents an "inner" self which has transcended the external world (material, social, or cultural) in a Buddhist sense, in which self-awareness is expanded beyond the tensions of subject–object differentiation. In becoming one with the objective world or nature, self absorbs the outer world into itself.

7 Kondo also examines how crafting of self is actually carried out in the social context of the workplace. She finds the creation of self to be accomplished through the creation of fine objects – all part of a hierarchy of power, making this possibility of self-realization largely unavailable to women. It appears that the potency of sacred power discussed by Rosenberger has been replaced by a power much closer to domination in certain spheres of the modern world. Thus women in the workplace are identified with the less bound, consolidating "inner" forces which are generative, and men with the outer differentiating forces which convey authority. The hierarchy of the Sato company consists of a "center" based on full-fledged, male artisans connected to and fulfilled in their work. The organizational peripheries are occupied by women, who are tied to the home and are structurally temporary members of the organization. Yet, ironically, the artisanal portrait of "crafting selves" is inappropriate even for artisans themselves, as their lives are increasingly defined by arenas outside themselves, such as management aspects of the companies who employ them.

8 To develop these distinctions between signs more thoroughly: an iconic sign resembles its object (as a diagram or picture, which may even momentarily make us forget the distinction between the real and the copy). An indexical sign has a direct relation to its object and qualifies its object by being really connected to it (Freeman 1937: 31). Indexes are dyads. Symbols have a joint relationship between the object denoted and the mind which makes them triads. This relationship is established by convention, and is arbitrary. For Peirce, symbols are the residual class of signs, in contrast to Saussure, for whom they are primary.

9 I do not wish to imply that the distinction between reference and indexing is absolute; this can be also viewed as organized along a continuum. Silverstein distinguishes between referential indexes, which include tense, locative deixis, and first and second pronominals, and non-referential indexes, which include social sex markers and deference indexes. "Referential ... indexes contribute to propositional description in discourse ... Nonreferential, relatively performative indexes [establish] the parameters of the interaction themselves, as in deference forms" (Silverstein 1976: 36).

10 These vignettes were also discussed, somewhat differently, in Bachnik 1992a.

11 The group anchorpoint is the counterpart of the individual "I" which anchors deictic discourse coordinates in Indo-European languages. Because the reference point is a group, the coordination of the reference point is a crucial facet of its organization, and this makes deictic organization part of social organization for Japanese. The significance of the group as a deictic anchorpoint is discussed in language by Wetzel (1984, in press); Bachnik (1982); in the organization of social life by Bachnik (1992b); Bachnik and Quinn (in press).

12 These axes correspond to Silverstein's description of "pure" or deference indexes. They are maximally creative, or performative, "establishing the parameters of the interaction themselves, as in deference forms, which ... establish overtly the social relations of the individuals ..." (1976: 36). Silverstein assumes propositional referential meaning to remain unaffected by deference indexes. But *omote/ura* affects this meaning as well, indexing what would constitute acceptable discourse topics. In fact, the implications of indexes like *omote/ura* in terms of indexing referential categories seem quite important.

13 The second son's outsidedness was due to the succession process of the *ie*, in which only one child (by preference the oldest son) succeeds. Yoshi, in this vignette, had established his own (new) household, which was considered a different reference point from his parents' household. This was a major basis of his outsidedness (see Bachnik and Quinn, in press).

14 The importance given to the Itōs in this situation was later reciprocated by them when they took considerable time and effort in introducing Nobu to the woman who eventually became his wife.

15 The weighting of the axis toward discipline, rather than self-expression is even evident in the design of the Katō house, where the *omote* area ranges from parlor 4 to parlor 1 and the *ura* from the kitchen to the house storeroom. The four *omote* rooms are not used by members unless guests are present (which means parlors 3 and 4 are used much less than 1 and 2). The four *ura* rooms are not accessible to outsiders (especially the bedroom and storeroom). But parlor 1 (an outside room) is often used by householders when they are relaxing, and the kitchen (an inside room) *can* be entered by outsiders when they are participating in household work (as the Itō wife did in vignette 3).

   The *omote* rooms, which are least used, have the best view, the best heating, sunlight, and furnishings and even the most tightly fitted construction. The guest rooms – particularly parlors 2–4 – are also most "empty" of expression of everyday life, and self-expression of house members. For everyday life the house members must use the *ura*, which are the darkest rooms, with worst furnishings and view, in which they are subject to constant drafts from loose-fitting doors and windows. This is also true of parlor 1, and even more so, of the kitchen.

Even the development of technology in Japan is weighted toward *omote* rather than *ura*, which is consistent with Kuwayama's argument. Farmhouses like the Katōs' commonly possess sophisticated video and camera equipment, including videotape machines, VCRs, *karaoke* machines, and color TV, all of which are related to *omote*, for they can be used to entertain guests. Technology for the *ura* is less developed, so that "ease" and "labor-saving" character-istics in technology and house designs, such as well-lit and heated kitchens, automatic washing machines, and/or ample hot water, are all less evident than the *omote* equipment in Nagano. *Kurō* seems a virtue for the Japanese housewife as well.

REFERENCES

Abu-Lughod, Lila. 1986. *Veiled Sentiments*. Berkeley: University of California Press.
Bachnik, Jane. 1982. Deixis and Self/Other Reference in Japanese Discourse. *Working Papers in Sociolinguistics* 99, Austin, Tex.: Southwest Educational Development Laboratory.
   1989. *Omote/Ura*: Indexes and the Organization of Self and Society in Japan. *Comparative Social Research*, Vol. XI (C. Calhoun, ed.), Greenwich, Conn.: JAI Press.
   1992a. The Two "Faces" of Self and Society in Japan, *Ethos* 20 (1).
   1992b. *Family, Self and Society in Modern Japan*. Stanford, Calif.: Stanford University Press.
Bachnik, Jane and Quinn, Charles J. (eds.). In press. *Inside and Outside: Defining a Situated Social Order in Japan*. Princeton, N.J.: Princeton University Press.
Benedict, Ruth. 1946. *The Chrysanthemum and the Sword: Patterns of Japanese Culture*. Boston, Mass.: Houghton Mifflin.
Crapanzano, Vincent. 1982. The Self, the Third, and Desire. *Psychosocial Theories of the Self* (B. Lee, ed.), New York: Plenum Press.
Doi, Takeo. 1973. *Omote* and *Ura*: Concepts Derived from the Japanese 2-fold Structure of Consciousness. *Journal of Nervous and Mental Disease* 157: 258–61.
   1986. *The Anatomy of Self*. Tokyo: Kodansha.
Edwards, Walter. 1989. *Modern Japan Through Its Weddings*. Stanford, Calif.: Stanford University Press.
Freeman, Eugene. 1937. *The Categories of Charles Peirce*. Chicago: private edition, distributed by the University of Chicago Libraries.
Gerlach, Michael. 1992. *Alliance Capitalism: The Social Organization of Japanese Business*. Berkeley: University of California Press.
Giddens, Anthony. 1979. *Central Problems in Social Theory: Action, Structure, and Contradiction in Social Analysis*. Berkeley: University of California Press.
   1984. *The Constitution of Society*. Berkeley: University of California Press.
Hamabata, Matthews. 1983. Women in Love and Power: Social Networks and Business Families in Modern Japanese Society. Ph.D. dissertation, Harvard University.

1990. *The Crested Kimono: Power and Love in the Japanese Business Family*. Ithaca, N.Y.: Cornell University Press.

Hardacre, Helen. 1986. *Kurozumikyō and the New Religions of Japan*. Princeton, N.J.: Princeton University Press.

Ikuta, Shoko. 1980. Ethnography and Discourse Cohesion: Aspects of Speech Level Shift in Japanese Discourse. M.A. thesis, Cornell University.

Ishida, Takeshi. 1984. Conflict and Its Accommodation: Omote–Ura and Uchi–Soto Relations. *Conflict in Japan* (E. Krauss, T. Rohlen, and P. G. Steinhoff, eds.), Honolulu: University of Hawaii Press.

Kondo, Dorinne. 1987. Creating an Ideal Self: Theories of Selfhood and Pedagogy at a Japanese Ethics Retreat. *Ethos* 15: 241–72.

1990. *Crafting Selves: Power, Gender, and Discourses of Identity in a Japanese Workplace*. Chicago: University of Chicago Press.

Lebra, Takie Sugiyama. 1976. *Japanese Patterns of Behavior*. Honolulu: University of Hawaii Press.

Ohnuki-Tierney, Emiko. 1984. *Illness and Culture in Contemporary Japan: An Anthropological View*. Cambridge: Cambridge University Press.

Peirce, Charles Sanders. 1931–5. *Collected Papers*, Vols. I–III (C. Hartshorne and P. Weiss, eds.), Cambridge, Mass.: Harvard University Press.

Rosaldo, Renato. 1980. *Ilongot Headhunting 1883–1974: A Study in Society and History*. Stanford, Calif.: Stanford University Press.

Rosenberger, Nancy R.. 1989. Dialectic Balance in the Polar Mode of Self: The Japan Case. *Ethos* 17: 88–113.

In press. Reversals in Japanese Gender Relations: Indexing Contexts and Universal Powers. *Inside and Outside: Defining a Situated Social Order in Japan* (J. Bachnik and C. J. Quinn, eds.), Princeton, N.J.: Princeton University Press.

Shore, Bradd, 1982. *Sala'ilua: A Samoan Mystery*. New York: Columbia University Press.

Silverstein, M. 1976. Shifters, Linguistic Categories, and Cultural Description. *Meaning in Anthropology* (K. Basso and H. Selby, eds.), Albuquerque: University of New Mexico Press.

1979. Language, Structure, and Linguistic Ideology. *The Elements: A Parasession on Linguistic Units and Levels* (P. R. Klyne et al., eds.), Chicago: Chicago Linguistic Society.

Singer, Milton. 1980. Signs of the Self: An Exploration in Semiotic Anthropology. *American Anthropologist* 82: 485–507.

Smith, Robert. 1983. *Japanese Society: Tradition, Self and the Social Order*. Cambridge: Cambridge University Press.

Stark, Werner. 1962. *The Fundamental Forms of Social Thought*. London: Routledge & Kegan Paul.

Wetzel, Patricia. 1984. *Uti* and *Soto* (In-Group and Out-Group): Social Deixis in Japanese. Ph.D. dissertation, Cornell University.

In press. *Uchi* and *Soto* in Linguistic Perspective. *Inside and Outside: Defining a Situated Social Order in Japan* (J. Bachnik and C. J. Quinn, eds.), Princeton, N.J.: Princeton University Press.

Index